CONEY

CONEY

THE OVERLOOK PRESS

WOODSTOCK & NEW YORK

First published in the United States in 2000 by
The Overlook Press, Peter Mayer Publishers, Inc.
Lewis Hollow Road
Woodstock, New York 12498
www.overlookpress.com

Library of Congress Cataloging-in-Publication Data

Ducovny, Amram M.
Coney / Amram Ducovny.
p.   cm.
1. Coney Island (New York, N.Y.)—Fiction. 2. Jewish teenagers—Fiction.
3. Amusement parks—Fiction. 4. Teenage boys—Fiction.   I. Title.
PS3554.U28 C6 2000   813'.54—dc21   00-042735

Type formatting by Bernard Schleifer Company
Manufactured in the United States of America
First Edition
1 3 5 7 9 8 6 4 2
ISBN 1-58567-067-7

For Moishe and Velia then . . .
For Varda now

In the Cherry Tree: August 30, 1937

Aba: *Heshele, what do you know of Franz Kafka?*

Harry: *I think he is a writer.*

Aba: *No, he is a journalist. A reporter of facts.*

Harry: *Like the ones in the movies who are looking for scoops? Like Clark Gable?*

Aba: *Exactly. Kafka is a Jewish Clark Gable. His soul is as handsome as Mr. Gable's face.*

Harry: *In what newspaper does he write? Is it the* Morning Journal? *Does my father know him?*

Aba: *Yes, your father knows him. But it is not Kafka who reports. It is his soul.*

Harry: *I don't understand.*

Aba: *All right, an example: A few days ago Kafka's soul reported on a meeting between Heinrich Himmler and Adolf Hitler. Himmler told his Führer of the results of a model reorganization plan of the concentration camps in Germany, to which the Nazis send Jews, Communists and homosexuals. Kafka faithfully recorded Himmler's gift for detail and pride in his management of the four camps: Dachau, Sachsenhausen, Buchenwald and Lichtenburg, a camp exclusively for women. Himmler was particularly expansive and meticulous in describing the latest, Buchenwald, a triumphant example of, and here Kafka gives Himmler's exact words, "functional unity and capacity." This philosophy requires little shelter, minimal food and no medical facilities. The goal is to have a prisoner lose at least fifty percent of his weight, with no reduction in his work output. Sickness is abolished. To guard these dangerous people, Colonel Karl Koch has fifteen hundred SS troops. Hitler was greatly pleased. He presented his master planner with a medal.*

Harry: *Why does Hitler hate the Jews?*

Aba: *It is a journalistic vendetta. Kafka wrote* Mein Kampf *before Hitler.*

Harry: *I don't understand.*

Aba: *I envy you.*

CHAPTER

1

HARRY TOOK THE HIGH GROUND. BELOW, THE PACK MOVED LIKE phantoms through the shadow cast by his perch.

He squinted to bring into focus his faulty vision. He wore no glasses because his mother insisted that he feigned myopia to cause her worry and expense. As he spotted each dog, he joyfully called its name. The roll call matched yesterday's. No carcass fed the scavengers of the sky.

The five dogs inched forward, huddled, fur blending, reminding Harry of the brown-black blotched brushes rhythmically stroked across customers' shoes by Negro shoeshine boys.

Bear was the leader, having ousted Smiley three weeks ago in a fight that had raged for more than two hours. Smiley had limped away, whimpering like a funeral mourner, yet maintaining the puffed cheeks and slight show of teeth that named him. Harry had laughed at this slapstick, then regretted callousness to a friend's pain. But it had been too late. How could you take back a laugh?

Bear's challenge had pleased Harry because it altered the rut of predictability. Bear was a female. Never before had there been a female leader of the pack.

Bear now crossed over the shadow line into the cold morning sunlight. Her stiff, stubble-short, black fur seemed raised in perpetual anger. Her flat bear's snout sniffed the ground. The others jockeyed for closeness to her.

Harry's favorite was The Weasel King. WK, as Harry affectionately called him, was a majestic dog, measuring at least seven handspans. The slightest breeze rippled his silky, charcoal-gray coat. A Great Dane's head and long, vicious teeth froze humans or changed their path. But the dog was an utter coward. He cringed at a nip by any of the others: Curly, a half-bald, two-hand spanner; Lindy, who was missing a hind leg; or Hauptman, the unlikely issue of surely a German shepherd and perhaps a spaniel. WK was the last to tear at kills.

Bear broke into a run. The prey was a fleshless cat whose mangy coat was a black-and-white pattern botched by a novice knitter. Its jowly male head probably outweighed its body.

The cat's hackles sprang. Body arched and hissing, it leapt straight up. Bear, jaws agape, left her feet and hurtled forward, clamping down on the slim neck before both hit the ground.

Harry strained to hear the mystical sounds of life on the brink of death. The cat's guttural shrieks and outraged hisses. The pack's low growls, punctuated by piercing whelps, as the victim sank claws and teeth into its executioners' flesh.

The pack ripped at close quarters. Had the prey been a rat, the dogs would have been wary, herding it at a safe distance from its feared teeth, until Bear saw a clear shot at breaking its neck. Harry preferred a rat battle. He could predict and second-guess strategy.

Bear let loose a coyote howl and began to eat. Not until her snout and mouth were layered with fur and blood did the others burrow into the entrails. WK held back, then discreetly nuzzled his head between bodies.

Giant waves crashing onto hard sand jerked Harry's attention to the horizon where he spotted a becalmed ship no larger than a bathtub toy. Harry was not fooled. The ship was huge. Stood on its bow or aft, it was the height of a Wall Street skyscraper. Each of its three funnels measured three times the diameter of a manhole cover. The wisps of black above it were actually billowing coal smoke, the residue of rapid locomotion whose wake swelled the ten-foot-high waves pounding the beach beneath him.

Planted on the bridge of the *Bremen*, Captain Heinz Ziegen-baum, the perpetrator of the ruse, scanned the shore through binoculars and smiled smugly at having tricked Harry, his hated adversary.

Harry leapt onto his new bicycle. As his legs pumped, he assured them that they could surpass the power of the golden pistons propelling the *Bremen*. He gained on the liner, dead even with the aft.

"Almost sneaked by me," he shouted to Ziegenbaum, "you Nazi rat!"

Ziegenbaum muttered, "*Ach du lieber.*" His binoculars fell to his chest. "More coal!" he screamed. "We can't let that little Jew beat us again."

All races against giant liners were grave tests. The gentlemanly British captains were overmatched. The French provided an astonished "*Sacre bleu,*" while the Italians spat a "*Va fangool.*" The Americans delighted in saluting a valiant victor. But he dared not lose to the Germans. If he did, what would Aba say when he and Aba sat together on the lowest thick branch of the cherry tree and spoke of important things?

He drew even with amidships. It would be close. He was running out of room. He wished for a racer instead of his fat Schwinn. The sharp January air stabbed at his throat. His panting exhalations hovered like personal clouds. He was gaining, gaining, gaining. He was winning!

The sparkle of a silver sun reflector warned him, but too late to brake. He wrenched the handle bars to the left and began to fly. He landed into darkness.

When light returned, two faces peered down at him. He recognized one. The other belonged in a dream. It was almost a perfect rectangle, the square chin about as wide as the forehead. Long cheeks flowed like overspreading pancake batter. A half-finger of flat nose and rust-colored eyes resembling BB gun pellets seemed tiny afterthoughts. Harry blinked.

An old woman tapped a heavily veined hand against her leathery cheek.

"*Oy*, he's alive." she said.

"No thanks to you," said the other, uncovering crowded yellow teeth. "Who the hell sits right in the middle of the boardwalk sunning? You either sit in the back or front."

"Listen, Mr. Midget, don't you tell me where to sit. I was living here by Coney before you was born."

Harry cocked his head for perspective. No, he was not a midget. He was a dwarf.

"Shove it lady," said the dwarf. "You OK kid?"

Harry mentally traveled his body. His right knee stung. His palms tingled. A bump on his head pulsated. He did not wish to touch it. He smiled at the dwarf.

"I think I'm alright. What happened?"

"Well kid you was peddlin' like to beat Georgiani in the six-day bike race and lookin' out to the ocean, so you don't see this dumb old crow sittin' right in the middle of the boardwalk, like she owned it. You skid and the bike bucks from the back like a horse and you take off like a big-assed bird. You ripped your knickers."

The woman stroked his forehead. Her palm was rough. He felt dirty. He did not like old people to touch him. They were rotting.

"I think you hit your head. Your Mama should take you by the hospital," she said.

The dwarf shoved her hand away and smoothed Harry's forehead and hair. His touch was warm, almost hot.

"They should take you to the hospital for crazy ladies," he said to the woman. "Why don't you haul your ass somewhere safe and let me talk to the kid." He winked a BB at Harry.

"Dirty-mouth midget. You belong by a hospital."

She walked away, shoulders alternately thrusting forward, expressing utter disdain.

Preparing to stand up, Harry rolled onto his side and spotted his bike. It had crashed into one of the ten-foot-high concrete, clam-shaped drinking fountains which were spaced along the boardwalk.

"Jesus, my bike," he said.

The dwarf's Mt. Rushmore head, set on a thin neck, jerked from side to side. It seemed in danger of falling off.

"Looks pretty bad," the dwarf said. "Front fender twisted, probably kaput. Front wheel bent. Useless. Chain housing pretzeled. Chain off. Could be OK. Looks like the handlebars survived. At least Schwinn can do one thing right."

The confident, professional diagnosis reminded Harry of a concession owner evaluating winter storm damage and the repairs needed to open a new season. The dwarf stroked his chin.

"Could cost as much as seven dollars, if it's worth fixin', which I personally wouldn't."

Inside Harry's forehead, where, Aba said, Harry saw important things, bikes leaned against a wall.

"Hey," he said, "don't you run the bike store near the Half-Moon Hotel? I ride by there to look at your racers."

"Own it."

"Could you take a look at my bike?"

"Sure kid. My name's Woody.

"Harry."

The dwarf offered Harry a hand to pull up on. Harry instinctively grabbed it but then began to release, fearing that his full weight would topple the dwarf. Suddenly his fingers were mashed as he was yanked to his feet. His knee throbbed.

Harry calculated Woody's height at about three and a half feet, two feet below him.

"Feel that strength," the dwarf said, releasing Harry's hand after a farewell knuckle squash.

"Yes," Harry answered to the wind, not to demean the dwarf by looking down at him.

"Hey, I'm down here," Woody directed, tugging at the waist of Harry's knickers. "This"—he outlined a short shape with his

hands, much like a man lustfully invoking a woman's figure—
"didn't just happen to me. I'm thirty-three years old. I'm used to it.
Yeah, I'm used to everything, except bein' patted on the head. I
quit bein' one of the moon men at Luna Park because of that. Six-
year-old kids pattin' me on the head. Like to take them across my
knee and teach 'em some manners."

The matted, sandy-colored hair, a square patch of tilled earth,
invited patting. It seemed unnatural not to. Aba instructed:
Sometimes the natural thing to do is not to do.

Rolling his bike on its unbent wheel, Harry followed the
dwarf's swayed back and protruding buttocks. Woody's arms, curved,
parenthesizing his body, were the twins of his bowed legs. He listed
left and right. Yet, from time to time, Harry skip-jumped to keep up.

They walked on the boardwalk toward the Half-Moon Hotel,
whose blue-tinged dome dominated the nonamusement section of
Coney; a pasha's palace among bungalows. Looming beyond, the
motionless Ferris Wheel anticipated summer lovers kissing while
the world turned upside down. Beneath it the Cyclone's sky-riding
wooden tracks formed a serpentine road to nowhere. Coney
awaited a warm wind to awaken it from its annual Ice Age.

In winter the boardwalk belonged to a tribe of ancient sun
worshippers who, steadying their beach chairs against the shut-
tered concessions, pressed silver sun reflectors under their chins,
channeling life into death masks.

Woody turned onto the 28th Street access ramp. The Norton's
Point trolley, bound for the Stillwell Avenue subway terminus, clat-
tered into view. Its one passenger sat in the rear of the car. In front,
a conductor calibrated the throttle bar. Low-wattage bare bulbs cast
a gray mist. A ghost trolley condemned to traverse Coney for eternity traveled endless tracks inside Harry's forehead.

"Hey," the dwarf called, "we're here."

A sandwich-board sign to the side of a glass storefront, read:
Woody's Bikes: New, Used, Rental, Repairs. Cash Only. Inside, the temperature remained below freezing.

"Hey, Soldier!" the dwarf yelled.

A man wearing blue overalls and an unraveling woolen khaki-colored hat emerged from behind a tangle of bikes, each missing a wheel or some other essential part.

"Damn, what is it Woody?" His voice was hoarse and strained as if bruised from fighting its way through his throat.

"Got a job for you." The dwarf pointed to Harry's bike.

Soldier stroked the handlebars. He smiled at Harry.

"Damn. Poor bike." He shook his head sadly.

"Wait," Harry said to Woody, "I never said . . . well, I really don't have any money."

The dwarf waved off further protest.

"Take the bike, Soldier. Fix it before anythin' else."

Harry relinquished his grip. Soldier cradled the bike's middle bar, gently lifted it off the ground and disappeared behind the bike graveyard.

"Don't worry, we can work something out," the dwarf assured Harry. "Let's talk."

Woody opened a door cut into the back wall which led into a windowless room containing an unmade, legless double bed, a worn morris chair and a free-standing Atwater-Kent radio. The dwarf sat at the edge of the bed, motioning Harry to the chair.

"So kid, you're scared."

"Scared?"

"Yeah, about what your old man and old lady is goin' to do to you about the bike. My old man used to beat the shit out of me."

Harry was not scared. He felt sorry for his father. The bike had been a present for his fifteenth birthday, three months ago. It represented much money to his parents. His mother had opposed the expenditure and boycotted the presentation. She would fill a year with recriminations.

"Yeah," Harry answered. Agreeing with adults, Harry knew, convinced them that you were smart.

He imagined his father given a choice by the Nazis: spank

your child or die. His father chose death.

"Well, like I said, don't worry. Soldier will fix your bike so Mr. Schwinn himself couldn't tell the difference."

The dwarf slid forward. His head was between Harry's knees. Harry wanted to cross his legs, but was unsure if he could swing his leg over the dwarf's head. Woody rested a hot hand on his thigh, just as Schnozz, the old barker, had done under the boardwalk. Harry checked that each button of his fly was secure in its hole.

"Got an itch?" the dwarf said. "I got some good stuff for that. I'll get you some later."

Woody's head swiveled up to engage Harry's eyes.

"Listen. I'll fix your bike, if you do somethin' for me."

Harry could not extract words from his dry throat. He nodded once to indicate understanding and then shook his head from side to side to decline the offer.

The dwarf imitated his yes-no and laughed.

Now he whispered, lips drawn to the right: "I'm a bookmaker, see, and a little numbers action too. Anyway, what I'm askin' in return for me fixin' your bike is that you ride around pickin' up bettin' slips. No big deal. Most of the cops are paid off by the guy I work for. But just in case, who would suspect a nice kid on a bike?"

"I go to school," Harry said.

"After school and weekends. And once you work off the bike, I'll start to pay you cash. Ten cents an hour."

Aba said: *Go wherever there is to go.*

Harry said: "Sure."

CHAPTER

2

HARRY LEFT THE STORE. THE WINTER SUN WAS EDGING INTO THE Atlantic. He zipped up his brown corduroy jacket to the last notch. Bending his chin to his chest and hunching his shoulders, he lengthened his stride to challenge the immobilizing wind, which retaliated by knifing into his exposed raw knee. The streetlights had not yet come on. Twilight settled on the rows of two-family houses, masking with neat silhouettes the distressed structures.

The few people in the streets walked briskly, purposefully, anticipating, Harry was certain, home and warmth. At his home there would be a note on the kitchen table: *Here's a quarter for supper. Don't eat hot dogs at Nathan's. Go to Kaplan's delicatessen.*

He decided to visit his grandparents, who lived in a small bungalow a five-minute walk from his home. He rang the bell. His grandmother leapt on his neck like a football player crunching a clothesline tackle. Her lips wet his cheeks and forehead. She smelled of the carp she ground by hand for the Friday night gefilte fish. The odor's intensity waxed and waned, but never completely deserted her or her house.

"*Kim arrine, Kim arrine.*" Her Yiddish offer of hospitality was delivered in a voice more appropriate for yelling "Fire!"

Bama, as two-year-old Harry had called her (the only name thereafter she would answer to), had arrived in the United States in 1919 and immediately sniffed a mean, godless country: a *medinah* to be ignored. She learned no English, guarding her illiteracy like a jewel. When Harry had asked her why she did not speak English, she summoned a tone of irrefutable logic:

"For what do I need English? Did they speak English in Warsaw?"

In the house, his grandfather, who insisted on Harry calling him Zadeh so the boy would not forget Yiddish, stood before a mirror adjusting his brown felt hat. When the brim was cocked over his right eye at precisely the correct rakish angle, he turned to Harry and asked:

"How many bowel movements have you had today?"

"Three," Harry lied, satisfying the minimum, immutable daily number prescribed by Zadeh for guaranteed longevity.

"Good," Zadeh said. "Do four or five. It's good to have some in the bank."

Zadeh turned back to the mirror for a last look, then walked to the door saying:

"I will be back in four hours, during which time I will have shown that amateur, Manny Edelberg, how a master plays chess."

He tapped his hat, confident that when Edleberg, his adversary in weekly chess marathons, beheld its jaunty confidence, he, Zadeh, would have gained a telling psychological advantage.

Bama zipped down Harry's jacket and removed it. Had he been wearing galoshes she would have pushed him into a chair and pulled them free. Bama's role in life was to turn men into invalids. She spotted the tear.

"*Oy*, the hurt of it. What happened?"

"I fell off my bike."

"A thousand curses on your mother for giving you one," she said on her way to the bathroom. Returning, brandishing a bottle of iodine, she knelt and removed his shoes, undid his belt and began to unbutton his knickers.

"Wait," she said, "you catch cold. I'll get you a bathrobe."

Stinging at the knee, Harry sat wrapped in his grandfather's stained tan wool bathrobe, which smelled of the Prince Albert tobacco he rolled into Zig-Zag cigarette paper, which when lit, flared, often singeing his nose.

"You do not bleed too much. That is because you are healthy, like I have made you,"

A shiver rode Harry's memory of the one American exception to Bama's Warsaw-enclosed world: the Polar Bear Club, whose members dived into the Atlantic each winter Sunday. In Warsaw, she similarly had defied the Vistula River.

Three-year old Harry, a conscripted cub, had been cradled in her arms and dunked. His body rapidly numbed, but not before he was cut by floating objects which, he realized years later, were chunks of frozen sewage, probably shit.

When he had turned sufficiently blue to ward off diseases for another week, he had been wrapped in a fiercely scratchy wool blanket and force-fed pumpernickel bread smeared with chicken fat. The regimen, she assured, guaranteed him longevity of at least one hundred years. Between them, Bama and Zadeh were raising Methuselah. The immersions ended when he was four and could outrun her.

"Here," Bama said, handing him a needle and thread, "make it for me."

Harry threaded the needle while Bama released awed sounds to celebrate Harry's needle-threading ability. He handed her the needle and she began to sew.

"*Nu*, Heshele, you learn good things in school?"

He decided to tease her.

"I learned about America. How good it is to live in such a free country among nice people."

Her America bristled with enemies: deliverers of catastrophic news like the mailman, who was in the pay of anti-Semites, as were the thieves at the electric and telephone companies. The unsavory band led by a master culprit named Meyer La Guardia.

She waved off education, a new enemy.

"Heshele," she said, "talk politics."

She leaned forward in her chair, her yellow-flecked, brown tartar eyes riveted on him as if he were a lone actor caught in a spotlight. He orated:

"Now that the British and French have deserted Czechoslovakia, Hitler will take what he wants. Already, he is doing it with Franco in Spain. The Poles have taken Tetschen from the Czechs. Jewish shops in Germany have been destroyed. The situation is bad. Sweet America is asleep."

Bama understood none of this except that it was bad for the Jews, as always. It also made little sense to him. Most was verbatim Aba sprinkled with Gabriel Heatter's radio commentary. Harry tried to interest himself in the world and how, according to Aba, a poet who boarded with the Catzkers, it was going to hell, but he couldn't get a handle on it. Too many performers; too many rings. Like Shnozz, the old spieler, dismissed the circus: *Lots of nothing*.

Bama inhaled his words through an open mouth, stretching her taut, leathery facial skin. High, thick cheekbones banished all wrinkles to her forehead. Harry thought she resembled the Indian on the buffalo nickel. With her lips parted, she became the "Indian Brave" coin bank sold at the five-and-ten.

"Heshele," she said, nodding her head in solemn agreement with his discourse, "you are out of the ordinary. And why should it not be? Are you not descendent from the genius of Vilna?"

Praise embarrassed Harry. He could not believe it. In class, he blushed. With Bama, as with his father, praise was automatic, meaningless, except as an expression of love. Harry also had trouble with love. As he hugged Bama before leaving, he hoped she could feel him straining for love.

The temperature had fallen. The few other pedestrians seemed on the verge of sprinting to escape the tormenting air. Harry moved slowly, in no hurry to reach home.

CHAPTER

3

AN HOUR AFTER HARRY HAD LEFT WOODY, A 1939 BLACK PACKARD
(the latest and most expensive model) driven by a chauffeur wearing gray livery pulled away from the Half-Moon Hotel and stopped
at the bike store. Woody climbed into the backseat beside Victor
Menter, who wore a double-breasted, blue pin-striped suit, white-
on-white shirt, gray silk tie seeded with tiny red crowns, black
patent leather pumps and gray spats. A box-backed camel's hair
overcoat lay on his lap. Woody, in sweater, frayed shirt, wrinkled
khaki pants, olive-drab army field jacket and black sneakers,
secured by dirty white laces, feared that he had missed a command.

"Vic, I'm sorry. Did you say this was a dress-up thing?"

"It is and it ain't. So I is and you ain't," Menter answered,
smiling at his own wit. "I don't know who we're going to meet. I
know one, but there might be others. Don't sweat it. Nobody
expects you to dress up. When you do, you look like a circus act.
Tom Thumb or something."

The car turned onto Surf Avenue and moved past rows of
tar-shingled bungalows that lay like Kafka's village under the
heaven-seeking rides of the amusement area. Grime-specked yellow windowshades seemed dreary symbols of common purpose,
perhaps a luckless fraternal order. The streets were abandoned to
the Atlantic's sadistic wind, save for the outdoor counters of Nathan's
Famous, a frigid oasis where a few men, turned turtle inside
upturned collars, wolfed down hot dogs in two bites and bolted.

"What a shithouse," Menter said. "Ain't nothing here worth a shit, except maybe Dr. Couney's premature baby hospital. And I ain't sure they ain't some kind of freak show neither."

His voice, tinged with a hint of a brogue, was high-pitched, as though yet uncracked by adolescence.

Woody nodded, saying:

"I was there once. You pay a quarter and they lift up those preemies behind a glass to show you. Christ, they don't weigh more'n a pound. Look like cigars with hair. You can't believe they're alive. Nobody can tell me they won't grow up to be freaks. Some chance."

Menter shook his head vigorously.

"Couldn't agree more. Don't know why you'd want to fuck with something that nature said should be dead. It's unnatural. Fact is, they'd be better off dead than growing up to be freaks."

The car glided past the borders of Coney and Brighton Beach and onto Ocean Parkway, a wide boulevard lined with tall trees, six-story apartment houses and neat two-family wooden and red-brick homes that ended at Prospect Park. Following the park's serpentine road, they exited at the Grand Army Plaza's replica of the Arc de Triomphe. From there, the red, green and white lights of the shops and movie palaces of Flatbush Avenue Extension marked a wide runway to the Manhattan Bridge.

Halfway across the lower deck of the bridge, the car skidded slightly on the snow-slick metal grating.

"Wheee," Menter laughed, "take us on the Bumper Car, Vince."

The chauffeur squared his back.

"Sorry, Mr. Menter," he said.

"It's OK Vince, I like it. Might even be fun to have a little accident so we could kick some kike's ass."

Woody put his hand on the chauffeur's shoulder, saying, "The right still dynamite?"

Vince lifted his right hand from the wheel and bent his arm

back, flexing his biceps. The dwarf hopped off the seat and stretched to feel the muscle.

"Wow. It's as hard as Papa Dionne's cock."

They all laughed.

"Papa Dionne's cock," Menter said, "that's pretty good. Where'd you hear it?"

"Made it up myself."

"Bullshit."

"I swear I did!"

"Woody, don't get too big for your short-ass britches. Nobody likes a smart-ass."

They drove on in silence through the gray-smudged late afternoon and parked in front of the Flatiron Building on Fifth Avenue and 23rd Street. The chauffeur unlocked the trunk and lifted out a wheelchair. Setting it beside the car, he opened the rear door, cradled Menter in his arms, eased him into the chair, and pushed him through the lobby to an elevator. Woody trotted to keep pace.

"Fourth floor," Menter said to the acne-ridden operator.

They stepped into a long, narrow corridor lined with identical wooden doors, halved by opaque glass. Wide black characters identified room numbers and sometimes the enterprise. The cracks of the narrow-slatted pine floor guarded years of miscellaneous dirt. Splattered ink stains suggested sooty snowflakes. The stagnant air smelled like a room which, opened after years of disuse, releases a hoarded mix of rancid odors.

Menter said: "four-oh-eight."

The chauffeur knocked on the door of *Acme Inc*.

"It's open," said a voice within.

The chauffeur and Woody pushed Menter into a dimly lit room containing a large mahogany desk and five scattered folding chairs. A tall man whose muscular body threatened to burst the seams of a double-breasted midnight blue suit stood in front of the desk. His flattened nose invoked the ring. His eyes, the color of a green traffic light, encouraged the ease of familiarity. Yet he displaced much air, leaving little for others.

"You stay," he said, pointing to Menter. "They wait in the hall."

"The dwarf stays. He's my muscle." Menter replied, motioning Vince out.

"I heard about you and your dwarf."

The man spoke carefully, like a stammerer ever wary of his affliction's spiteful maliciousness. He smiled, revealing a chipped front tooth.

"You think you're some kind of ancient potentate with a royal jester. Does he do tricks?"

Menter feigned sleep. The pose accentuated his mongoloid features. Only at the last moment had fate veered away from inflicting Down's syndrome. Nature's arsenal of errant genes was evident in the ruddy face, egg-shaped head, and half-open, pig-pink eyes. Above these, mundane heredity had triumphed, shaping a canopy of fine, blond curly hair.

"I'm Victor Joseph Menter. And he is Mr. Woodrow Winston. And you must be Tom Noonan. You want to talk or can I nap some more?"

Noonan pursed his lips and said:

"Don't push too hard."

"It's your nickel."

"As you say. The subject is Coney Island. But first I'll show you something."

He lifted from the desk a poster-sized scroll and unfurled it against his chest. It showed two sketches of Orchard Beach in the Bronx. The left was captioned *Orchard Beach then*, the right *Orchard Beach now*. *Then* put Orchard Beach in its geographical context, a dot on Long Island Sound, alongside Rodman's Neck and Hunter's Island. The *now* portion enlarged it as the focal point of the area. A boardwalk, parking facility, play and game areas and a picnic grove were identified in large letters. Noonan's index finger traced the facilities.

"Commissioner Robert Moses did that. He created clean, white beaches, ample bathhouses where families change in comfort and then swim. He gave kids room to play, wholesome places where families picnic under beautiful trees. I had the privilege of working with him."

"Hooray for him and you," Menter interrupted.

Noonan ignored him.

"Recently Commissioner Moses has turned his attention to Coney Island. He wishes to create a park there. I believe this is only the beginning and that eventually he will want to do for Coney Island what he did for Orchard Beach. When he does, my principals wish to own the real estate that the city will be obliged to purchase."

"Sounds good to me. Where do I come in?"

"You are President of the Coney Island Chamber of Commerce and Coney Island Businessmen's Association. An out-side buyer would arouse too much attention. Prices would rise. Therefore you will be the buyer. Everyone will get a fair price for selling. You will receive a fifteen percent commission for each sale."

"And if they don't want to sell?"

Noonan lifted the back of his hand to his lips and kissed a clear diamond set in a wide gold band.

"You are here because I have been told that you have great powers of persuasion. Use them. If persuasion doesn't work, there are other options. I don't care what condition the property is in when we get it. It'll be razed anyway."

Menter nodded and winked. Noonan continued.

"The bank I represent will handle all the financial arrange-ments. Besides commission there will be bonuses. The less money we spend, the more for you. Understood?"

"Understood."

"It is my estimation that Commissioner Moses will want to move soon. I want the property by September."

"By September it is."

In the hallway, Menter rubbed his hands in glee.

"Some sweet deal!"

He crossed himself and, with a continuing flourish, goosed the air.

In the car, Menter screwed a cigarette into a silver holder and lit up. He clamped the holder between his teeth, elevating it to the jaunty angle favored by President Franklin Roosevelt

"Remind you of someone, Woody?"

"Sure Vic, like I always say, FDR."

"I wonder where he got his infantile paralysis. For sure, not like me, from swimmin' in the Gowanus Canal. And he didn't have no kike doctor who stopped coming round when he sniffed no more dough."

"How old were you?"

"Seventeen. You shouldda' seen me before. I was the best shortstop in Brooklyn."

"Tough."

"Yeah, now I'm like you, lookin' at the world through assholes."

"Livin' in fart air."

"Smell much pussy?"

"All the time."

Menter smiled.

"Woody, you think FDR screws his old lady?"

"They got a shitload a' kids."

"Jesus Christ, you're a dummy," Menter said, patting Woody's head lightly, then increasing the force until he drew sound, "they had those kids before he got the paralysis."

"Oh."

Menter cupped his hand under his genitals and said:

"I don't know about FDR, but this can still do plenty damage."

Woody knew different. The whores at Rosie's (owned by Menter) had told him that Menter would have them up to his apartment, sometimes two and three at a time, working for hours on his limp piece of meat.

"Sure thing, Vic," he said, forming a circle with his thumb and forefinger.

"You understand what Noonan told us, Woody?"

"Sure. Buy the Midway property and then some."

Menter grimaced.

"Dumb. Dumb. Dumb. You got a dwarf brain. He covered his ass in case anything fucks up, but he told us to burn it, then pick up the ruins for nothing. That way, him and we make the most money and he figures it will give Moses the idea to step in quick, like a prince, to save Coney."

"Geez."

"What geez! Ain't you never seen a Coney fire before? The kikes set them all the time to collect insurance."

"Sure, but the whole Midway . . ."

The car passed a truck that had been pulled over by a police officer.

"Hey," Menter said, "wasn't that Jamie, the ambidextrous cop?"

"Yeah," Woody answered, "still takin' money with both hands. Jamie can figure a shakedown from his grandmother. I wonder how much he'll get from that driver?"

"Pennies compared to the old days," Menter replied, blowing smoke toward the roof of the car and tilting his head to watch it curl upward.

"Yeah," he continued, "those were the days when Coney was *the* place. All that wide-open beach and all those speedboats grabbing mother lodes of real booze from mother ships."

Menter laughed.

"Once Jamie forgot to check out the Coast Guard on a hot weekend. Speedboats so low in the water with hootch that the booze is makin' mixed drinks with the ocean. They're just about to land at Norton's Point when they spot this Coast Guard cutter. They turn ass and head back to open sea, flying right along the beach. The people on the beach think it's some kind of race until the Coast Guard opens fire. Then it begins to dawn what's happening.

"Jamie, who was on the Steeplechase pier, knows exactly what's happening. So quick, he figures a way to cover his ass. He runs to the end of the pier, pulls his gun and fires at the speedboats which are maybe a hundred yards out of his range. He was even yelling: *Halt, police!* By now the crowd is rooting for the runners. A million people screaming. Then the motor of the Coast Guard ship conks out and it drifts while the runners disappear. Later, Jamie tells the Feds he's sure he hit something and they ask to see the Big Bertha he was lugging with him."

"I heard about that," Woody said.

"Yeah, that was when Frankie Yale was Mr. Coney Island. Frankie gave me my start. He was related to me on my mother's side. When I got the paralysis he said not to worry. Told me to work with my brain. He was right."

"I seen his funeral. Wasn't it the biggest ever in Coney?"

"Yeah. People came from all over. Frankie was a travelin' man. Frankie goes to Chicago and Big Jim Colosimo dies. Frankie shakes hands with Dean O'Banion and Dean gets a great funeral. Al Capone used to work as a bartender in one of Frankie's Coney joints. Frankie never trusted him. He was right. Frankie got shot to pieces on Al's orders."

In Menter's penthouse apartment atop the Half-Moon Hotel, Woody mixed two glasses of rye and Coke.

"Who can we get for torches?" Menter said as much to himself as to Woody. "Good outside pros will cut the profit. Any local talent?"

"There ain't nothing here but dumb working stiffs and horny freaks," Woody snapped.

"Freaks? In winter?"

"Yeah, Vic, there's a whole house of 'em livin' here now. The ones who work the sideshows in the summer. Fifi, she's French, a Frog fat lady, bought a house on West Eighth and rents out to her freak buddies. Makes a good buck, too."

"Who lives there?"

"Let's see. There's Olga, the World's Ugliest Woman; Jo-Jo,

the Dog-Faced Boy; Albert-Alberta, the Half-Man Half-Woman; the Blue Man; the boy with two mouths; Otto, the Strongman and, oh yeah, Lohu and Mohu, the Japanese Siamese Twins, and maybe some more."

"They're the torches," Menter said, grinning.

"Are you kiddin'? Those geeks couldn't light a cigarette."

"I can teach 'em."

"What makes you think they'll do it?"

Menter squared himself against the back of his wheelchair.

"In Coney, they do anything Victor Menter tells 'em to do. They're nothing but a bunch of prick suckers, thieves and fags. And them that ain't, my cops will say they are. Freaks don't talk back to Victor Menter. They do as told."

"But after, Vic, they could squeal."

Menter smiled.

"We'll make sure they can't."

"Huh?"

Menter clapped his hands loudly.

"I hate freaks! Almost as much as kike doctors!"

In the Cherry Tree: February 1, 1936

Aba: *Ivan Pavlov has died.*

Harry: *Who was he?*

Aba: *He was a Russian who tortured dogs.*

Harry: *Was he punished?*

Aba: *On the contrary, he was greatly honored all over the world.*

Harry: *By people who hate dogs?*

Aba: *Probably most deeply by those, but everyone declared him a genius for proving that a human being can fool a dog into thinking that it is about to be fed, not by showing it food, but by ringing a bell.*

Harry: *All dogs?*

Aba: *Up till now, only the dogs he tortured. But there is no reason to believe that any dog could stand up to Comrade Pavlov's methods.*

Harry: *What about cats?*

Aba: *What about human beings?*

Harry: *They are different from dogs.*

Aba: *How so?*

Harry: *Well . . . they speak. They would tell each other: Don't let Pavlov fool you, there is no food.*

Aba: *And what if they were so hungry that they wanted to believe there was food, even if they knew there was not?*

Harry: *I would never believe it.*

Aba: *And what about God?*

Harry: *Ha. I know that one. A boy in school told me. Dog is God spelled backward.*

Aba: *That is not what I meant, wonderful American boy. Now listen carefully: On Sunday bells ring all over the world and when goyim hear them they believe there is a God. Correct?*

Harry: *Yes.*

Aba: *And on Saturday, Jews believe there is a God. Correct?*

Harry: *Yes.*

Aba: *So who is the right God: the Sunday God or the Saturday God?*

Harry: *The Saturday God. The God of the Jews.*

Aba: *Heshele, did you hear a bell ring?*

Harry: *No.*

Aba: *You must listen more carefully.*

CHAPTER
4

A DISTANT PHONE RANG, INSISTENT AND ANGRY, LIKE A BABY'S hunger wail. The governor was calling to commute Harry's death sentence for an unspecified crime Harry had not committed. Harry strained against the straps that lashed him into the electric chair. Only he could answer the phone and save himself. He tried to call for help, but his lips would not part.

He awoke screaming but heard no sound. Wet, fuzzy cotton coated his pillow-buried lips. The ringing went on. He stumbled toward the phone in the living room.

"Hello," he said.

"Allo, Meester Kaatz."

"The name is Catzker."

"No. No. Ze name is Kaatz. Believe me."

"OK. But this is not he. I'm his son."

"Is ze fadder by home?"

"No, he's not."

"Vell, I'm sure you could help me. You see I'm a loyal reader of ze fadder, Meester Kaatz. And all yesterday, *Shabbes,* I vas terrible vorried about vat vass to befall Soorkaleh. Of course I couldn't call on *Shabbos.*"

"Of course."

"So tell me, does Soorkaleh find out dat dat fine young man vat loves her and vants to marry her did not perish in a pogrom in Russia and right now is by steerage in a shiff on his vay to America?"

"I really don't . . . "

"And vill she call off dat terrible match dat lousy *shadchan* made for her with dat kosher butcher vat is old enough to be her fadder and alvays has bloody hands, yet?"

"My father doesn't tell anyone what the next installment is, not even my mother."

"You a good son. But, if you'll please, in my case to make a exceptional. You see it's not only Soorkaleh vat vorries me. Vat about Chaim? Vorking eighteen hours a day for dat rotten sveatshop owner to bring over his beloved Miriam and zere two beautiful daughters, Rachel and Esther. How can he save enough money? And even if he does, vill ze goyim at Ellis Island discover Esther's sickness—vouldn't even mention it for somevone to hear—and send her back to Poland?"

"I'm sure everything will turn out OK."

"Tank you. I knew you knew."

"No. I just said . . . "

"So vat is goink to happen to dat nogoodnik, Soorkaleh's brother, Schmelik? He's goink to abandon his vife and children for dat *kurveh*, you should pardon ze expression, Malka, vat now calls herself Margery yet?"

"I'm sure by Monday or Tuesday everything will be all right."

"So tell me how?"

"I don't know. Only my father knows."

"You not a nice boy."

"Sorry."

"In fact, rotten."

Click.

Harry replaced the receiver. The phone rang.

"Allo, Mr. Kaatzen."

"Wrong number."

He laid the disconnected receiver beside the phone. Harry was not supposed to do that. It was his responsibility to speak to readers who were following his father's novel, which was serialized on weekdays in the Yiddish newspaper *The Morning Journal*. The paper catered to Orthodox Jews, whose religion barred the use of phones on Saturday. By Sunday, many could no longer bear the worry over the perils afflicting the characters.

Today's first call had been relatively short. Often readers invented intricate solutions, demanding that he confirm or deny. Harry enjoyed telling his father the more imaginative scenarios. If his father nodded, it was not because the reader had hit upon the truth. There was no truth until his father wrote that day's install- ment during the one-hour subway ride from Stillwell Avenue to the Canal Street office of the *Morning Journal*. However, the nods often signaled that the reader had become a coauthor.

Harry returned to his room and laid a record on the turntable of a box-shaped portable phonograph. He watched the disc move in perfect circles, stretching the golden letters until they lost mean- ing and snaked, as if poured, onto the black label. Harry bent over the record, trying to circle his head to match the seventy-eight- revolutions-per-minute and determine whether a perfect synchro- nization would unscramble the letters. It was an experiment in relativity. Harry was interested in relativity because his grandfather resembled greatly Albert Einstein.

Harry grooved the needle on the smooth outer rim of the record. Billie Holiday's freakish voice rose from the shiny surface.

"Must you play that junk?"

Harry's mother, palms dug into her hips, stood in the door- way. The light cast through the windows by the low January sun dabbed a blush of orange on her ivory facial skin that clung tightly to the cheekbones and a long, thin, dipping nose. Her large, oval- shaped eyes, lightly rinsed by a translucent blue, blinked often as if accepting endless curtain calls. Thick yellow hair, the color of a Van Gogh haystack, was bunched into a tight bun at the back while loose strands fell at random angles onto her forehead. She was con- sidered strikingly beautiful. Harry did not agree, even though he owed most of his features to her.

"It's Billie Holiday," he replied reverentially, a calculated irritant.

"It's a sick cat. And why is the phone off the hook?"

"I already had two or three calls. What's so bad if they get a busy signal?"

"What's so bad if . . ." she mimicked his singsong speech, "your father's son . . . so bad is that we need the two pennies he makes from that paper, that's so bad."

"Oh, Mom, how will they know we're not talking to someone?"

"Those Jews"—she distorted her face by puffing her cheeks and spreading her nostrils—"those Jews! Don't worry, they'll know."

She thrust her face toward him.

"Pliss, Miss Op-er-at-or, if you'll be so kind, you could check dis number to see anyone is talking. It's ah terrible emergency. Off ze hook. Dank you so very much . . . Allo, Mr. Editor, what kind of person is it you have to write by your paper what vouldn't talk to readers? Such an insult!"

Harry walked past her and replaced the receiver.Immediately, the phone rang.

The caller had discovered blanket salvation: the Irish Sweepstakes. At his sixth sweepstakes winner, Harry's father plunged through the front door, rushed past him, grabbed a book from the crammed bookshelf and flopped onto the couch. He turned the pages ferociously until his small brown eyes alit on wisdom.

As he read, the broad Slavic face, dominated by a wide, flat nose and a massive forehead lined with furrows resembling the Palmer Method exercises for good penmanship, expressed puzzlement, then tentative agreement and finally epiphany.

Harry was not sure of the book's title, but he knew its author: Sigmund Freud. Dr. Freud was being consulted for psychological insight into whatever mishap had befallen Moshe Catzker during this morning's battle with a 1934 Model T Ford.

The Ford was a present given to his father a year ago by a reader, who had bought a new car, and rewarded the writer for years of happy endings.

At the time of the gift, Moses Catzker was thirty-six and had never driven a car. His relationship with things mechanical was adversarial. A single victory, the use of a can opener, was a talent he preferred not to test often.

Immediately, the car had inspired him to consult with John Dos Passos, Sherwood Anderson and Theodore Dreiser in planning trips across America. He, Aba, and other friends would circle the parked vehicle like unhorsed Indians, first touching, then entering. All eyes swept the road for danger, cheering as his father wrenched the steering wheel of the stationary vehicle.

The Negro delivery boy from a local grocery, hired to teach him to drive, quit after the first lesson, actually ten minutes into it. His successor, an off-duty cop, lasted a bit longer by insisting that lessons begin at five AM, with the understanding that the appearance of another moving vehicle automatically ended the session. Eventually, the cop suggested a driving school, which was expensive but guaranteed a license.

Two weeks later Moses Catzker had been licensed by the State of New York to operate a motor vehicle. He told Harry that he had passed the test with flying colors, quoting the inspector: "I've seen enough. Wow! But a deal is a deal. You pass, buddy."

America beckoned, but leaving Brooklyn presented a formidable obstacle. On the first attempt to make Manhattan, his passengers, the same three who had cheered his stationary heroics, convinced him to turn back and try again on a cloudy day so as to avoid the sun's glare that was distorting his vision. Thereafter, they declined to accompany him, citing the joys of "soloing" à la James Cagney and Pat O'Brien.

After much pleading, he had agreed to take Harry, but only for a drive limited to around the block. As the ignition sparked the engine, Harry lost the father he knew. The usual hunched, slack shoulders turned as square as Frankenstein's monster. White knuckles strangled the steering wheel. He eyed the empty street for five minutes before bucking away from the curb. At the first intersection, a pedestrian, glancing through the windshield, had been moved to say: *Mister, mister, take it easy.*

Soon dents of unexplained origin began to appear. Upon examination, Harry concluded that most were the results of contact with pushcarts, trees, fences and fire hydrants.

Eventually, the car was becalmed except for his father's dawn drives which always provoked consultation with Dr. Freud.

Freud was his father's family physician, seemingly a phone call away. The same familiarity extended to other residents of the book-shelves. A discussion between his father and Aba drew no distinction between Mani Leib, a Yiddish poet living in California, and Dostoyevsky, Tolstoy or Proust. All were spoken of as if they were friends who happened to be out of town for the moment.

His father closed the book with a triumphant clap, winking as he walked past Harry, who offered the receiver to share a torrent of Yiddish. His father circled the air with his index finger, poked the side of his head, whispered "meshugah" and disappeared into the kitchen.

The caller was saying: "So after Muttel wins the sweepstakes he has enough money for Leah's operation, isn't it?"

"Sure," Harry said. "I sure hope it all turns out the way you say."

"Trust me, *boychik*, it will. I am a man what knows life. Give your father a greeting from me and tell him David Mersky prays for him."

In the kitchen, his parents sat at a table protected by a covering of blue oilcloth. His father dunked toast into a cup of coffee, bent his head to the rim and slurped the soaked dough. His mother strained her coffee through an oblong of white sugar clamped between her front teeth. Both dragged on cigarettes, swallowing smoke with liquid.

"Ah, Heshele," his father said, wiping his mouth on the sleeve of his tweed jacket, "there is something I must tell you." His father's English was cemented under the dual coat of Yiddish and Russian.

A year ago, when his mother became convinced that money could be made speaking in English on Yiddish culture to synagogue men's clubs and assimilated fraternal groups, his father, at her insistence, had enrolled in a diction school which guaranteed to denude all foreign elements. After three weeks he had quit, saying: "I did it for my teacher. He was starting to sound like me."

His father laid a hand on Harry's shoulder, and with the other beckoned his wife to pay close attention. She moved her chair farther away.

"Listen to what happened this morning. I was driving on the Belt Parkway when all of a sudden I see a crazy man who stands in the middle of the road and is waving for me to go off the road and onto the grass. Since I have had much trouble staying off the grass and trained myself very well not to, I cannot follow this crazy man's instructions, even though the car in front of me does so. When I get closer I see that this man is a policeman who is looking at me like I am crazy, while I am looking at him like he is crazy for asking me to do such an illegal thing. All the time we are getting closer and I am thinking about my driver's manual and what it says about right-of-way so I forget about the policeman until I see him dive headfirst onto the grass as I go by and hit a large metal garbage can that is blocking the road.

"I stop to see what damage there is and the policeman runs up to me and shouts, 'What's wrong with you buddy? If you would have killed me, I would have beat the hell out of you.'"

Harry and his father laughed, rolling their eyes at each other to visually Ping-Pong the punch line and keep the moment going.

"Jokes, always jokes," his mother said.

"Velia," his father said, "we must—"

She cut him off.

"We must, we must, we must do this and we must do that. So do it! No, *we must* means me, while you sit on East Broadway with the rest of the geniuses and say *we must*."

"Now, Leah . . ."

"The name is Velia."

"So. And what am I today, still Maurice or maybe we are back to Mike?"

She offered him a derisive smile.

"The Mikes of this country make a living."

His father feigned adjusting a monocle. He picked up a napkin and read:

"Mike Catzker, American tycoon, also odd jobs."

"A regular Eddie Cantor, without his fortune."

"Ah, Eddie does not know the nobility of failure. I have observed the heavy burden a successful father places on the life of his children. I am making sure that this does not happen to Heshele."

"Well, we must . . ." his mother said, shrugging her shoulders to indicate helplessness, "we must get going. We are meeting them for brunch before the theater. Harry, you will clean up."

After washing the cups and saucers, he sat on the couch in the living room and covered his face with an open volume of Freud. As his parents entered, he lowered the book slowly, revealing awestruck eyes. His father laughed. His mother sighed and adjusted a black seal fur hat, then smoothed the collar of a matching coat. His father's gray slouch hat was circled by a blue band that held a small red feather, The brim was snapped down, front and back. Under a tweed overcoat, a red wool tie lay on a gray corduroy shirt. She chose his clothes.

Harry walked toward them. His mother turned her cheek toward his lips, retrieving it at first touch. His father lightly scratched Harry's scalp.

"See you, Heshele," he said.

It might be as long as a week before Harry saw either of them, unless he got up before seven when his mother left for work or his father awakened before Harry left for school at eight-thirty. His parents spent their nights at the Cafe Royal on Second Avenue in Manhattan, where Yiddish writers and actors ate and argued. For Harry, there were notes and coins.

"'Bye," Harry said.

His father snapped his fingers.

"I almost forgot. Your friend Aba is coming back tomorrow from his great triumph in Philadelphia where he read his poetry to more people than greeted Charles Lindbergh in Paris."

They turned and walked to the door. She, unsteady on three-inch heels, slid her arm under his and said:

"Always jokes . . . what's so funny?"

CHAPTER

5

AFTER SCHOOL THE NEXT DAY, HARRY TURNED DOWN FRED KRAUSE'S offer of joint Joe Baker stalking. Fred was Harry's only regular friend at school and that was less friendship than a shared interest in the mystery of Joe Baker.

Joe was the most amazing human machine in the penny arcade. He could add, divide or multiply any amount of numbers as quickly as they were thrown at him. Once Harry, answer in hand, had fired at Joe fifty numbers ranging from billions to fractions. The correct answer immediately had tumbled out of Joe's almost toothless mouth. Since then, Harry had conceded that Joe was never wrong and had been content to fill the void between Joe's gums with spur-of-the-moment random numbers.

When not mashing numbers, Joe spoke scatology, parroting for the most part statements taught him by the whores at Rosie's. He introduced himself to all passersby with never-varying words:

"My name is Joe Baker. My prick is a faker. My balls weigh a thousand pounds."

The revelation oozed spittle, while his right hand performed masturbatory motions on the dangling end of a clothesline rope holding up his patched trousers. Women, new to the neighborhood or visiting, shrieked or swung heavy pocketbooks to ward him off, while Joe's widening eyes beheld mad assailants.

Once Fred had reported a Joe statement: "No eat, no shit. No cat, no fuck." Harry had tailed Joe for a week to see if he really did.

Eventually Fred's older brother had pointed out that Joe's *cat* was a synonym of his own making that did not serve.

Although Harry had no close friends, he did not consider himself a loner. He simply preferred the company of adults, who understood things such as his discovery that if he unplugged a playing radio, for a moment afterward the disconnection, sound continued. Fred had pleaded for the secret to this magic trick. Aba had put a name to it: *limbo*.

The word had dazzled Harry. The sound was as mysterious as the phenomenon it described. Onomatopoetic words had excited him since he was six, when, at Hebrew school, the formless void that was the world before the Creation was described in Genesis as *Sohoo V'Vohoo*. Harry had seen and heard *Sohoo V'Vohoo* in the dark, shapeless anger of the Atlantic. *Limbo* was also at hand since Coney was a gigantic radio plugged in every spring and unplugged each fall, yet the sound went on. When, in the cherry tree, he had told Aba that they lived in *limbo* surrounded by *Sohoo V'Vohoo*, the poet had hugged him, almost causing both to topple from the thick branch.

"You are five thousand years old," Aba had exulted, "you have inherited the sad history of your people."

Harry scuffed at yesterday's snow. It was not packed tight enough for belly flopping on his sled. He decided to check at Woody's on the condition of his bike.

A tingling bell attached to the door announced his entrance, but no one appeared. At the spot at which Soldier had materialized, he found a door and knocked. There was no answer. He tried the knob and beheld a graveyard of dismembered bikes. Handlebars, fenders, chains, wheels and seats lay scattered like debris following an explosion. The only light in the windowless room was cast by a small, bare bulb hanging from a knotted wire.

Something moved. On a cot in the corner farthest away from him, Soldier, lying prone, slowly rose from the waist to a seated position.

"Hello Soldier, " Harry said.

Soldier did not acknowledge him. He swung off the cot, walked stiff-legged to the wall opposite and pounded his forehead against it. After some thirty seconds of violent collisions and soft cries, he placed his right leg behind his left, executed a smart military about-face, marched back to the cot and lay down. Blood streaked his forehead.

The bulb suddenly flashed brightly, crackled and went dark. Harry jumped backward, brushing against something.

"Hey, kind o' goosey, ain't ya?"

Harry looked down at Woody.

"No, it's just that . . ."

"Soldier have one of his spells?"

"I guess."

"Has to do with the war. Pay it no mind. No one else does."

"Doesn't he hurt himself."

"Soldier? Nothin' hurts him anymore. Hey, I'm glad you come by. Got some business to talk over with you."

They picked their way among haphazardly stacked bikes. Woody stopped in front of a green racer.

"Kid, I'm sorry to tell ya that your bike is kaput. I know that's terrible for ya' and since I seen how it wasn't your fault that it happened, I figured out a deal. I'll let you have this one, even up for yours. I can get some dough for your good parts, and if I don't break even . . . hell, what are friends for?"

Harry stared at the bike of his dreams. Inside his forehead he was hunched over, squeezing the curled-back handlebars and pumping the slender wheels, while Captain Ziegenbaum spit apoplectic German curses.

"Hey kid, you look like Soldier. Whaddya say?"

"Yes! Yes! Yes!"

"Good. You can ride it outta here."

Harry grabbed the handlebars.

"Hey, wait. Remember, we got a deal. You're on the payroll now. A nickel an hour. Let's go in the back and talk it over."

As they neared the door to Woody's room, it opened and a dwarf emerged. Neither dwarf spoke, avoiding eye contact. Woody lay down on the unmade bed and spoke to the ceiling.

"That was my brother, Teddy. He's a shit. Still works as a Moon Man at Luna. Sucks up to anyone who pats him on the head. Even tries to look like a midget so he can hook on with that *Call for Philip Morris* crap."

Woody anticipated the questions racing through Harry's mind.

"I know, I know. No, my parents weren't dwarfs. My father was close to six foot."

"Are you twins?" Harry blurted out.

Woody sighed.

"I'm thirty-three. Teddy's a year younger."

"Does he live near here?

"He lives *right* here. We don't speak to each other, but we sleep in the same bed. Plenty of room for the two of us. But I don't talk to that ass-kisser."

Harry sensed that further questions were unnecessary. Answers would be given, as when Aba gulped a water glass of vodka, looked at him, but spoke to himself.

"Why do I let him live here? Because he's my brother. He's Theodore Roosevelt Winston. He owes that moniker to me. I scared my folks so that they picked a name six months before he was born that couldn't possibly fit a dwarf. I keep him around for another reason too: he's a reminder that you can beat the odds. Figure the odds on my parents coming up with two dwarfs. They brought home a million-to-one shot. And now let me tell ya somethin'. It's a relief to be a dwarf. Everybody's got a dwarf inside o' him waitin' to come out and worried shitless that it will. But I'm out already. Nothin' to worry about."

In the thick silence, Harry visualized himself as a dwarf. Suddenly, Bama's respect for the evil eye did not seem so crazy.

Woody jumped off the bed and sang while tapping a time step:

When you're smilin', when you're smilin', the whole world smiles with you. When you're laughin', when you're laughin', the sun comes smilin' through. But when you're cryin' you bring on the rain. So stop your cryin' and be happy again. Just keep on smilin', cause when you're smilin', the whole world smiles with you.

The voice was naive and squeaky, like Betty Boop's.

"Like it?"

"Sure."

"Could have done it professionally. Got offers. We'll bill you as *The Dwarf Troubador* or *Wee Bonnie Woody*. No thanks. No pats on the head. I ain't no freak."

Woody pointed his index finger at Harry.

"You'll see what ass-kissin' freaks are. Can you work tomorrow?"

"Yes."

"OK. We'll start you off with the house of freaks on West Eighth. A bunch of them live together since about three years ago. Now everyone hates everyone else. Serves 'em right. Anyway you pick up their slips and you also tell 'em that Woody's got a job for them and they'll be hearin' from me. Then you come here and drop off the slips. Got it?"

"Sure do."

"OK. Grab your bike."

Woody lay down and closed his eyes. He looked dead, his grotesque features the residue of a fatal disease.

Harry walked the green racer toward the boardwalk. He held its handlebars lightly, removing one finger at a time until only his thumbs controlled it. Its tires drew a slim, graceful line in the snow. He tilted the bike from thumb to thumb, enjoying its lightness before gripping the handlebars, setting his right foot on the pedal and, on the run, vaulting his left leg over the seat and landing on hard leather.

He pedaled toward the boardwalk, skidding on patches of snow and shifting his weight to right himself. The chain began to slip. On the incline of the boardwalk ramp, it disengaged completely.

He dismounted and for the first time examined the bike. It was a creature of Soldier's junk: rims dented by hammer marks, different-size chain links, the seat stem too thin for its holder.

He sat down on a bench facing the ocean and tried to occupy his mind with piercing the horizon until he could see Europe. Behind him he heard the clatter of a rolling metal door shuttering a boardwalk concession. Moments later a hand gently touched on his shoulder.

"Hello Harry."

He did not answer.

Fingers kneaded the flesh between his neck and shoulders He shivered like a puppy drying itself.

The probing fingers belonged to Schnozz, one of the few penny arcade owners who remained open the year round. His nickname did not derive from an unremarkable nose, but from his claim to have played the piano for Jimmy Durante at Coney beer gardens around 1910. Schnozz had no use for the current incarnation of the people's playground, obliterating it with Proustian recall of Coney's golden age.

A month ago Harry had sat on the same bench anticipating Schnozz's next story. The wind, as now, had burrowed under the sand and the sun had made its first touch on the ocean, like a fat bather testing temperature with his big toe. Schnozz, seated beside him, had transported them to his beloved Dreamland Park.

"Can you picture it?" Schnozz had demanded, leaving no doubt that Harry could not fully imagine the required majesty. "A million electric lights. One million!"

In the smooth cadence of the sideshow spieler he had been, he daubed like a pointilist, dotting white buildings on expanses of grace and pleasure. A derisive hand dismissed the vulgarity of Luna Park's *Trip to the Moon,* where one was greeted by midgets dressed as Moon Men. Dreamland, a place of taste, had offered three hundred midgets in a life-scale replica of Jonathan Swift's *Lilliput,* augmented by a few giants from *Brobdingnag*.

Dreamland had opened in 1905 and burned to the ground in 1911. Schnozz's words brought back to short life birds unable to escape the inferno with flightless singed wings and crazed lions and tigers shot to death by policemen suddenly on safari in Coney.

After the tale, Schnozz had suggested a walk on the beach. The strong wind had reddened Schnozz's pockmarked face, lodging sand in the crevices. He had guided Harry under the boardwalk, where they could rest and talk.

They sat on the cold sand. Schnozz's words slowed and fell to a whisper. His right hand smoothed Harry's cheek, moved across his chest and found the buckle of his belt. His fly was parted, button by button. Schnozz dug for his penis which popped out like a released jack-in-the-box. Harry had watched Schnozz's naked pate move over his penis and dip like the arcade game's miniature crane that descended, metal jaws spread wide, to claim a prize. Soon Harry had filled Schnozz's mouth. The old man swallowed and wiped his white-specked lips with the back of his hand. Harry, nauseated, had run to the ocean's edge to submerge his face in the jarring cold. When he had turned around, Schnozz was gone.

Schnozz sat down beside Harry. Their knees touched under the bar of the bike. Harry slid out of contact. Schnozz mocked him by widening the gap with a shimmylike thrust of his buttocks. His knee hit a wheel.

"Where did you get this bike?" he asked.

"Woody."

"What! You brought it from that lousy dwarf?"

"Sort of a trade."

"For that beauty you had!"

"I had an accident and it was all busted. Woody took it for parts and gave me this one."

Schnozz gripped Harry's shoulder.

"He's a crook and worse. Let's you and me go over to that store and have it out with him right now."

"No, Schnozz. I sort of like Woody, and with people you like . . . "

Schnozz squeezed Harry's hand.

"Want to take a walk on the beach?" he said, smiling shyly, like an unsure child attempting to cajole an adult.

Harry returned the pressure to show friendship, but shook his head. They were even now. Harry had paid a fair price for permanent admission to Schnozz's fabulous spiels.

CHAPTER
6

ABA STOLZ, NÉ AVRAM STEIN, WINNER OF PRESTIGIOUS PRIZES FOR Yiddish poetry, illegal alien, having entered the country three years ago on a two-month visa to cover the 1936 US presidential election for a defunct Polish publication, sighed and lowered himself onto the outside steps of the house on West 35th Street, where he boarded with the Catzkers.

He had just returned from an odyssey that had begun with a phone call from Samuel Modell, a wealthy Philadelphia textile manufacturer.

"Hello, is that Aba Stolz?"

"Yes."

"Aba Stolz, the poet?"

"The same."

"Good. I would like you to come to Philadelphia."

"Why?"

"To read your poetry. Why else?"

"Indeed, why else?"

Train tickets were sent. On a Sunday evening, Stolz had arrived at the Modell home, where a group of affluent Philadelphia Jews were gathered for dessert, coffee and culture.

Modell, a man in his fifties who proudly displayed a paunch of affluence under a tight vest spanned by a gold chain, took him aside.

"All the people in the room have contributed funds for you."

"Thank you."

Modell's bland brown eyes darted left and right. He whispered:

"You don't write anything dirty, do you? Some of the people understand Yiddish."

"I will keep it clean. You may be the judge."

"I don't understand Yiddish."

"Then, why . . . ?

"My mother . . ."

"Ah, she is here tonight?

"No, she died twenty-five years ago. She spoke Yiddish. Especially when she didn't want me to understand what she was telling my father."

Before the reading, he mingled and explained poetry.

"How do you know so many words that rhyme?"

"There is a secret way to use a dictionary. Kabbalistic."

In the salon, amid couches and chairs upholstered in an explosion of foliage, Modell introduced him:

"We are proud to have with us tonight Aba Stolz, a Yiddish poet whose gifts have brought joy to millions of our coreligionists from coast to coast."

While reciting the first poem, he scanned the faces for comprehension. Some twenty men and women somehow had managed to assume identical frozen expressions, as if staring at a tiny dot indicated by an optometrist. He wondered if there had been group practice. The only exception was Modell, who, from the first word, wept.

Following the last poem there was a long silence until the audience realized the recitation had concluded. He received discreetly muffled applause. Modell, red-eyed, waved a thick envelope.

"Poet Stolz," he said, his arm sweeping the room and catching Stolz in the neck, "all these good people have contributed funds to help you continue your wonderful work."

He handed Stolz the envelope, which Stolz accepted while transforming his benefactor into as an organ grinder and himself an ingratiating monkey.

Stolz had come away with twenty single-dollar bills. He rubbed at the roll in his pocket, accepting as just irony the possibility that he might never enjoy spending it since he was sentenced to freeze to death on the stoop for the recidivist crime of losing his key.

Snow began to fall. To pump heat into his veins, he imagined the *Jewish Daily Forward* running a skimpy obituary on him. Enraged, he punched Schrage, the editor, bloodying his nose, and triumphantly shouting: "Ha, you thought dead was the end of me."

Harry, head down, his forlorn eyes fixed on his bike's useless chain, did not see Aba.

"Hey, *boychik*," Aba shouted, "all the gold in the *Goldeneh Medinah* has been found. You can stop looking."

"Aba!" Harry dropped the bike and leapt into an embrace.

"Hoo-hah, such a welcome. In Philadelphia, they were slightly more restrained. Anyway Heshele, you saved my life. I lost my key—don't say *what again*—and was within an icicle of death, when you, my savior, arrived."

Harry ran up the steps to open the door.

"Heshele, the bike. It seems to be a different one. Don't come down. I'll get it."

Inside they sat in the kitchen. Aba poured himself half a water glass of vodka and gulped the colorless liquid.

Harry thought of Aba as a man on fire. His carrot-colored, uncombed hair stood up like licks of flame. The matching beard was a brush fire scorching albino-white skin and menacing a thin hooked nose. His green eyes were saved from incineration by their luminous wetness. Chapped lips, however, had been seared into permanent parting, revealing yellow teeth that rooted at any available angle like trees desperately clinging to a mountainside.

"*Nu*, Heshele," Aba asked, "what is new in this America of yours?"

"And not yours?"

"Good, Heshele. Answering a question with a question will never get you in trouble. Answers are dangerous. Once, in Warsaw, a *pogromchik* asked me the time. Foolishly, I told it to him. He slapped me for thinking that he did not know the time of day. I should have said: *What time would your excellency wish it to be?* For this he would have also slapped me but with the force of a question, not an answer."

"Is that true?"

"Does it matter? If it is not true it will be. Everything will be true and false by turns."

"Did they like your poetry in Philadelphia?"

"Poetry had nothing to do with it. They liked patting themselves on the back because they were supporting a Yiddish poet. If they could have done so without listening to his poetry, they would have been much happier."

Aba's eyes did not dance now. They were elsewhere, collecting sadness. It was a harvest common to Harry's father and his friends when they considered the rapidly shrinking number of Yiddish-speaking people on earth.

Once Fred Krause had come by the house to pick him up. Ackerman, the playwright, and Aba were arguing, in Yiddish, as to whether it was in fact true that Tolstoy believed that Anna Karenina could see her own eyes glowing in the dark. As was normal for an important conversation, it provoked derisive finger pointing and fist shaking, while the decibel levels rose apace. Fred had been riveted, absolutely certain he was witnessing a prelude to mayhem. Ackerman, catching Fred's intense interest, had asked him in English:

"Do you understand Yiddish?"

"No."

Ackerman had sighed: "*Oy,* I should be so lucky"

"I should be in Palestine," Aba said. "The Arabs are killing Jews, the Jews are killing Arabs and the British are killing everyone. It must be a land of poets. And furthermore, if Palestine becomes a Jewish homeland, it could save the Yiddish language."

"That would be great. You would be a great poet there."

"But that will not be, my optimistic American friend. In fact, a Jewish homeland will deliver the last rites for Yiddish."

"I don't understand."

"Of course you don't. You see straight ahead, in your wonderful American way. The facts are these: If there is a Jewish homeland, the official language will be Hebrew, a biblical language about as relevant to the modern world as the Bible. Yet preferable to Yiddish."

"Why?"

"Because Yiddish is the enemy of all nations. Actually, if Yiddish were proclaimed the language of a Jewish homeland, it would be the fulfillment of a millennial Jewish dream—the creation of a perfect paradox: a nation born and committing suicide simultaneously. Consider a country running on Yiddish. If you wish to call a man an idiot, you call him *a soldier*. If you wish to promote him to super idiot, you label him *a prime minister*. To identify vulgarians or worse, look to designations for men who drive trucks or till the soil . . . and so it goes. So what you have is a nation whose heroes, leaders and builders receive simultaneously medals and dunce caps. No state could survive that lingua franca."

"Will there be a Jewish homeland, Aba?"

"I doubt it. The goyim need Jews to beat up and borrow money from. There doesn't seem to be any replacement for these necessities of goyishe life."

The front door opened and closed. His mother, who despite dedication to lightness and delicacy retained a floor-shaking, flat-footed planting of one definite foot after another, entered the kitchen.

Aba rose and embraced her.

"So, how was Philadelphia?" she asked.

"It was Philadelphia."

"Don't I know it. The first three years of Harry's life we lived there. Do you remember, Harry?"

"No."

"Of course you do. I wheeled you everywhere. People looked into the carriage and said how beautiful you and I were. Don't you remember that?"

"No."

"Anything to be contrary. He begins everything with *no* and his father with *we must* Between them I have no luck."

"Where is Moishe?" Aba asked.

"Who knows? Playing cards in that dive, or discussing something he knows nothing about, like making money. I didn't feel well, so I came home."

She turned to Harry.

"Did you eat?"

Harry held up his quarter.

"So what are you waiting for? I'm surely not cooking."

"I was talking to Aba. I saved his life."

"Absolutely . . ."

His mother cut Aba short.

"I have no doubt. Have you gone completely crazy, Aba? Now, you are riding a bike."

"Excuse me, but I don't know how to ride a bike. Wherever did you get that idea?"

"From the bike in the hall that I almost killed myself on. It looks like it's been in an accident."

"As far as I know, it belongs to this American boy."

"Nonsense. He has a beautiful bike that cost a fortune."

The silence was Harry's to fill. He looked at Aba, wishing magic: Couldn't a poet, a man who knew the secret meanings of words, know to say simple words: *It was a joke, Velia. It is my bike.* Aba was silent.

His mother, excited by the scent of catastrophe, pressed her lips together, draining the blood. Harry mumbled: "It's my bike, sort of."

"Sort of!"

He told the story, ending with a defense of the bike as a beauty worth much more than the other, but in need of a few repairs.

"A beauty! Worth more! If it's worth a nickel, it's a lot."

"Oh, Mom . . ."

"Don't oh Mom me. Do you know how long I had to sit at a typewriter to earn enough money for your bike? Do you know!"

Aba held up his hand.

"Velia, easy, slowly. We must . . ."

"Another *we must* country heard from. Harry, we are going to see that thief."

"The store is closed."

She stomped toward the hall.

"Closed, ha. We'll see."

Harry's eyes pleaded with Aba, who rose shakily and scratched Harry's scalp.

"Don't worry, American boy, we'll find a way. Velia," he called, "I will come with you. In matters of commerce, I am a regular J.P. Morgan."

"Come if you want. But no jokes. It is not funny."

His mother's pounding brought Soldier to the door. Harry wheeled in the bike, as she demanded:

"Is that your bike?"

Soldier, fulfilling an informational request, examined the bike.

"Damn, yes, Ma'am, that's one of mine all right."

"It's a piece of junk."

"Damn, no Ma'am."

"It's all crooked!"

Soldier slid his palms over the handlebars.

"Damn, you see, Ma'am, once something is broken you can never make it like it was. Even if you take a piece of wood and saw it perfectly into two pieces and then glue it together, it looks perfect, but it ain't. There's the sawdust you lost. Things never mend back to the way they was."

"What do I care for two pieces of wood!"

Harry's dread was diverted by his mother playing Margaret Dumont to Soldier's earnest Chico Marx.

His mother was now demanding to see the owner, a bill of sale, which in any case would be invalid because Harry was a minor, and the establishment's license to do business. Soldier, in the presence of a lady, sincerely apologized for the owner's absence and his ignorance as to the answers to the other questions. He suggested two possible actions: return tomorrow during the day or walk over to the Half-Moon Hotel and look for Woody, who couldn't be missed because he was a dwarf.

"A dwarf!" his mother screamed. "Leave it to my genius to get me mixed up with an evil eye. How could you get mixed up with a dwarf!"

"What's wrong with . . ." Harry's answer tailed off, as he spotted a black Packard stopping in front of the store. Woody and a chauffeur pushing a man a wheel chair entered.

"Hi, kid," Woody said.

"Hi."

"What's going on?" Woody asked.

"Did you sell him this piece of junk!" his mother demanded.

Before Woody could answer, Menter pointed his finger at Aba and said:

"I know you. Weren't you at Druckman's house in Sea Gate?"

"Yes. And I recall you too."

Menter smirked.

"Out of the ten other cripples in wheelchairs who were there."

"I meant no offense."

Harry never had heard Aba speak so softly.

"Ain't you some kind of Jew poet?"

"Yes."

"I can talk Jew."

He bent forward, stared as Harry's mother's backside and smacked his lips.

"*Tookas*," he said.

His mother looked to Aba for defense. Aba smiled at Menter.

"Your Yiddish pronunciation is very good."

"Yeah. Well tell me: how do you say 'whore' in Jew?"

"How dare . . ." his mother began.

Aba hooked his mother's arm with his and crushed it against his body. He spoke over her.

"*Kurveh.*"

"Yeah. Well, you recite me a Jew poem."

Aba, in the cadence of a poem, intoned, in Yiddish:

"Be very calm. Do not make a fuss. These are very bad, dangerous people."

Menter screwed a cigarette in his holder and lit it.

"That was very good monkey talk. What does it mean?"

"Oh, it speaks of the flowers and the birds, as do all poems."

"Hear that, Vince"—he poked the chauffeur—"birds and flowers. Sounds like a cemetery."

Vince nodded.

"Now, Vince here deals with all complaints. You got a complaint lady?"

Soldier spoke: "Damn, it's this, Vic. I fixed this bike, but it can't never be the way it was. Lady, I did my best."

Menter glanced at the bike.

"Looks perfect to me. How about you, Vince?"

Vince nodded.

"What about you, poet?"

"As you say. I think we should go now. Harry, take the bike."

Harry grasped the handlebars. Aba, pulling his mother, took small steps toward the door. Soldier rushed past them to hold it open.

"Some *tookas*, huh Vince," Menter said, outlining buttocks with his palms.

His mother's sobs were the only sound in the cold-afflicted streets. At home, she plunged facedown onto the living room couch. Between gulps of breath, she screamed:

"A curse, that's what that boy is, a curse."

"Now Velia," Aba said, "you don't mean that."

"Why is it," she shouted, "why is it men always feel obliged to tell me what I mean?"

Harry wanted to escape to his room, but couldn't. He watched his mother, thinking: If I look at her with love, it will be better.

"Why are you staring at me like an idiot?" she shouted at him. "Are you admiring the state you put me in!"

The phone rang. Harry answered it.

"Hello."

"Hey, kid." It was Woody. Harry said nothing.

"Hey, kid. I'm sorry. It was all a mistake. You took the wrong bike. There was a brand new racer, the same color, right next to it, and I didn't see you take the other one. Hey, kid."

Harry looked at the receiver.

"Listen, kid, come by tomorrow and pick up the new one. OK? Hey, kid, OK?"

Harry hung up. He wished he could tell his mother how much she had done for him. But it would be of no use. Once born, disasters were eternal, immune to change.

The next morning Harry was drinking a glass of milk when Aba appeared clad in his poetry-reading outfit: a gray ascot, brocaded formal shirt and black trousers. A gray blazer and black beret would complete the ensemble. Harry could not remember Aba in uniform in the morning. The poet yawned the odor of liquor.

"Good morning American boy, drinking American milk, in this healthiest of all *medinahs*."

"Good morning."

Last night hung over them. Harry studied the white latticework film coating the empty half of his glass, wondering why some things disappeared without leaving a clue as to their former presence, while others were reluctant to entrust themselves only to memory. Aba cleared his throat.

"You see," he said, as if summing up a lengthy discourse, "there are situations where there is physical danger just below the surface that must be avoided, almost at any cost."

"Even in wonderful, free America."

"Unfortunately this is so. Beasts are in the majority every-where. In Germany their claws are the law. In America the law is on your side, but you may not be in a position to enjoy the privilege."

"Were you afraid, Aba?"

"Heshele, American boy, fear is always my first reaction. No, more than that. Fear is an essential part of my personality, as inte-gral as laughter. You, American boy, cannot understand that because your free land has freed you of this Jewish sickness."

It was not true. But Harry was ashamed to tell even Aba.

"Have you ever hit anyone, Aba?"

Aba's head twitched, as if suddenly afflicted with a tic. He closed his eyes and nodded.

"Tell me about it," Harry asked.

Aba faced the window, hands locked behind him. He rocked back and forth, bending at the knees and pushing his pelvis for-ward, like in the newsreel he had seen of Jews praying at the Wailing Wall.

"It was a long time ago. And perhaps one day I will tell you how it came about . . . how it came about." His voice slid softly inward. .

"Well, I have to go to school."

Aba draped his arm around Harry's shoulder and walked him to the door.

"Study hard," he said. "I expect you to be the first Jewish president."

As Harry walked down 36th Street to the Norton's Point trol-ley, on which he would sneak a ride to school by flattening himself against the rear end, he was surprised to see Aba at the entrance to Sea Gate, the private community that bordered the southern end of Coney. It was not uncommon for Aba to give poetry readings there, but these recitations had always taken place at night or on Sunday afternoons. He would ask Aba if he had inaugurated a cheap early morning show, like the one for a quarter at the Paramount on Broadway.

CHAPTER
7

A BROAD, WHITE WOODEN SLAT BARRED UNAUTHORIZED VEHICLES AND pedestrians from entering Sea Gate, which held off Coney with a twelve-foot-high chain-link fence. Aba informed a private guard that he was visiting Ben Druckman. After confirmation by phone, he was admitted.

The borderlike separation was appropriate. A different country unfolded. Coney's shacks and bungalows disappeared, replaced by rows of neat two-family houses, set back from the sidewalk by generous lawns. Neatly clipped hedges and enormous hydrangeas marked property boundaries.

No littered, concession-smothered boardwalk blocked the wide, immaculate beach, accessible only to holders of resident cards and their guests.

Sea Gate was America's Land's End. The ocean curled around its tip to a bay which led into the Narrows, a seventeen-mile stretch past the Statue of Liberty to the piers of New York Harbor. In summer its crowded marina boasted oceangoing yachts and majestic three-masters. Once a commuter ferry had run year-round between the marina and the Battery, the southern end of Manhattan Island. Three-year-old Harry had established, in his father's eyes, credentials as a poet by saying of the ferry: "The *Belle Island* is coming back from going away."

Private police, rarely hesitant to mark interlopers with a memento of a billy club, cruised day and night, stopping any unfamiliar face.

Aba rang the bell of a two-family red brick house. A Negro wearing a white cloth jacket and black trousers opened the door, took Aba's coat and led him to a large living room that forcefully proclaimed the decorator's preference for white objects. Ben Druckman rose from a white couch. He wore a white silk bathrobe over a white turtleneck sweater and green plaid trousers. Argyle socks breached open-toed bedroom slippers.

A short, thick man, his broad-boned face dotted with brown age spots expressed a perpetual pout, as if sagging under a backlog of disappointment. He moved on tiny, shuffling steps, not entrusting equilibrium to one leg.

Aba accepted his extended hand, surprised by the weakness of the grip. Aba, who was anticipating the crushing fingers of their first meeting, realized that wishful memory had created a powerful Druckman, a superman who met his needs.

"Good to see you, Aba." Druckman mumbled, chin down.

"A pleasure, Ben."

They sat on the couch. Neither spoke. Druckman shrugged.

"I read Nick Kenney in the *Mirror*, he's a helluva poet."

"I don't know how . . ." Aba cut himself off. Ignorant of the protocol of this strange land, he feared a disastrous misstep.

"I don't drink, but if you want a schnapps," Druckman said, nodding to confirm knowledge of Aba's weakness.

"Plain vodka, please."

"James," Druckman called.

The Negro appeared.

"A shot . . . a glass of vodka."

Aba gulped. Warmth passed through his throat, igniting a welcome flame in his stomach. He had written a poem about interior scourging with alcohol. He hiccupped. He floated on pleasant dizziness. He smiled.

"You really like the stuff," Druckman said.

"Yes. It lifts a lot of weight off the brain."

"Givin' guys like you your medicine made me a rich man."

Druckman held out a silver cigarette case. Sucking the flame of Druckman's matching lighter, Aba inhaled deeply, increasing his lightheadedness. He laughed.

"You offer all sorts of poisons," he said, holding out the glass and cigarette, but take none yourself. Is that how you gang . . . Sorry."

Druckman laughed.

"Don't be so pussyfoot. I did what I had to do in my life. No regrets. But, let's get one thing straight: I'm not a gangster . . ."

"Of course not," Aba interrupted.

Druckman overrode his words.

"I'm a retired gangster."

Druckman brushed a gentle fist past Aba's jaw. A stroke of friendship or a warning touch, Aba wondered.

"Now, let's stop the bullshit," Druckman said, settling back into the softness of the couch. "Shit me easy, I'm a white man."

Aba looked into blank eyes, thinking: I am putting my life in the hands of a gangster. What a disciple of Benya Krik! What a schmuck! If he screws me I blame you, friend Babel.

"As I told you at our previous meeting, I thought you could be helpful to me. The fact is this: I am in this country illegally." Aba gulped more vodka. "With what is going on in Europe, the FBI is cracking down on all aliens. I'm afraid they will find me out and deport me to Poland."

"And you think I can put the kibosh on the FBI?"

"I don't know. I just thought . . . since you were so friendly to me . . . didn't you say you would like to hear me recite . . . I could do a poem now."

"Don't," Druckman said, crinkling his nose in displeasure. "I ain't got a gun to your head."

"I don't have any money. I offer what I can. Dog-eat-dog is no less true for being a cliché. Although I feel dog-eat-cat would shed more truth."

"You got trouble with animals too?"

"No. it was a figure of speech . . ."

"You remind me of my father," Druckman interrupted.

"I'm glad."

"Don't be so glad. He was a *putz*. He gave money to poor people in Russia when we didn't have what to eat. My mother was different. Never asked what I did. If I made dough, it was OK."

"You remind me of a poem by Halpern: *My mother is still crying in me.*

"I didn't say she was bawlin' . . ." Druckman put his left hand over his mouth, creased his brow and closed his eyes.

"Halpern, Halpern," he whispered like a medium calling up a spirit, "I remember her readin' that name in that newspaper . . ."

"Der Freiheit."

"Yeah Fry . . . whatever you said. She really liked him. Could you set up a meet with him and me?"

"Unfortunately, he is dead."

"Maybe me too, soon."

Druckman laughed at Aba's undisguised disappointment.

"At least I got one guy prayin' for me. What I got is circulation problems. My doctor says there's new medicines comin'."

"Permanent cats have need of friendly dogs."

"What is it with you and animals?"

"Sorry."

"The doc says the new medicines, it could help my memory too."

"Your memory?"

"Yeah, it's funny, Sometimes I even forget where I am. Jerome has to tell me."

"Jerome?"

"Yeah, the nigger."

"You called him James."

"See what I mean. But what the hell's the difference, he'd answer if I called him Alice. Now, what were we talkin' about?"

Oy, Aba thought, *yes, oy*, he repeated to the poet accusing him of banality. *Oy, and all it entails.*

"Let's see . . . ," Aba said.

"Never mind, I remember," Druckman interrupted. "I wanted to test you, and you flunked. You didn't come clean."

"What do you mean?"

"Yeah, you're in the U.S. not legal. If that was the only problem, I could fix it with a phone call."

"But . . ."

Druckman shook his head. .

"Come on, I know it all. Your name ain't Stolz and you're wanted for murder in Poland."

"How . . ."

"After you talked to me last time, I had a friend of mine, an expert, dig up stuff on you. When you got friends in the right spots it's easy. Get me?"

Stolz drained the vodka.

"Right. If I know the invented Raskolnikov, you know the real one."

I don't know no Raskolnikov, but I got the police report. Wanna see it?"

"From Poland!"

"No, from Hoboken."

Druckman held out a sheet of paper, saying:

"I got it translated by a professor at my grandson's Columbia College."

The black symbols lay on the white paper like a cover of filth. Stolz reached out. Druckman released his hold, but Stolz's fingers turned rigid, unbendable. The sheet fluttered like a child's paper airplane onto the couch.

"You got arthritis. You should wear a copper bracelet like me." Druckman displayed the cure.

Stolz retrieved the paper He wondered: Will I remember it as it was or will it be the dream? He preferred the nightmare which compressed time and ended in screaming relief. He closed his eyes.

Cries of anguish in the street had warned of their coming. Hoofbeats confirmed it. He had slammed into place the wood bolt.

His mother tugged at him, shouting, "Under the bed, under the bed! They will kill you, not me." He had resisted, screaming, "No, I must be with you!" But the fear in his stomach, gnawing, threatening to devour his entrails, had weakened him. He had allowed himself to be pushed to the floor, where he lay motionless until his mother had placed her hands on his shoulders and shoved him under the bed, like a stored thing.

The door splintered. A drunken phlegm soaked voice shouted: "Ha, a Jewess, will I rape her or kill her?" His mother fell to the floor. He could see her.

As in the nightmare, his eyes opened. Druckman stared at him.

"Don't you wanna read it?"

Stolz read:

On April 7, 1935, in a house on Parysow Street in the town of Miasto, the body of Pavel Sienkewicz, age 22, was found. Cause of death was a bread knife that punctured his heart. Testimony of witnesses, including the Jew known as Beryl, the blacksmith, whose place of business is next door to the scene of the murder, has established conclusively that Sienkewicz was murdered by the Jew, Avram Stein, age 24, who resided in the house with his mother, Malkah Stein, exact age undetermined. Malkah Stein was also found dead, apparently of natural causes. The murderer has fled. There are reports that he has entered the United States illegally.

Stolz looked up and spoke to the universe:

"In Poland a crushed skull inflicted by a *pogromchik* is rightfully identified as natural causes."

"You a lawyer, too," Druckman said, taking back the paper. "My grandson goes to the Columbia College. He might be a lawyer. He's the star football player, even though he's the only Jew on the team. I could get you tickets to see him." He pointed to an eight-by-ten glass-framed photo of a young man wearing a football helmet that rested on a white grand piano.

"Will you help me?"

Druckman nodded.

"I'll try."

"I have no money."

"Christ, I don't need no money."

"What do you want?"

"Nothing. Nothing like money. It's tough to explain. My wife's dead. My son got his own family. I think about dyin'. I want to be Jewish.

"But you are . . ."

"No. No. No. I mean real Jewish."

"You want to become an Orthodox Jew!"

"Who said that? I don't wanna be alone. I wanna be attached. Especially when I don't know where I am. Am I gettin' through to you?"

"Yes," Aba said. "Jews as they become older become more Jewish. It is as if a dormant gene activates a racial wisdom tooth."

Druckman shook his head vigorously.

"There, that's it! I don't understand a word you said, but listenin' to you made me feel Jewish."

"So what you want of me is . . ."

"Just see me. Talk to me."

"A Jewish Scherherezade."

"Is that a Jewish word?"

"No. An idiotic one. Please forget it."

"That ain't hard for me."

Druckman's face hardened. "Now, I gotta tell you somethin'. There's a nigger in this woodpile.

"A nigger?"

"No, a white man. His name is Victor Menter . . ."

"I have met him," Aba interrupted. "First here in your house, then yesterday in a most unpleasant situation. I believe he is a virulent anti-Semite."

"You bet your sweet Jew ass he is. Before I retired, Menter worked for me."

"Why did you employ an anti-Semite?"

"Christ, can you think of a sweeter way to screw a Jew hater than to make him take orders from a Jew? If I'd told him to get circumcised, he whips it out and starts slicin'. Sorry I didn't."

"What has he to do with all this?"

"I'm retired now and he's got a lotta power. He's well-connected by his *goomba* Italian mother's family to very powerful people. By street talk he could find out what I'm tryin' to do for you. If that happens, you and the people you live with, are up shit creek."

"The Catzkers! But why?"

"The Catzkers harbored you, a criminal. That's a crime. If Menter ratted on you, they go to prison, could be deported too. Their kid is in good shape because he was born here. He'd go to a orphan home."

Aba dug his fingernails into his scalp. The demons who mocked his attempts to expose them in poetry now laughed out loud, taking credit.

"Well, then, let's forget it."

"Too late."

"My God! Why? Does he know about me already?"

"I don't know. He likes to torture. He may be watchin' you like a cat with a mouse. Hey, now you got me doin' animals. But gettin' that report took some doin'. Maybe he knows already. If he don't by now, he probably won't find about it when I make your record disappear from the Polish police files."

The demons smirked, discounting everything but doom.

"I suppose . . . you will do your best . . . I mean to hide the report."

"I always do my best. Hey, I'd like it if you wrote a poem for me, even maybe about me."

"I don't write poetry in English."

"Do it in Jewish."

"Do you understand Yiddish?"

"Nah, but it don't make no difference. I got a feelin' I wouldn't understand what you wrote in any language."

CHAPTER
8

BY NOON, HARRY COULD NO LONGER WAIT TO GRIP HIS NEW BIKE. He cut the rest of his classes and sprinted to the bike store. Woody greeted him warmly and handed him the racer, saying, "Ride over to the house of the freaks, pick up the slips and bring 'em back."

Doubled over, clutching the sleek, curved handlebars, Harry pedaled slowly along the boardwalk, admiring his reflection in glass storefronts. A midday sun had called to prayer the ancient sun worshippers who, in a state of sweating grace, were not the audience he desired. When school let out, there would be slit-eyed jealousy.

At Stillwell Avenue he left the boardwalk and stopped at Nathan's for a hot dog, French fries and an orange drink. He remained perched on his bike, a sultan on a throne, mashing the food and liquid into one magnificent taste. He flipped a quarter onto the counter.

"Nice bike," said the counterman, stretching out his arm to hand Harry a nickel change.

Harry grudged a haughty nod, playing William Powell in *My Man Godfrey*.

He slalomed through the traffic under the elevated train tracks, then turned right, moving past the arches and turrets of Luna Amusement Park. Beyond was the spot where, according to Schnozz, once stood a 150-foot-high hotel in the exact shape of an elephant. At night its eyes had glowed yellow.

He turned onto West Eighth, a street of two-family wooden shacks, more peeled than painted. In the distance, soaring on the wings of Schnozz's word pictures, the four hundred-foot white tower of Dreamland Amusement Park dazzled his eyes with a million light bulbs, illuminating The Creation, Pompeii, gondolas floating by The Doge's Palace in Venice, and Captain Jack Bonavita, the bravest lion tamer ever, who lost two fingers and then his right arm, but always returned to the cage to stare down rogue beasts.

Dismounting, he carried the bike up the wooden steps of number 39, pressed the black tit bell and, hearing no ring, tried the door, which scraped the floor as it gave way. He wheeled the bike toward a smell of cooked cabbage and the murmur of conversation.

"*Merde*," a woman's voice chastised, "you bring tires with ze shit of *chien* in ze house."

The speaker was Queen Fifi, the fat lady at a sideshow in Coney's Bowery section. Her eyes, nose and lips were tiny islands in a rippling sea of flesh. Yet, rosy coloring on delicate white cheeks evoked Renaissance cherubs. A golden cardboard tiara indented her curly blond hair.

The queen, overflowing a piano bench at the head of a long oblong table, presided over a court of freaks whom Harry recognized from the large posters that lined the Bowery:

Jamie, *the boy with two mouths*, who, lacking makeup, presented a simple hole in his cheek. Olga, *the world's ugliest woman*, whose thickened face and massive shoulders suggested a punch-drunk boxer. Lohu and Mohu, the Japanese Siamese twins, seated in one chair, eating with their outside hands. Jo-Jo, *the dog-faced boy*, a dispirited beagle.

Blue Man, skin glowing as if phosphorescent. Albert-Alberta, *the half-man, half-woman*, bereft of sweater bulges, and Otto, *the strongman*, whose shaved bullet head, bull neck, pendulous purplish lips and filed teeth were, in this company, havens of human familiarity.

Otto strode toward Harry, arms extended, fingers curled to strangle.

"You come see freaks? *Ach*, I show you."

Harry wheeled his bike between them.

"Woody!" he shouted.

Otto stopped.

"Voody?"

"The slips."

"*Ach*, now a boy he sends. You hear Fifi, a boy."

"I like boys," Fifi said, tilting her massive head at Harry. "I like them same like you, Otto."

The diners laughed. The Siamese twins turned toward each other. Harry wondered if they used each other as a mirror. Schnozz said that some Siamese twins were fakes: regular twins yoked together in a tight corset. He scanned Lohu and Mohu, searching for a clue in their identical brown suits, white shirts and green plaid ties.

"Nice' boys not stare," Fifi said. "How is your name?"

"Harry."

"'Arry is most pleasurable name. Sit wiz us, 'Arry. We like nice visitor."

Otto placed a chair next to his.

"No, Otto," Fifi said, waggling her index finger, "no under-ze table *dalliance*. Between Albert-Alberta and me will be his place."

Seated, Harry fought a terrible urge to stare. He bowed his head as if partaking in a solemn ceremony.

"Young boy," Olga bass voice boomed, "ven I vass ah beauty I vass ballerina. Nijinsky loffed me. All Moskva and St. Petersburg vass at my feets. Ven is vite nights, I dance in streets. Tsar and tsarina chav see me, invite me to Vinter Palace. Den"—she punched her shoulder—"den dis."

Fifi lip-farted.

"Nijinsky, tsar, hah. Ven you vass ah beauty," Fifi mimicked, "you be a kootch dancer. You slide on ze *fesse* on ze stage and push out ping pong ball from ze *trou*, one after one. One is told zat at zat you ze best. Zoot! like from a cannon. Also lights in zere for ze shining *con*."

Olga wiped her lips delicately with a food-soiled paper napkin.

"I not answer fot, degenerate peasant. Vonce I vass ah beauty. Vat vass you effer, but fot stink."

Blue Man stood up and crashed his fist onto the table, rattling plates.

"I not understand," he shouted. "In Prague circus we did not speak so terrible t'ings!"

Fifi cupped one breast with both hands and jiggled it at him, saying:

"But it is all family fight, *monsieur sacre bleu*. It not mean *rien*. We family. You *envie?*"

"You vood drown him vit dose mountains," Olga said and waited for laughs that did not arrive.

Fifi dropped her chin over her right breast and kissed it loudly.

"Mine are soft, full of life, where armies nurse to *gloire*. You *seins* give muscles and sweat. Ze odor of a man."

"And what, pray tell O rotund oracle, is wrong with the odor of a man?" Albert-Alberta said, cocking his head coquettishly. "It is a sign of manhood, just as shit and semen are the smells of a boy."

Otto stood up and flexed his biceps which rose like a camel's hump from the hem of his short-sleeved shirt.

"*Ach*," he said, pointing to Albert-Alberta, "this call itself man. A man has strength. You say you half-woman. I say you all woman."

Albert-Alberta nodded and replied: "Ergo of no possible use to you." He sang: *'Tell me Lord Montague, How many hairy assholes did you screw? Was it one or ninety-two? Oh, tell me, Lord Montague.'*

Fifi applauded vigorously, requiring her to extend her arms so that her palms could collide beyond her breasts.

Harry slowly lifted his head and, receiving no reprimand, swiveled his neck.

Lohu raised his hand and shook it like a schoolboy bursting with the right answer.

"I pity all of you," he said.

His brother added: "All of you understand nothing."

The others took no notice, except for Albert-Alberta, who made the sign of the Cross, and whispered:

"Buddha two, Jesus nothing. But it's a great match, folks."

"But we forget our guest," Fifi said. "'Arry, you like Otto do strong trick for you?"

Harry remembered Mike Mazurki in a movie.

"Could you tear a telephone book in two?"

Everyone laughed. Fifi patted him on the head.

"*Mon petit,* zat is wonderful. *Alors,* Otto, our guest make request."

"Zere is no book in zis shithouse."

Albert-Alberta ran to the foyer and returned with a Brooklyn phone directory. He bounded up to Otto, bowed low and, sweeping his arm grandly in the style of a Shakespearean fop, laid the book on his lap. Otto, staring straight ahead, spread his knees. The book fell to the floor.

Jo-Jo slid off his chair, disappearing under the table, and surfaced back at his seat holding the book. He opened it and, whelping with strain, tore it in half along the binding, Everyone but Otto applauded. Tensing his biceps, the strong man said:

"Yah, yah, is funny. Now we go out and lift cars."

"Why is to be ashamed of trick? If not tricks, how we make living?"

Otto chomped on his cheeks.

"'Arry, *écoute*, Otto, he can tear book like in show. But he is like chef. He need time to bake book in oven. Zen is *très simple.*"

"Lie," Otto shouted.

"Fifi," Jamie said, rolling his eyes, "you promised us the Boze Art today."

The room froze. Harry thought of the wax museum. Fifi patted Harry's head.

"*Alors, porquoi pas,* ze boy needs education. I explain:

"'Arry, in *Paris*, once in ze year, we have *Beaux Arts Ball*. All *étudiants* of ze arts invited. At midnight all doors locked and each must remove clothes. Of course one can depart before midnight, but who do such *faux pas*? The doors locked till six *matin*. Not even *gendarmes* can enter, and ze *étudiants* amuse zemself with much pleasure. I tell *mes amis* zis and they have *envie* for Beaux Arts even more zan once in year. You go with us. Zere is no harm, *mon petit*, I promise. Because you ze one *vrai étudiant* here, you have honor to disrobing *moi, la reine*."

She turned her palms in a lifting motion. Otto tugged her to her feet. The others savagely tore at their clothes. Shirts, underwear and socks flew and floated over agitated inmates of a madhouse.

Olga, on all fours and gasping like a breath-starved football player, wiggled while accepting leisurely strokes from a kneeling Albert-Alberta, whose hands conducted a symphony orchestra. Spotting Otto sitting sullenly, he pointed to the twins, joined at the hip by what resembled a large fish scale, who were masturbating each other, as if a coxswain were setting a frenetic beat, and shrieked:

"Take a lesson from them, Otto!"

Jamie, seemingly guided by an enormous erection, came to a kneeling rest before Olga, who licked his penis with a pitted tongue.

A lion roared. Olga collapsed.

"Glad to have been of service," Albert-Alberta said, turning his conducting to Lohu and Mohu, who were watching parabolas of semen land like disabled parachutes.

Fifi moved in front of Harry. She was about his height. A white cotton blouse hung loose over a pleated blue ankle-length skirt. Her bare feet, astonishingly small, seemed inadequate to their task.

"Alors, gentil gosse, is not polite to refuse hospitality. Disrobe me and you, zen do as you wish. No harm will come."

She placed his hand on the top button of her blouse. He unbuttoned her. His penis was stiff. Otto, behind her, removed the blouse. She wore no brassiere. Her skirt fell. Her hand on his head guided him to his knees. He tugged her pink panties to her ankles. She kicked them away. His eyes were level with a tiny patch of blond pubic hair barely visible against the milky dunes of flesh. The odor of Woolworth perfume burned his nostrils like the vaporized mists Bama unleashed to cure his cold.

"Now remove you clothes. Ze *règles* of *fête*."

Harry piled his clothes before him like a sandbag. His erection throbbed with virginal ecstasy of finally *knowing*, but nausea claimed his stomach.

Fifi turned a sweating face toward Harry, shut her tiny blue eyes, and nodded understanding.

"Such fear, *mon petit*, is only life. You do not wish, you may go now, if zat please you."

Harry grabbed his clothes and ran through laughter. He was desperate to wash. On the steps, wearing only his knickers, he finished dressing. The door opened. Fifi, nude, held out the betting slips. Her other hand gripped his bike.

Harry stretched out his hand to accept the papers. Fifi squeezed it gently.

"Not forget ze *cheval,* brave knight."

He caught his bike as it bumped down the stairs.

In the Cherry Tree: January 16, 1937

Aba: *American boy, tell me about America.*

Harry: *It has forty-eight states.*

Aba: *Is it the land of the free and the home of the brave?*

Harry: *Yes.*

Aba: *Then explain to me, American boy, why, a few days ago, the American government said that Americans cannot fight against Hitler in Spain.*

Harry: *But Hitler is in Germany.*

Aba: *He is also in Spain.*

Harry: *What is he doing there?*

Aba: *There is a civil war in Spain. He is helping one side.*

Harry: *Is it like the American Civil War? Are they fighting to free the slaves?*

Aba: *That is almost true. They are fighting so there will be no slaves.*

Harry: *I think I understand. If Hitler's side wins, it will be like the South won the Civil War, and all the black people in Spain will be slaves.*

Aba: *The white people too.*

Harry: *But white people have never been slaves.*

Aba: *At the Passover Seder, do we not say: "We were slaves to Pharaoh in Egypt"?*

Harry: *Yes . . . You know, Aba, I never thought about that because I knew the whole story, and the Jews are the ones who are winning all the time. Moses is like Joe Louis. He knocks out Pharaoh in every round.*

Aba: *You like Joe Louis.*

Harry: *Oh, yes. I listen to his fights on the radio, and the next morning on the way to school I stop at candy stores to look at the big picture of him standing over the man he has knocked out which is always on the back page of the* Daily News.

Aba: *The* Daily News *is a fascist newspaper. It is on Hitler's side.*

Harry: *Then I must not look at its pictures of Joe Louis?*

Aba: *No, Heshele, look to your heart's desire, but know that on the front page Joe Louis is knocked out.*

CHAPTER
9

STANDING ON THE PEDALS OF HIS BIKE, PUMPING AND ROCKING VIOLENTLY, Harry measured speed by the pain of the cutting wind. He flashed over the grave of Dreamland and skidded onto the sand beneath the boardwalk. Carrying his bike to the ocean's edge, he eased into a prone position and submerged his face in the lapping residue of once-surly waves. The frigid salt water stung his eyes and pricked his skin. The scourging, he hoped, would unclog his mind and allow it to answer questions that were lodged there.

Why had he wanted to bury his head in Fifi's sweating breasts?

Why had he wanted to bite her pubic hair?

Why, during his panicked flight from the room, had he cursed himself for the loss of Fifi's stinking mystery?

Why, in a world that encompassed many worlds as different from each other as day from night, did freaks, poets, dwarfs, his mother, his father, share a common obsession?

He remembered a joke he had overheard his father tell:

The grandmother of a large family dies. The grandfather, who worshipped her, is grief-stricken and dazed. The family, sitting shivah at home, notices that the grandfather has disappeared. Alarmed that in his confused state he may have wandered off and come to harm, they frantically search for him. He is discovered in a bedroom atop the young housemaid.

"Zadeh," the family screams, "how could you?"

The grandfather replies: "Oy, in such a terrible time, do I know what I'm doing?"

Harry tried to visualize his grandfather in that position, but couldn't get his clothes off. He laughed. Another question relieved him of the unanswerable ones: *Was his grandfather crazy and, if so, how did that affect his own sanity?*

Lifting his head from the water, he looked toward the twenty-five-yard-long fishing pier that jutted into the Atlantic from Steeple Chase Amusement Park. There, memory placed his grandfather, whose resemblance to Albert Einstein provoked double takes, standing beside seven-year-old Harry.

Though twenty feet above the nearest water, Zadeh wore hip-high rubber boots. He was furiously reeling in a line. When the hook breached, it might hold a bait worm, but nothing more. Zadeh had never had caught a fish.

Harry began a sanity inquiry.

Zadeh worked as a tanner in a leather factory, a trade he had learned in his native Poland. The profession was temporary, to be endured only until the world recognized his stature as a Talmudic scholar. His approach to fishing was properly Talmudic: *If idiots can catch, surely I can.* The premise was lost on the ignorant fish.

He escalated the battle, drafting seven-year-old Harry as aide and purchasing sophisticated rods, reels and lures. The fish were unimpressed. He became a nuisance to anyone on the pier with a catch in a bucket.

"What bait you use?" he would demand.

"Worms."

"Special?"

"Worms is worms."

"How far you cast?"

"Who knows?"

"You got a favorite spot?"

"Where they're biting."

Eventually his Talmudic mind informed him that Harry's baited hook alongside his presented a choice that confused and immobilized stupid fish. He ordered Harry to withdraw his line, but to stand poised to plunge a gleaming scaling knife into a catch. It was now eight years that Harry had been at the ready but never challenged, for which Harry was thankful, because neither he nor Zadeh had the vaguest idea of how to clean a fish.

The end of the first nibbleless day set the pattern for all subsequent catchless expeditions. Lifting his eyes to the heavens, Zadeh gloomily conceded by reciting Goethe's rhymed German: "Man thinks and God laughs." He then leapt up, brought the heels of his boots together and added: "Sometimes man can laugh at God."

At a fish store specializing in *just-caught fish*, Zadeh bought the last laugh.

Appropriately bloody catch in bucket, they had insisted that Bama immediately clean and fry the hard-won prize. None of them particularly liked fish, but they were no less vengefully ravenous than cannibals at the flesh of captured enemies.

The last bite cued a bowel movement lecture, followed by the lecturer's long absence that taught by example. When Zadeh, glowing with health, returned from the bathroom, he would head for his desk and open his Old Testament. Harry would pull up a chair beside him.

Zadeh maintained an unblinking stare while reading the black Hebrew letters of the Torah, moving his head, rather than his eyes, from right to left. Harry considered those fixed eyes as unfathomably powerful as Buck Rogers's ray gun.

Soon Zadeh would sound a salivaless expectoration and reach for his shiny, black Waterman pen, whose circumference nearly matched the fat Upmann cigars he sometimes smoked. Unscrewing the cover and jabbing the point downward to loosen the flow of ink, he would launch a closed-mouthed vibrato growl of disgust for the offending passage. The fourteen-carat gold-plaited nib then glided along the margins of the Torah, leaving hairline strokes of blue ink which at first seemed a meticulously copied musical score but, when completed, formed a perfectly even block of a midget Hebrew army commanded to attention. The error set right, he would again spit it out and swivel his head in search of the next abomination.

When turning a page, Zadeh would bid it good-bye with an exasperated "Enough already." This habit had alerted Harry, at age ten, to his family's general failure to draw distinctions between the animate and inanimate. His father, reading Freud, would mumble, "Thank you." His mother praised or cursed her mascara brush. Bama's intimacy with the evil eye empowered her to chase it from the room by brandishing a straw broom and cursing.

His father explained that Zadeh and Bama and perhaps to a lesser extent, his mother, were victims of Polish romanticism, an aberration which drew no distinction between fantasy and reality. The results could be as relatively benign as electing of the concert pianist Paderewski Poland's first president, or as life-threatening as centuries of insistence that Poland could subdue Russia.

The explanation had shed sense on some of Zadeh's eccentricities: when he came across a picture of Stalin in a newspaper, he would obliterate him with a punch that put a hole in the paper, then brush his right palm over his left to bid good riddance to the Russian tyrant. Or the time in a local candy store when Harry, age twelve, had been drawn to a large group surrounding the pinball machine and egging on the player with: "Go get 'em, Pop." On tiptoes, Harry had watched Zadeh barking commands in English and Yiddish to the silver balls as they collided with the bumpers.

Playing pinball was a sop to Zadeh's passion for gambling. Lacking funds, he usually was relegated to kibitzing. More than one black eye had confirmed the stupidity of some who resented his advice.

Eventually he had been picked up in a raid on a gambling casino. Bailed out and brought home by Bama and Harry's parents, he ignored their questions, fuming over the duplicity of the number 16, which had lied to him.

"Sixteen," his mother repeated, adding with a derisive laugh. "Wasn't that the age you said I was too young to go out with boys? Some lucky number."

"Leah," Bama shouted, "you must not speak to Mr. Fishman that way."

"Mr. Fishman, Mr. Fishman, can't you call him anything else? He's your husband, my father, for Christ's sake."

"In Warsaw . . ." Bama began, but deferred to her husband, who abandoned the number 16 and pointed a stiff finger at Harry's mother, arcing it through the air like a pendulum.

"You must never say that name. How do you know who is listening?"

"Say something to him!" his mother yelled at Harry's father. "You're a big mind, a writer, maybe he'll listen to you."

Harry's father long ago had certified his in-laws as insane. He avoided them whenever possible, cautioning Harry: "If you listen to a madman long enough, he starts to sound sane."

"Velia," he pleaded, moving toward his coat, "I must go to the paper. Europe is about to blow up."

"Oh no you don't! Europe can blow up tomorrow. Say something. The next time he'll go to jail for God knows what."

"That's better," Zadeh complimented his daughter.

"Listen, Fishman"—his father's overly sweet voice had reminded Harry of a Coney Island barker buttering up a mark— "do you think it is wise for a Talmudist like yourself to be in the company of people who go to such places?"

"Catzker, don't be too quick to judge. There are Kabbalists among them."

"Of course," his father agreed, pursing his lips at received valuable information, "there are Kabbalists everywhere. But the others . . . it is not right for a man like you."

"Catzker, you call yourself a writer and you know so little. There are not Kabbalists everywhere. If there were, the world would be on the verge of heaven. Is that what you are telling me?"

"Surely not. Let us forget the Kabbala. Let us speak of the police. If they do not want these games to go on, don't you think you should obey them?"

"Obey the police? You are crazy. They are goyim. Do you ask me to agree with goyim!"

"But many of those who were arrested with you were goyim."

Zadeh found this a telling point. He stroked his chin, analyzing. His father claimed triumph by grabbing his coat.

"Aha," Zadeh shouted, "spies!"

"Papa," his mother said, "they are going to put you away one day. Where, I don't know."

"In the cemetery, of course."

Bama chased the evil eye with her fists.

And there was chess, which was not exactly relevant evidence. Or was it?

Zadeh had taught chess to four-year-old Harry, who had picked up the game in a couple of sessions. Bama had proclaimed him a prodigy, feeding him candy as he sat on two telephone books across from Zadeh, who was oblivious to everything except plotting a winning strategy.

The prodigy's chess game, however, had a chronic failing. When Zadeh captured Harry's first piece, a pawn, he proudly placed it along the edge of the board on his side of the table. The isolated warrior appeared so lonely and forlorn that Harry was impelled to provide it with company. As quickly as possible, he would position another piece in fatal jeopardy. The bizarre moves raised Zadeh's suspicion that a subtle trap was in progress . He would study the board for as long as ten minutes, searching for the intent of the bold sacrifice, until deciding that it was just an idiotic blunder, and pouncing.

After being beaten in every contest during his fourth year, Harry began to cry in defeat. Three years later, cured of his lonely-pawn syndrome, but still having experienced only hot tears over a chessboard, Harry won his first chess game, not against Zadeh but a schoolmate, who succumbed to a four-move checkmate. Much to Harry's disappointment, his victim did not cry, but merely shrugged his shoulders and said:

"You're too good for me. Wanna try box ball?"

By age eight Harry was bored with chess; however, his frenzy to defeat Zadeh never subsided, though he had learned to hold back the tears until he had locked himself in the bathroom. It was still so.

Eight almost had been the last year of Harry's life. Zadeh had tried to cure him of an acute stomachache with the all-purpose high colonic. Harry had fled the greased nozzle which had been introduced into him many times. When pulled from under a bed by his father and Dr. Bluestone, the immediate diagnosis had been a burst appendix. The operation was performed just in time. Zadeh pooh-poohed the idea that had he caught up with Harry, he would have killed him, and further maintained that Bluestone was a quack who had ordered surgery when a good bowel movement was all that was needed.

The random bin of facts housed two competing considerations as to hereditary insanity: On the corroborative side was Zadeh's father, who one evening had left his house in Warsaw to buy a newspaper and disappeared for fifteen years. During that time, it was fairly well documented, he had established families in South Africa and elsewhere. Returning to Warsaw, he entered his house, sat down at the table from which he had risen fifteen years previously, and demanded supper. His wife complied wordlessly,

On the nay side of the madness ledger was Harry's own relationship with inanimate objects. Treasured jazz records spoke words that were not imbedded in the grooves. Each school-day morning he said good-bye to his father's hat. He even spoke to God, but only to secure a pennant for the Brooklyn Dodgers. Certainly there was nothing abnormal in all that.

No, neither his grandfather nor he nor anyone in his family was crazy.

As Harry's father said: "A Jew needs all the friends he can get."

10

SOMEONE TUGGED AT HARRY'S KNICKERS. SOLDIER, STOOPED OVER him, was wiping sand from the bike.

"Damn, you shouldn't let sand get in, it's like . . . Damn, especially this brand new one." His fingertips glided along the handlebars, as if rimming fine crystal.

"What are you doing on the beach, Soldier?"

Soldier slid his hands inside his torn-at-the-elbows army field jacket to hitch up grease-stained khaki pants. The wind lifted and let fall the threads of his unraveling wool cap. He shrugged.

"Damn, I got a room on West Sixth for when I don't stay at Woody's and I like to walk along the beach to Woody's. You headed that way?"

"Yes."

"Damn, wanna walk together? You can roll the bike in the hard sand, not to clog up the chain."

"Sure, Soldier, I'd like that."

"Damn, you like the beach, Harry?"

An automatic shrug prefaced all Soldier's speech, triggering the *damn* which hung by itself, unconnected.

"Yes, I do. It makes me feel clean."

"Damn, I coulda said that. There weren't no beach where I was brung up. The first one I seen was in France, at the hospital they sent me to. It was a town called Deauville, but we called it Doughboy."

Soldier laughed, provoking a tic in his right cheek. He slapped it.

"Does it hurt?" Harry asked.

"Damn, no. My grandpa had it. Said it weren't no different from a yawn, except you done it with your cheek instead of your mouth. In church he'd point to folk yawnin' and say, 'If they done like me, it'd be more polite.'"

Harry imagined little Soldier in church with his grandfather. Everyone looked like Judge and Mrs. Hardy, Mickey Rooney and Judy Garland, except for a miniature Soldier, ragged in khaki. The congregation sang the favorite hymn of the Irish kids at school: *Onward Christian Soldiers and leave the Jews behind.*

Soldier kicked at the sand.

"Damn, I did like that beach in Doughboy. They'd come and pull me off it, like I had got lost. I hadn't. I just wanted to feel the soft sand and look at the water that never ended. I like things that never end. Like sometimes just before you fall asleep you think it's forever. I don't mean die. Just sleep happy forever."

A barefooted, bent-over beachcomber, scarred shoes dangling from laces tied around his neck, slowly approached.

"Hey, Soldier," he said, "how's it go?"

"Damn, any luck, Robbie?" Soldier asked.

The man straightened, unfurling into a six-foot-nine-inch stick figure, covered from neck to ankle by a pepper-and-salt overcoat. Between the lapels of the upturned collar, his nose, like a turtle's head, tested danger. He took from his pocket a few pennies and nickels.

"Not much," he said, offering examination of the oxidized booty, "but I think I got an Indian head nickel. If I can clean it proper, it should be worth something."

He doubled over as if hinged at the stomach and fought his way against the wind. Soldier angrily kicked a divot of sand into the ocean.

"Damn, that was Robbie. He used to be *The Human Skeleton* 'till he got a rash all over him. Folk don't like to look at rashes. So now he looks for Indian heads. I hope he found one."

Soldier began a dry, choking cough. His body shook like a pummeled rag doll. He bit for air. Harry feared that he could literally break apart. He sank to his knees. Tears squiggled crystalline worms on his cheeks. A high-pitched inhalation gradually subdued the cough.

"Soldier. Is there anything I can do?"

"Damn, it's past now. I once won a medal in a track meet. Now my lungs are full of . . . damn, sometimes I get mad."

Grabbing Harry's offered hand, Soldier pulled himself up, then jumped to retrieve the bike that had fallen and was being decorated by blowing ocean foam.

"Damn, it ain't new no more. It'll never be new again."

"You like new bikes, huh Soldier?"

"Damn, yeah. I never had one when I was a kid, but I can't say I really missed it. I loved puttin' bikes together from parts I got at the town dump. I was better at fixin' bikes then. Had more patience. Now it's sort of, if it don't fit perfect, it's the best I know how."

"You do a good job, Soldier. Bikes aren't easy to fix."

"Damn, thanks Harry, but I know better. You know when I got my first new bike?"

"When?"

"Damn, it was in Doughboy. I was walkin' in the town and I spot this bike store. I point to a black job, and hold out a fistful of *parley-vous* money. This old guy with a mustache who looked like a walrus goes bug-eyed, grabs most of the dough and shoves the bike at me.

"I went tearin' through that town like a bat outta hell. I recollect people pointin' at me and shoutin' somethin' like *'ooh law lee.'* There was a lot of carriages pulled by horses with women with big hats in 'em. The horses whinnied when I went by and God help me if the drivers didn't sort of salute me by raisin' their whips over their head and yellin' somethin' in *parley-vous*. Behind me I could feel my bathrobe flyin' and my slippers was almost comin' off. I guess I rode like that for fifteen minutes before the hospital folk caught up with me. They told the walrus to give me back my money. Oh, was he mad! And he was right. He sold me a new bike and now it would never be new again. They kept on askin' me if he gave back all my money. Now how was I supposed to know that? But I said yes, hopin' he had pocketed a few bucks for what he deserved.

"When we got back to the hospital they took all my money and put it where I couldn't get at it. But, whoa-eee that was a ride!"

"I'd like to go to France on the *Ile de France*. I see her out there, coming in and going, "Harry said.

Soldier followed Harry's eyes to an empty horizon cut short by a curtain of low black clouds.

"Damn, how can you tell it's this Frenchy ship? You got spyglasses that could read the name?"

"Nah, I got a book with pictures of all the ocean liners—front, sideways, how many stacks, their record time for crossing the Atlantic, how many passengers and crew. Once you read that, you can spot a ship easy."

"Damn, I'd like to see a book like that."

"I'll lend it to you, Soldier. I know it all by heart anyway."

"Damn, would ya Harry? I'll give it back, I promise. But you gotta remind me. My memory ain't no good no more."

Harry suddenly felt as if he were meeting Soldier for the first time. Previously he had been a tool to fix his bike, a head-banging spectacle, another deformed Coney freak. Everyone, it seemed to Harry, played chess using everyone else as designated pieces. The king and queen of England were coming to the U.S. on the *Queen Mary*. Soldier, his proud military uniform become a mourner's sack-cloth, his once eager face rubbed with ash-gray beard stubble, was the undefended, lonely pawn, sacrificed for all the kings and queens of Europe.

A swirling black cloud smothered the sun. The wind asserted primacy as nature's messenger. Harry shivered. He looked at Soldier's knuckles, joined to his by the handlebar. He felt close, empowered to ask a friend's question.

"Is that because of what happened to you in the war?"

Soldier's peach-pit–shaped eyes blinked slowly, trying to focus or perhaps forget.

"Damn, it was that mustard gas. I was always crazy about mustard too, could eat it with a spoon, and the doctors tellin' me that it was burnin' my lungs and givin' me spells. I asked how come I didn't smell it. They told me it didn't smell like mustard. Didn't smell, not at all. But that don't make no difference in the way I feel about mustard. When I go by Nathan's, I like to puke. I can't even try and eat mustard, even though I think I'm still crazy for it."

"I'm sorry, Soldier."

"Damn, it's OK, Harry. I'm alive. There's plenty who ain't."

"Did you kill any Germans?"

"Damn, no, and I'm glad for that. I didn't join up to kill anyone. It was to get the war over. That's what the president and everyone was sayin': *it was up to us Yanks to get the war over.* Damn, killin' was never a part of it."

"I'd kill Germans."

"Damn, would ya. I got some German blood in me."

Harry tightened his grip on the handlebar.

"I'm Jewish," he said, making amends for not defending his mother in the bike store.

"Damn, that's nice. The army was the first place I met Jew people. A lot different from what I was taught. I was lookin' for their horns. In the hospital there was one just like me with the mustard sickness. Never talked, not one word. Just hummed songs I didn't know. Wonder where he is."

Soldier stared at the bike quizzically, scratching the back of his neck.

"Damn, how long did Woody say you could keep this one?"

"Woody gave it to me."

"Damn, gave?"

"Yes, gave!"

"Damn, watch out."

"I'm not lying!"

Soldier put his hand on top of Harry's.

"Damn, I didn't mean that. Give it back."

"Never!"

"Damn, Harry, what does he want you to do for it?"

"Nothing."

"Damn . . . Please, Harry."

Soldier shook. Harry, anticipating another coughing spell, took the slips from his pocket.

"Collect these."

"Damn, don't do it Harry! It ain't the slips. I done that. It's Woody. He wants to mess people up."

"How do you mean?"

"Damn, Harry, I'm sick. But not as sick as everyone thinks. I hear things because people talk like I ain't there. Woody wants to make everyone like him."

"Soldier, that's crazy."

"Damn. No it ain't Harry. He . . ." Soldier shook his head violently, trying to dislodge the elusive words. "He gets you so you have to live his life. I seen it. I heard him say: "'Now they're screwed like me.'"

Harry decided not to listen too long to a madman.

"Soldier, I'll think about it . . . Soldier, would you give Woody the slips for me? It's cold and I'd like to get home."

"Damn, Harry, sure."

Standing on the boardwalk, Harry watched Soldier's back grow smaller. Every six steps, he would skip and almost lose his balance.

Some track medal, Harry thought.

11

HARRY PEDALED FRENETICALLY TO ESCAPE THE DAY, SPEED DISTANCING him from the freaks' bodies, Soldier's tics and the human skeleton's rash and toward a cleansing antidote: Bama's warm, kneading hands and cat-wet kisses. Before he could ring her bell, the door flew open. She pulled him into the house.

"*Oy*, Heshele, precious one, it is the Papa. He is sick. Come see," she wailed.

Zadeh lay on his back on the bedroom floor, his blood-drained face twisted into a lopsided Halloween terror mask. Spittle dribbled out of the corner of his mouth and fell to his chest like a Lilliputian waterfall.

"Bama, did you call an ambulance!"

"I call the police."

"Did you speak English? Did you tell them your address in English?"

"I think yes. I am not sure."

Harry ran to the phone and demanded Coney Island Hospital emergency. The doorbell rang. Bama led two cops into the bedroom. The hospital answered. Harry shouted: "Emergency! Forty-nine Neptune Avenue, ground floor, a man is very sick."

The receiver was jerked from his hand. One of the cops whispered into it: "This is officer Dunn. It's a stroke. He's alive, just. Bring emergency equipment."

He laid a fat index finger that smelled of cigars over Harry's lips. Harry nodded.

The other cop was having little luck in moving Bama out of the bedroom. He motioned to Harry for help.

"Now, Ma'am," he said, "you mustn't touch him. The ambulance is on the way and everything will be all right. This nice boy here—your grandson?—called the hospital. Why don't you go sit with him until the doctors come."

She widened the spread of her feet. She would not do as he asked. He was the enemy, an anti-Semite. Yet she had called the cops. Harry wondered how that worked in her mind.

"Call the Mama!" she screamed at Harry.

He dialed.

"Hello, Mom?"

"What's wrong?"

"Zadeh," he said—the name was suddenly silly, not carrying the necessary official gravity—"your father . . ."

"Yes, yes! What! Arrested again?"

"No, sick. A stroke."

A short shriek.

"How do you know?"

"There are cops here."

Bama plunged toward him and grabbed the phone.

"Leah, the Papa, the Papa!"

Bat squeals escaped the receiver.

"Leah, Leah, what will I do? The Papa, the Papa!"

He heard the line go dead and tried to wrest the phone from her, but she would not give it up. A cop tugged at him. "Listen, kid, let her have the phone. It'll keep her out of the room."

An ambulance siren grew closer and louder, a finger of noise pointed at Jacob Simon Fishman, a stranger become an intimate because he was wrestling with mortality. Men showing white garments under their overcoats wheeled a stretcher into the bedroom. Through the closed door Harry heard loud voices, which he tried to decode to life or death. A cop emerged. He led Harry away from Bama, who still clutched the phone, moaning *the Papa, the Papa* to a busy signal, and dropped a heavy arm around Harry's shoulders.

"Kid, your grandfather is dead. They did all that they could, but it was a very serious stroke. Look at it this way: even if he had lived, he would have been a vegetable. So maybe he's better off."

Harry saw Zadeh at his unvarying morning ritual: biting into the raw onion that assured bowel movements and longevity. But it was not the face he had watched licking the stinking juice off his chin. It was the stony, sculpted agony of the bedroom. He tried to blink it away, but he could not. He ran through memories: hand-in-hand walks; being shown off to fellow workers at the leather factory; standing poised at the fishing pier; staring across a chessboard. No use. Zadeh was contorted flesh, bubbles of spittle. Harry sobbed, frightened by his mind's impotence.

The cop drew Harry's face onto his blue-coated chest. Cigar odor clogged his nostrils. Harry gagged. He tried to pull away but the cop increased the pressure, crushing his nose.

"That's it, kid. Get it out here. I know your folks are coming. But till then you've got to take care of your grandmother. Now, stop crying and we'll go and tell her."

He released his pressure. Harry inhaled deeply.

"You ready?" the cop asked.

Harry nodded. But for what he was ready, he did not know. They were about to tell a woman who could not imagine life without her husband to start imagining it. In India, wives burned themselves with their dead husbands. Maybe they were right. They approached Bama, who squinted at the cop, slowly nodding her head.

"He has died," she whispered to Harry.

Harry did not answer. Silence sufficed.

The cop began to break the news.

"Ma'am, your husband . . ."

Bama dropped the phone, doubled her fists, and pounded at the cop's chest. Particles of dust rose between them. Instinctively, the cop reached for his billy club. His hand rested on it as spat Yiddish crackled at him.

"Assassin, maker of pogroms, killer of Jews, Cossack, may your entire family die horribly in a plague!"

The cop nodded his head. He understood her grieving and the spoken memories of her dead husband. He stepped back. Bama's fists continued, chopping air.

The bedroom door opened. Like a figurehead, the other cop led a furled white sail past them. Bama leapt toward it, ripping away the sheet.

"Yakov Shimon, Yakov Shimon," she wailed, shaking the corpse's shoulders to awaken him.

It was the first time Harry had heard Bama call Zadeh by his given names. She sounded like one of the lost little girls sobbing forlornly into millions of wrong faces on a summer Sunday on the beach.

One cop pulled her off as she cursed his forefathers and their whores. The other grabbed her around the waist. They held her, wriggling and cursing, as the white lump disappeared and the sound of ignition guaranteed its inaccessibility.

One of the cops shouted to Harry:

"Hey kid! Come on. She's your grandmother. Do something! We can't stay here all day."

Harry offered Bama his hands. She placed her cold palms in his. He led her to a couch. She would not release his hands. They sat like bashful lovers, frozen before petting.

The cops opened the entrance door.

"Sorry, Ma'am," one said.

"Murderers," Bama hissed.

Bama lifted Harry's hands and kissed each finger.

"Heshele, the Zadeh loved you."

"I know, Bama."

"He was a man who thought big, important things."

"Yes, Bama."

She jumped up, ran to Zadeh's desk and snatched his Bible, which was protected by a plastic red-and-white cover more fitting for a barber's manual. She sat next to Harry and opened it to a page whose margins were completely covered by tiny, thin Hebrew calligraphy. Her tears smudged the blue ink. She lifted her head and hardened her jaw.

"What good is all your scribbling now? Hah! Tell me." She let the desk know that the challenge was unanswerable.

"Heshele, such a man . . . such a man who wrote things about God, must clean toilets to bring us to America after."

After designated all time following the news in Warsaw of the outbreak of the World War. In Bama's world, life was divided between the *after* or *before* of that event.

In 1913, *Zadeh* had sailed to America alone to earn money quickly in the Golden Land to bring over Bama and their two daughters. His first job had been cleaning toilets on the Third Avenue Elevated Line.

When war broke out in 1914, he had not yet earned the fare. They could not communicate for five years. Esther, their younger daughter, died of influenza. Bama and Harry's mother almost starved to death.

Bama waved a derisive arm at the desk.

"How can you blame him for not being there when we came to Ellis Island? A man with such big thoughts."

In 1919, he had sent money. From Warsaw, Bama and his mother had traveled to the port of Antwerp, only to discover that they had insufficient funds to cover the passage. In Danzig, it was the same story. Finally in Le Havre, they had found passage on an ancient tanker. After five weeks on an open deck, tossed violently by the winter Atlantic, they had arrived at Ellis Island dehydrated and near delirium.

On that day, Zadeh stood on the dock in Houston, Texas, which, he had been informed—by whom he could not remember, but it was a reliable source—was their port of debarkation.

The Hebrew Immigrant Aid Society had rescued Bama and his mother, housing them in a shelter. A week later Zadeh had returned, insisting then and always, that the ship had altered course.

"Heshele, precious one, let us play chess."

Harry was surprised that Bama knew the game. During his matches with Zadeh, she had not even paused to watch while delivering milk, cookies and tea.

He placed the chessboard between them and set up the pieces. He put a black pawn in one fist and a white one in the other and held them out for her to choose. She looked at the fists and smiled. He set the pawns in place. He had given her the white pieces to play, but she did not begin the game. He turned the board around and made the first move.

She duplicated it. Five more moves were copied. He pushed a piece that blocked duplication. She followed suit anyway, placing two pawns on the same square.

"Bama, you can't . . ."

"Have you won, Heshele?"

"No."

He moved. She crowded another square.

"That's it, Bama. I win."

She spoke to the board:

"That's all I ever wanted him to do! But no. Big man!"

She swept her arm through the pieces, scattering them to the floor. "We will play again, Heshele."

"Yes, Bama."

"But you won, Heshele. Why are you crying?"

"Yes, I know."

He put his arms around her neck and hugged. He kissed the taut skin of her cheek, his lips slipping like worn suction cups on the wetness.

Harry's mother rushed into the room. His father followed, shuffling, head down, a gray felt hat held forward to shield him from incalculable madness. Bama ran to her daughter, gripped her shoulders and shook her violently.

"The Papa has died! The Papa has died! What kind of God? What kind of God?"

His mother's fur hat fell between them. She bent at the knees to retrieve it. Bama grabbed for her shoulders, knocking her off balance. She fell backward onto the floor. His father's terrified eyes peeked out from under the brim of his hat. His mother sat up and rubbed the back of her head.

"What happened, Mama," she screamed, "what happened?"

"The Papa has died!"

She rushed at Harry's father, who crooked his arm in front of his body.

"He was a big man. Is it not true, Catzker?"

"Yes, a big, a great man," his father mumbled.

Bama collapsed onto the couch, as Harry leapt up to avoid her hurtling body. She buried her face in a pillow, moaning: "*Oy, oy, oy.*"

His mother was crying. Her left palm covered her mouth. She turned to her husband and spoke through her fingers:

"We must make arrangements."

He nodded.

"Put the notice in the papers. He has a plot in the Workman Circle cemetery in New Jersey. I want him to lay in Gutterman's on Second Avenue."

"All right. I will call the Workman Circle."

He went to the phone, began dialing, then stopped.

"But where is he?"

He looked toward the bedroom, eyes widening in panic.

"Coney Island Hospital," Harry said.

"Where you were born, precious Heshele," Bama screamed.

While his father spoke on the phone, his mother sat beside Bama, stroking her hair.

"Mama," she asked, "how did it happen?"

Bama turned to face to her.

"Of course, you were not here."

She pointed to the bedroom.

"He was standing in that doorway, scratching his back against the wood, like he did ten times a day. Then he said: 'I have a terrific headache,' and walked to the bed. Then he fell. Just fell down. Such a man, just fell down and said a terrible word. I wouldn't repeat it. Why should he say such a word? A man like that. *That* is the word he leaves me with."

Harry knew the word: it was *fuck*. Zadeh liked the sound of it. Sometimes he would sing a song softly to himself using only "fuck" to replace the entire lyric.

"He didn't know what he was saying, Mama."

"Oh, yes he did. He cursed. Such a man knows when he curses."

The two, their faces no more than three inches apart, flared identical nostrils.

His mother said: "Hate, only hate you know."

"What else is there for a daughter who runs away at sixteen?"

"To get married is not to run away."

"Hah!"

"Velia," his father shouted, "for God sake. Are you crazy?"

Moving to a chair, his mother sat straight-backed, gripping the armrests. She stared at nothing or at her mind's projection. She reminded Harry of the Wax Museum model of Ruth Snyder strapped into the electric chair.

"Mama," she said, "come home with us. You can't be alone."

"I will not be. I will stay with the Papa."

"How will you get to Gutterman's? It's in New York."

"You could sit with me."

"No, Mama, I could not."

"Run away again. Then Heshele will take me. My precious one will sit with me and the Papa."

His mother nodded.

"Bama," he said, " I'll go with you."

"And you too," his mother said to his father, cutting short his obvious relief.

He began to plead the imminent blowup of Europe that had to be reported.

"Just take them to Gutterman's," his mother snapped. "Then you can go play cards. I just want to be by myself."

12

HARRY, HIS FATHER AND BAMA EMERGED FROM THE SUBWAY AND WALKED toward the blue canopy of Gutterman Funeral Home.

"Mrs. Fishman," his father said when they had reached the entrance, "I must go to the newspaper now. I will make sure the obituary notice says all the right things."

"That he was a big man who thought big things," she said.

"Of course."

"You all think big thoughts, no? Big philosophers!"

She grabbed Harry's hand and pulled him. He turned to say good-bye to his father, who waved like a dockside friend wishing passengers bon voyage.

Death, wearing a black suit, black tie and black skullcap, greeted Harry and Bama in the vestibule. Hands linked behind his back, he bowed slightly from the waist, like a maître d'hôtel.

"Yes, may I help you."

"Yakov Shimon Fishman," Bama announced, leaving no doubt as to the importance of the name.

"Yes. The deceased is not yet ready."

"We will go to the room," she said.

"Of course," Death replied. "You know there is no need for you to spend the night. We have a very reliable *shomer*, who will sit with him. A most dedicated individual. A member of the *Chevra Kadisha*. A most pious Jew."

"We will spend the night with my husband."

"As you wish. Follow me."

Death led them into a pea-green room upon which dusky light lay like thin smoke. Five wooden folding chairs labeled *Gutterman* were randomly scattered. On a tiny side table, three tall yellow brass holders sprouted milk-white votive candles.

Through another entrance a man supporting at least three hundred pounds on his five-foot frame wheeled in a closed pine-wood coffin. Behind him, like an afterthought, a tiny man hidden from neck to ankles by a gray overcoat, whose upturned collar brushed against the back brim of a black felt hat, moved cautiously, placing one foot delicately forward and shuffling the other parallel. His croaking voice singsonged prayers read from a book toward which he inclined his head, so that the tip of his triangular, wiry black beard seemed a reading pointer.

"Adam la hevel damah, yomeen katzail ohvayra."

Bama pounced on the casket, propelling it into the stomach of the pusher, who jumped backward, knocking the book from the hands of the prayer sayer.

"Yakov Shimon! Yakov Shimon!" she screamed, kissing the wood.

The fat man took from his jacket pocket a three-by-five card, examined it and scratched his head.

"Madam," he said, "in this casket is Phivele Wolf Litovsky. Is Yakov Shimon perhaps a personal name of endearment?"

"Fat one, are you crazy?"

The prayer sayer had picked up his book and was kissing it loudly.

"*Oy*," he moaned, "such a desecration. That a holy book should fall to the floor."

"What is that stuttering frog doing here?" she shouted at the fat man.

"He is the *shomer*, the watcher, who will sit the night with your beloved Phivele Wolf Litovsky."

"Madman! You have Litovsky on the brain. My husband's

name is Yakov Shimon Fishman and I have no need of this cripple. Get rid of him."

"One moment, madam." He backed out of the room.

"You too, deformed one," she directed, pointing at the prayer sayer, who was rocking back and forth over the casket, rasping in Hebrew. "You will not dribble your phlegm on my Yakov Shimon."

"Woman," he answered, "have you no respect for the dead? From what part of hell have you come here, anyway?"

She was lunging for his throat when the fat man reappeared and plunged between them, grabbing her wrists.

"Wait, wait, Mrs. Fishman. Please. Listen to me."

He tapped the coffin with his fingertips.

"Here, indeed, lies Phivele Wolf Litovsky. Your Yakov Shimon Fishman is almost ready. He will be here in no more than ten minutes, probably less."

"Houston," Bama said

"What?"

"What, what? So wheel Litovsky out and take that hunchback with him."

"Mrs. Fishman, I cannot do that. We have only one room available."

"What! You mean I must spend my last night with Yakov Shimon in the company of an unclaimed corpse and that clubfoot?"

"Mrs. Fishman, Mr. Litovsky is not unclaimed. He has many grieving close ones. But they prefer the *shomer* to watch over him. They are not strong like you."

"How many more orphans do you intend to wheel in here?"

"Please, Mrs. Fishman. There will be only the two. Calm yourself. It is not uncommon."

Bama's eyes narrowed. Her lips drew together tightly until they looked scourged. It was an expression of derisive understanding Harry often had seen. She poked a finger into the fat man's chest, thrusting and retrieving to punctuate her words:

"You do a good business here, hah!"

The fat man led her to a chair. She bowed her head and sniffled.

"Good, Mrs. Fishman, you understand. And Mr. Pincus will say prayers for your husband too. He is a pious Jew and his prayers are heard."

The fat man left the room. Pincus closed his book, placed a candle beside the end of the coffin and lit it. The flame spluttered like a Fourth of July sparkler and then straightened into a yellow and blue raindrop. Pincus spoke to Harry:

"The candle is at the head. The feet of the deceased must always face the door."

"Big philosopher," Bama interrupted.

"Why do you insult me?" Pincus whined. "I am a member of the *Chevra Kadisha*. We make sure that the dead are treated with honor and dignity. It is one of the great mitzvahs of the Jewish faith. We wash the dead in the manner that is commanded by ancient laws. Our society even washes the head with the white of a raw egg mixed with vinegar. There are few Jews left who maintain such fidelity to our ancient tradition."

Harry closed his eyes but could not erase the picture of Pincus cracking an egg on his grandfather's white hair, the yolk gliding like a life raft through the twisted flesh. He sat down next to Bama, putting his head between his legs, as per the instructions of Mr. Brown, his gym teacher, to ward off vomiting or fainting. Bitter bile filled his mouth. He wished for Harry Carey's spittoon. He swallowed the stench and vomited.

Bama's hand smoothed his nape, while she screamed at Pincus:

"Good, holy one. See what you did. So, doer of mitzvahs, clean it up!"

Pincus ran from the room and returned with the fat man and a man in overalls who mopped the mess into a bucket. The fat man sprayed a pine-scented mist around the room by pumping a long plunger attached to a round metal container, lettered *Flit Insect Killer*.

"Are you all right now?" he said to Harry. "Mrs. Fishman, do you think the boy should be here?"

"Heshele, maybe you should go."

Harry, his head weightless and tingling, saw in Bama's eyes the panic of a freshly abandoned dog.

"It's OK, Bama. I want to be with you."

She kissed the top of his head.

The far door opened. Another pine box was placed side by side with Litovsky.

"Are you sure it is my husband?" She sneered at the fat man. "Look at your cards."

"Yes, madam, I am certain."

He left.

The thick pine odor had clogged the air. Pincus could hardly pray for coughing. Bama took a candle, lit it with Litovsky's flame and placed it at the head of Zadeh's coffin. Pincus's face turned scarlet.

"Woman, do you think it is Chanukah? Those are sacred flames. To disturb them is a sin beyond imagining."

"So, imagine it," she said, placing her palms gently on the coffin, like a doctor examining a child's chest.

Pincus read from his book:

"*Shimar tam v'ray yashor, key anchareet l'eesh shalom.*"

"What are you spitting, holy one?"

"I am saying to the Lord: *Look at the good man and see the upright. For there is immortality for the man of peace.*"

"And God is listening?"

"It is my hope."

"Hope away."

"I pray for your husband also, may peace be with him."

"He has no need of your croakings. He was a big man. He thought big thoughts."

"That is not enough for the Lord."

"So let the Lord sue him. Leave me in peace, deformed one."

"Fortunately, the Lord understands that it is the grief of an *onen* that speaks blasphemy and not the true person. I will pray for him, despite you. And you should adhere to our tradition and ask forgiveness of the deceased for any harm or discomfort you may have caused him during his lifetime."

"*Azoy!* Harm or discomfort. And when I am in the box, how will he ask my forgiveness?"

"It is for the living to ask and for God to hear."

"Always such neat arrangements. Big men, thinking big thoughts. Nothing with nothing."

"Woman, I will pray for your husband, may peace be with him. He is in need."

"You will soon be sleeping like a child."

"How dare you! You know as well as I that from the moment of death to the burial the deceased may not be left alone and must be watched. I must be awake at Mr. Litovsky's side until there is someone else. If I fall asleep, may God take me."

"But I am here."

"Women can only be a *shomer* for another woman, not for a man."

"So I have met with good luck! Without you who knows what plague would be sent for only a woman sitting with her husband."

"The boy is with you. He is Bar Mitzvah."

"As a matter of fact, he is not."

Pincus yipped like a dog whose paw had been stepped on.

"*Oy*, the Holy One, blessed be his name, works miracles. He has placed me here to avoid a terrible sin. I am now a *shomer* for two."

"But, believe me, you'll get paid for only one. So croak away and don't stop for a second, because I will not sleep and if you do, the Lord will hear from me."

Pincus babbled. Harry caught "David," and thought: *Little David was small, but, oh my, he smote Goliath, who lay down and dieth. Little David was small but oh my.* He sought to translate the lyric into Hebrew, but could find no equivalent for *oh my.* He searched his mind for incidents from the Bible in which someone is taken by surprise and says it. No use. People didn't say *oh my* to God.

Pincus pulled a chair between the two coffins. His words receded deeper within him and fell from his lips as a hum. Silhouetted by candlelight, Pincus was a rocking overcoat and hat. Harry saw Claude Rains as the Invisible Man and Zadeh as the Mummy.

"Heshele," Bama whispered, "come closer to me."

Their chairs touched. She tilted his head onto her shoulder. His lips touched her neck. Through smell, he tasted *gefilte* fish.

"Heshele, I was remembering in Warsaw, before, when my grandfather died. I was a girl, like you are a boy, and my grandmother was crying and telling me how terrible it was when her grandfather died, and her grandmother and . . ."

Harry watched a movie of calendar pages exfoliating. Years flashed and disappeared. He figured: It is now 1939; she was, say, thirteen, we're back to about 1889. Two more grandmothers back, now it's 1769. *I am hearing words that were spoken before there was electricity, before there was America. Where we're sitting, Indians powwowed, while in Warsaw, my great-great-great-grandmother cried.*

The room began to fill: George Washington; Errol Flynn as General Custer; Maimonides; Attila the Hun, sword raised; regiments of Cossacks; bearded prophets wearing sandals and carrying staffs; dinosaurs in combat; and then grandmother after grandmother, all with Bama's face, telling boys about grandfathers, until there was David, fussing with a slingshot, being told of his grandfather's death. A white pillar of smoke became a swirling blackness. It was before the Creation, *Sohoo V'Vohoo.* Harry said: *oh my.*

The swirl was buffeting his shoulders, jerking him back and forth. He heard God call his name. He answered as did Adam:

"Heneni."

God said: "Heshele, wake up."

He opened his eyes, as commanded. God was his father. His mother stood beside him. As deities, they wore black.

"Heshele, it is morning," God said.

"Of which day?"

God smiled.

"Come out of the dream, Heshele. You are in Gutterman's, where you fell asleep last night. They said you were sick."

Harry looked around the room. Mr. Litovsky, Pincus and Zadeh were gone.

"Are you hungry?" his father asked. "We brought you a peanut butter sandwich."

He handed Harry a square of wax paper.

Harry's need to eat went beyond hunger. He ripped away the wax paper and, using both hands, shoved the pumpernickel bread in his mouth, cramming in the entire sandwich as if packing an overstuffed suitcase. The peanut butter stuck to his palate, immobilizing his tongue. His cheekbones cracked as he widened his mouth to gain leverage.

"I assume you are no longer sick," his father said.

His mother turned away, registering disgust.

His father handed him a black overcoat with a velvet collar.

"Here, put this on. Lazar the tailor said it would fit. A Hasid left it there last year."

He wiggled into it. It rested on his sneakers.

"Lazar is no bespoke tailor," his father said.

He walked beside his parents and Bama into the chapel. Faces, vaguely familiar but too fleeting to identify, floated by like balloons on strings. On the raised stage Pincus sat beside a coffin.

Rabbi Elfenbein, an old friend of Zadeh's, walked onto the stage, faced the audience and cleared his throat.

Elfenbein and Zadeh had been chess and Talmudic adversaries. Their jousts, held at his grandparents' home, invariably provoked shouted insults. In chess, the loser claimed unfair, disturbing tactics such as lighting a pipe, clearing the throat or breathing too hard at a crucial juncture. Differences in Talmudic interpretations led to mutual charges of idiocy which, if let loose upon the world, would visit irreparable harm on the Jewish people. At the appropriate moment, Bama would enter with tea and honey cakes which they slurped in renewed friendship.

Elfenbein began to speak. His Adam's apple, a large nugget, glided up and down like the gonger on the high striker. The eulogy tumbled past Harry's ears which were filled with a chorus of thousands of crickets. He grasped at familiar phrases:

"The Lord is my shepherd . . ."

Harry saw his grandfather as a sheep, layers of wool expanding him to the size of a cow. The beast turned. Its face was another layer of wool.

"Under the cover of His wings forever . . ."

The Lord, an eagle with the face of Paul Muni, swooped and snatched the sheep-cow in its talons. They soared up, up, up, the bird's wings blotting out the sky until they became the sky. The sheep dangled like a magician's assistant, levitated.

On the ride to the interment, Harry sat next to his father on the jump seats of the limousine facing his mother and Bama. The women stared straight ahead, clamped teeth protruding identical cheekbones, eyes firing hate. His father slumped, hat tipped forward, but unable to disappear completely. Harry wished him a sombrero.

As the coffin was being lowered into the grave, Bama leapt forward to kiss it, teetering at the hole until a gravedigger grabbed her.

Harry noticed a group of his parents' friends gathered in a circle like a huddled football team. Lockerman, the playwright, whispered something. The others strained to keep from laughing. Harry remembered that Lockerman, in answer to a request from the management of the *Jewish Daily Forward* to its employees for money-saving ideas, had suggested the elimination of toilet paper from bathrooms since all the writers had no use for it due to piles.

As dirt covered the coffin, Zadeh, dead at fifty, spoke to Harry, promising long life, the reward for ever-empty bowels.

In the Cherry Tree: November 5, 1938

Aba: *Did you hear the radio broadcast of* The War of the Worlds?

Harry: *No. But everyone at school was talking about it.*

Aba: *What did they say?*

Harry: *Many said they heard it and were not afraid.*

Aba: *Do you believe them?*

Harry: *Yes. We know that radio is made-up stories.*

Aba: *Don't they ever frighten you?*

Harry: *Yes, but not in a real way. They just make me afraid of things that I am afraid of, like the dark or a creaking floor. They make me remember what I am afraid of.*

Aba: *What do you think of all those people who ran into the streets with handkerchiefs over their mouths to protect themselves from Martian poison gas?*

Harry: *They are like my mother.*

Aba: *How is that?*

Harry: *They are sure everything bad will happen.*

Aba: *One person called a newspaper and asked, "What time will the world come to an end?" Could that have been your mother?*

Harry: *No. If the world were coming to an end, she would already know the time.*

Aba: *The world is coming to an end, Heshele.*

Harry: *When?*

Aba: *In a few months, maybe a year.*

Harry: *How do you know?*

Aba: *I heard it on the radio.*

Harry: *You believe* The War of the Worlds *could come true?*

Aba: *No, but I did hear it on the radio, a few weeks before.*

Harry: *On what program?*

Aba: *It was a voice describing how the Nazis marched into Czechoslovakia and the people threw flowers at Hitler.*

Harry: *But that is not a made-up radio program. It is true.*

Aba: *Yes, Heshele, and no one ran into the streets and screamed.*

CHAPTER

13

DURING THE RIDE BACK FROM THE CEMETERY, BAMA TURNED CATZKER
into a caterer, demanding to know how many mourners would
return to the house from the cemetery. How many at the chapel,
who had not gone to the cemetery, would show up? How many
schnorrers would read the notice and arrive for free food and
drink? What was the grand total? How quickly could he get to the
A&P on Mermaid Avenue and return with the quantities of food
necessary to feed that number, which she would increase by twenty-
five percent, because he knew absolutely nothing about such matters?

Each question received a mumbled number or protestation of
ignorance.

"Such a big man with such big thoughts can't remember a few
pieces of bread."

"No, no, Mrs. Fishman. It is just that I want everything to be
perfect. Therefore, Heshele will come with me. He has a memory
like a genius elephant."

His father had kicked him gently in the ankle to alert him to
start him remembering.

Now, as they pressured perfect footprints into the snow that
had been accumulating all day, his father took Harry's hand.

"Heshele, how are you?"

"OK, I guess."

"Are you very sad?"

"I don't know. I know I should be. But what does it mean to
be sad?"

His father stopped. He cupped his free hand to let the snow gather. It quickly turned from an inviting white coating to black-specked gray water.

"Sadness is in my hand. In a second, a thing of beauty becomes dirty water; innocence leaves a child's eyes; he who strived for immortality lies forgotten under weeds. Sad is missing the love that death has sealed in the ground or that life has denied life to."

"Then I'm sad. When you took my hand, I remembered how he took my hand when we went to the pier to fish. And I thought: *That will never happen again.* And then I thought: *Up until now I never understood the word never,* and there was a lump in my throat."

His father pulled him into a bear hug. "Heshele," he said, "Aba once began a poem like this: '*Make simple God, the words I make.*'"

He pushed Harry to arm's length to be admired, and laughed.

"*Oy,* Heshele, that coat. Lazar has some idea of fit. You look dressed for a *Purimspiel.* A dimwit Hasid."

Harry looked himself up and down in the storefront glass of Maslow's Insurance Company. He curled imaginary *payess.* They hugged, laughing.

The return to Bama's house, each clutching to his side two heavy bags of groceries, was a dangerous passage through slippery streets. After two near-tumbles, his father abandoned the sidewalk for the gutter and slid his shoes though the snow as if he were ice-skating, at which he was expert. He began to "la la" *Over the Waves.* Laughing and singing off-key, they glided side by side.

Half a block from Bama's house, his father eased to a halt.

"Now, Heshele, we must stop laughing. The dead demand respect."

"Can't you respect someone and still laugh? There were a lot of funny things about Zadeh."

"Yes, Heshele. And you keep them and laugh about them. Laughter with the dead is the only living quality we can share with them. Sadness, regret, pain, are all one-sided. But now we must as T.S. Eliot, an anti-Semite, but yet a poet of some value, has written: "prepare a face to meet a face."

"Is that the right thing to do?"

"No, but it is *the thing* to do, even though we are aware that it is against our nature "

Crushing the bags to his sides, Harry spanned the three outside steps in one stretch of legs and twisted the knob of the front door so that it flew open before his weight. He staggered wildly, trying to stop his momentum by finding a stable center of gravity. The eyes of small groups in hushed conversation fixed on him, wondering whether he was merely a disturber of decorum or an unhinged bereaved about to wail the raw emotion which would link this shivah to the millennia of Jewish sadness.

Harry stumbled into the kitchen, almost flattening his mother against the refrigerator. The wet bottoms of the bags parted, disgorging jars and cans.

"Klutz," his mother said. "Well, just don't stand there. Pick it up."

On his knees amid the pickles, tuna fish, crackers and cookies, he watched Bama rush at his father.

"Did you see the hunchback?" she screamed. "Such an evil eye for the Papa's shivah! Catzker, throw him out."

"Mrs. Fishman, I must continue a conversation with Rabbi Elfenbein . . ."

"To hell with Elfenbein. All he knows is to eat cake and fart. Throw out that angel of death."

"Mrs. Fishman, as much as I respect your wishes in your own home, I cannot do as you ask. The gentleman you speak of is Label Feinschriber, a talented poet."

"Another big man with big thoughts. So why can't he think away his hump?"

His father's small Tartar eyes darted like panicked gerbils before beginning to blink rapidly. Now, Harry knew, his father would use words—any words—like defensive fists, to ward off the unpleasant or boring.

"Mrs. Fishman, we should not be so hard on other people's infirmities. After all, we are all God's creatures, and it is his wisdom

that made us what we are. I realize there are superstitions surrounding such deformities and they continue to carry a tribal message, but intelligent people, like yourself, Mrs. Fishman, cannot be
governed by mystical powers that have their basis in the luck of the
genetic draw."

"Shit in the ocean," Bama spat.

Bama pulled Harry to her. "Don't look at the hunchback," she
whispered. "You have not finished growing yet."

His mother pleaded a headache that demanded air, and fled
the shivah. She entered the candy store where her father had tasted
the joys of pinball and waited outside a phone booth while a fat
man ended an agitated conversation with a slammed receiver and
a volcanic eruption of smoke. He ripped at the metal handle on the
wooden-framed glass door, which folded inward and momentarily
wedged against his belly.

"It's all yours," he said to Velia, covering her face with cigar
smoke.

Velia waited outside the booth, letting it air out. The cigar
smoker, now sitting at the counter slurping an egg cream, jerked
his head toward her.

"Cigar smoke's good for you, lady. It puts hair on your chest."

A group of teenagers gathered around the pinball howled
appreciative wolf calls. Velia stepped into the booth.

"Amalgamated Clothing Workers of America." The voice was
drained of energy, barely audible.

Marie, Velia thought. What a greeting!

"Mr. Barbetta, please."

"I'll connect you," Marie said, as if responding to a request for
a favor.

"Mr. Barbetta's office," Sybil sang in operatic high spirits.

"Sybil, this is Velia. Is Mr. Barbetta in?"

"Oh Velia, I'm so sorry about your father."

"Thank you, Sybil."

"I'll connect you."

"Hello Velia. I am sorry I could not get to the funeral service. But as you know, today was a day of critical negotiations."

The voice leaked a trickle of hoarseness through a timbre that caressed like a blanket of penetrating steam in a Turkish bath. The words were formed carefully. Barbetta never spoke rapidly or used contractions. Like a stammerer who avoids the terrors of *m* and *t*, he feared the speed and compression of his boyhood Neapolitan that lurked, champing for outlet.

"That's all right, Lu . . ." She wondered if Sybil, hand smothering the mouthpiece, was listening. Maybe even Marie was allowing the switchboard to blink and buzz while plugging her ears into Luigi's line. The hell with it.

"It's really OK, Luigi. I understand. But now I need you."

"Where is the shivah? I will come as soon as I am finished here."

"That's not what I meant."

"I do not understand."

"I want to be alone with you."

The receiver crushing her ear, a habit of a childhood in which privacy was an admission of sin, fell silent. She saw Luigi's shinning, soothing black eyes, immobilized by the failure of a stock answer to carry a situation. He would be staring at the phone as if the correct words were about to wriggle through its holes like angel hair pasta. Sniffs of air, bowed on the black hair curled inside his wide nostrils, rasped in her ear.

"But Velia, today. How . . . ?"

"Luigi, I must see you. Isn't that enough?"

"Of course. Of course. Let me see . . ."

Now, she knew, his free hand patted his thick black-and-white hair, an even split, as if landscaped by a compulsive gardener.

"I could be at the . . . I can be there by seven-thirty, maybe a little later."

"You are a wonderful man."

"Yes."

She looked at her watch: Five-thirty. Where to go? The shivah was out of the question. She and her mother were a word away from a screaming match. Moishe's friends—they were hers too, but she always thought of them as his—were settled into their high-toned drivel and probably, no, definitely, ridiculing her father. Yes, he was ridiculous. But she gave them—no less ridiculous—no right to maul him on their rotting gums.

She left the candy store as a teenager whistled *The Bear Came Over the Mountain* to the rhythm of her buttocks. The snow had begun to freeze. She took small steps, testing her high heels before committing her full weight. Climbing the ramp to the boardwalk, she could see over her shoulder the window of the room at the Half-Moon, rented by the Amalgamated, that would be her sanctuary. Her heel hit an icy patch. She slipped to her knees, sliding part-way down the ramp until a pair of hands on her buttocks stopped her. She heard Joe Baker's usual greeting.

She was not afraid of Joe. He was like Aaron, the idiot milkman in Warsaw, whose deliveries included a proud exposure to which housewives had learned to say, "How nice," whereupon Aaron would carefully stow his treasure until the next admirer.

Her shredded stockings lay on reddened knees. A mirror, she imagined, would reflect a snot-ridged face and the hairdo of an anarchist. All in all a fitting companion for Joe Baker, who was something to prevent her from falling again.

"Hello Joe."

Accustomed to blows and screams, Joe instinctively jumped backward at the sound of a female voice.

"Don't be afraid, Joe. I like you."

She slipped her arm in his and tugged him forward. He smiled and began his introduction:

"My name is Joe Baker, my prick is a . . ."

"Now Joe, you've already told me that."

She squeezed his biceps.

"Numbers," he said.

"Two Tolstoys, One Dostoyevsky and seven Chekhovs."

Joe jerked his head from side to side, as if slapped. He wailed. A cloud of stink covered her face. She quickly shouted:

"2,474, 5,356, 17."

He gave the answer. They walked arm in arm. At the ramp leading to the Half-Moon, she sought to disengage. He crushed her arm to his side.

"Rosie's," he said.

"Rosie's? I don't understand."

"Rosie's, Rosie's," he shouted, sliding his free fist up and down the dangling end of the rope that held up his pants.

He dragged her beyond the hotel.

"Rosie's!" Velia shrieked. *My God, he wants to take me to Rosie's whorehouse. He thinks I'm . . .*

"2,000, 4,000, 6,000," she yelled.

"12,000," he answered, still dragging her.

She sank to her knees, trying to wriggle free. He crouched and pulled her like a sled. She grabbed at his ankle. He tripped and flew forward, landing on his forehead, then skidding about three feet.

She ran slipping and sliding toward the hotel. At the ramp she looked back. He hadn't moved. Had she killed him? She didn't care.

She sat on the radiator in the hotel bathroom for half an hour, moving to a stall when anyone entered. Finally warm, she tugged her hair into some kind of order.

At the newsstand in the lobby she bought a *Daily Mirror* and a Milky Way candy bar and fell into in a leather chair that allowed a view of the entrance. She chewed the chocolate and caramel into a stream of sweetness that soothed her throat and stomach.

It was six-fifty. The only other people in the lobby were a group of old men and women, sitting on the edge of their chairs like birds on a perch and swiveling their heads toward any movement. Their eyes, Velia thought, suck you up, like Luigi inhaling oysters. Suddenly they all rose and, each limping or listing at differing angle, shuffled to the elevator. It was time to switch on the radio and wait for Gabriel Heatter's assurance: *Ah, there's good news tonight.*

She read the front page headline: *Pope Dies*. Below was a photograph. Could that worn-out man be the same one who looked down at her from the walls of the convent? She read the report:

"Pope Pius XI, 261st head of the Catholic Church, died early this morning. His heart, weakened by two years of illness, stopped beating. The 'Pope of Peace' was 81 years old and had ruled for 17 years."

He was not the one. They all looked the same.

She reread: "His heart, weakened by two years of illness, stopped beating." She imagined that gentle death: a wistful sigh, the eyelids closing slowly. Not a Jewish death. Jews scream to the grave, as they scream in life. Their brains explode and leave a mess, like Papa.

Closing her eyes, she traveled to the convent which she had entered when she was eleven. She wore a white blouse and blue jumper skirt, surrounded by identically dressed girls. Nuns, reflecting the sun off their gleaming white hats, glided to their chores.

In the vestry, she lovingly beheld her white, alabaster angels, with whom she shared a blush of rose on the cheeks. She once again slid her fingers slowly, like a novice Braille reader, over the fluted wings that promised soaring flight—to anywhere.

The Warsaw convent was a place, the nun had told her, where a girl, even a Jewish girl sent there by her mother to plead for sanctuary because her family was starving, could meet God and the Son of God. She had been introduced to the Son of God, eaten his flesh, drunk his blood. She preferred the pure angels, in whose faces she saw her own.

Then, after more than a year of days that were neatly parceled out to be spent with the Father, the Son and the Virgin, the Mother Superior had told her that she was to return to the bearded men who stank, spat and prayed to an invisible God who, she was certain, also stank and spat.

She had pleaded that the convent was her home and all the girls more sister to her than her real one. She wanted to be like them: a Catholic. The nun had answered that these were not decisions for a child, but when grown-up, she could do as she wished—even become a nun.

The closest she ever came to that goal was Shrafft's. There, scrubbed women wearing white gloves were led to tables covered with fresh white linen, to be served by blond waitresses, corseted in schoolmarm black-and-white uniforms. If the decor did not include angels, she could imagine them hovering over the white food.

At age fifteen she had applied for a job as a waitress, even though it was no secret that Jews were not hired. Leah became Velia and Poland moved to Russia and hints of the Romanovs. The interviewer, sure of his instinctive ability to spot Jews, demanded no credentials from this blond cherub.

She lasted two wonderful weeks, until her father, alerted that she had not been attending school, tracked her down, burst in during lunchtime and yelled at her in Yiddish. She fled in her uniform, never returning to pick up the pay due her. The uniform still hung in her closet, a testimonial to the limitless possibilities of lying.

A disturbance at the entrance ended her reverie. She watched in terror as Joe Baker, shouting, "Rosie's!" was thrown out. Then he was back, allowed in under the protection of the creature in the wheelchair and the chauffeur. The three surrounded her.

"Rosie's!" Joe shouted over and over, until it sounded like the a cheer.

The house detective waddled over.

"What's up, Vic?," he asked.

"Don't know. Joe is saying he knows this one from Rosie's."

The house detective squinted professional eyes at her:

"Ain't I seen you here before?"

"Probably. I often take dinner here with dear friends," she answered in the sanitized accent taught at Schrafft's.

"These whores are really something," Menter said. "Hoity-toity, and all that."

119

Velia lunged forward, missing a slap at his face.

"Hold that whore!" Menter shouted, brandishing a fist, "I'll see to it she never works again."

Joe put an armlock on her neck. His other hand pawed at her breasts. The house detective interposed himself between her and Menter.

"Vic," he said, "we can't have that here. Get her outside some-time."

Menter nodded, now more interested in Joe's vigorous squeezing of Velia's breast.

"Nice feel, huh Joe?"

Baker's cracked tongue slid rapidly between the corners of his mouth.

Menter laughed.

"Vince," he said, "give Joe a couple of bucks for Rosie's, and let's get away from this cunt so she can go back to work." His fist masturbated the air.

Joe skipped across the lobby, pulling at his rope, almost col-liding with Luigi Barbetta, who ignored her as he walked to the elevator, where Menter and Vince waited.

"Hey, Luigi," Menter said, "what the hell are you doing here this time of night?"

"A business conference. You know how it is, Vic, we work for our brothers and sisters twenty-four hours a day."

Menter's eyes swung from Luigi to Velia and back again.

"Sure, Luigi," he said. "Sure . . . Luigi. Brothers and *sisters.*"

Velia bolted to the elevator. She knocked softly on the door of room 612. Inside, Barbetta was ill at ease. Her phone call had been an open admission of their affair to the eavesdropping staff. She was becoming dangerous.

He sensed a prelude to a campaign for a double divorce. He wanted rid of her, but her fantasy-driven reaction loomed too unpredictable.

He opened the door, flattening himself behind it. She threw

off her coat, directing his attention to her torn stocking and scraped knees. She sobbed out her experience.

"You know that crippled animal," she concluded, "I want you to give him what he deserves."

"Of course," he answered. "My God, that is all you needed. Leave Menter to me."

He poured two glasses of wine.

"My deepest sympathies on your great and tragic loss."

It was the exact phrase she had heard countless times after handing him a note bearing the name of the deceased and the bereaved's name and relationship. She merited only the mechanical, phony solemnity.

"I suppose," she said, "he was not a bad man. Although he made my life miserable anytime he could."

"Why speak ill of the dead? As your people say: *Alov ha Shalom*. May peace be with him."

She looked at her savior from the black beards. He might as well be Jewish. But he wasn't, and his skin was the color of her angels. She could close her eyes in the arms of an alabaster angel.

He unknotted his tie and began to unbutton his shirt.

"Draw the curtains and shut the light," she said.

"Still, after all this time?"

"Still. I don't want to see you naked or you to see me. It's dirty."

He sighed resigned exasperation.

As she lay down beside him, she spoke to her purpose, seizing the latitude conferred by her grief.

"A husband I never loved or wanted. A child I never wanted. I got pregnant to get out of the house," she lied, having faith only in embellishment. "Pregnancy was a solution. I didn't think beyond it."

"Velia, there is no need to tell me all this. I do not believe you, in any case. You are distraught with your loss. In such a state you are liable to say anything."

"Believe me, Luigi, believe me. I am telling you a truth I have never told anyone. Now you are closer to me than my husband. And that is how it should be."

They made passionless love, Velia thinking, *He is mine as never before*, and Luigi panicking because he could not see clearly how, in an orderly fashion, to rid his professional and personal life of this threat.

As they dressed, she reminded him:

"Don't forget that gangster Menter."

"Of course."

Menter, it suddenly came to him, was the solution. *I looked the other way on some renegade, nonunion shops he operates in. Now he can repay me.*

CHAPTER
14

AFTER ATTENDING THE CHAPEL CEREMONY, ABA TOOK THE SUBWAY to his favorite Harlem whorehouse.

Proximity to death was one of life's many stimuli that agitated his desire to handle a woman, to wander his hands over all the grab bags of pleasure with which God had endowed his afterthought perhaps as recompense for chronological neglect.

When a psychiatrist friend had explained that the orgasm was the closest living approximation of death, therefore *la petite mort*, Aba, who believed that demons crafted all enigmas of life, had accused him of consorting with the French, convicted overintellectualizers.

In truth it was not the pursuit of orgasm that possessed him, but the yearning for tides of warmth his fingertips could capture and let flow through his body.

Once at a poetry reading he had watched a young Negro maid wearing a white serving outfit dole out food from a buffet table. Her icy, cocoa-colored skin, not completely covered by the uniform, promised a tactile romp of savagery and tenderness. He had held out his plate while his eyes swooned and his hands itched.

That evening he had made his first trip to a Harlem whorehouse, a path well traveled by Yiddish writers and actors seeking the thrills of unJewish, African abandon and elevation to the level of just another white man.

The Madam had asked him, "You want anything special?"

"They're all special," he had answered, watching the black

flesh covered only by blacker bras and panties parade by.

In a tiny room, the whore, a chunky woman of indeterminate age, quickly threw off her underclothes and lay down on the lumpy bed. She twitched her wide nostrils as if preparing them for something, then shut her sad eyes and said, "Masie say you just want it straight"—a finger descended to her pubic hair—"but maybe it ain't so. The mouth is extra."

Without removing his clothes, he lay down beside her to examine his first Negro woman. At once he thought oneness, harmony. The brown nipples on the brown breasts, the dark pubic hair curling under the dark thighs, blended into an uninterrupted expanse of sexual nourishment. No wonder Solomon, that experienced archsensualist, had turned boy in the hands of Sheba.

He asked her to lie on her side. He lay one palm on her back and slid the other under her onto a breast. He slowly smoothed his way down. The distinct sensations lifted from each contour vied for attention, confusing his brain into a drunken dizziness. By the time his fingers found her clitoris and the other hand savagely spread her buttocks, a long orgasm had wet his underpants.

Now, following a more conventional act, he reboarded the subway: He looked at his watch: seven-fifteen, still time to make the shivah.

At the 96th Street subway stop another favorite of his erotic gallery boarded: a scrubbed-sterile, button-nosed, ghostly white blonde, directly off the American assembly line. The product that had scored a direct hit on Celine's gonads.

She sat and read *How to Win Friends and Influence People*. Calling on Kafka to metamorphose him into a spider, he sat down beside her.

"You've won," he said.

She looked up, averting his eyes, scanning the car for possible help.

"You have won a friend and I am ready to be influenced."

She was relieved. It was only a pickup, not a madman. She blew air onto the book.

"Clever. Now leave me alone."

A Bronx accent wafted on currents of drugstore perfume and

powder. He wished for the sickly, sweet odor of Juicy Fruit gum to increase his pleasure.

"Wouldn't you like to practice what is being preached?" he said. "Mr. Carnegie himself once said to me: *All reading and no playing make Jack and Jill wallflowers.*"

She finally looked at him but only to make plain that what followed were her final words:

"You sure like to talk. Why don't you get off at Union Square and stand on a soapbox."

He had misjudged. She was an informed person. Good conversation was the way to her heart.

"I don't like to approach you in this vulgar way," he pleaded, "but what does one do in America? In Europe, where I come from, as you can tell by my Charles Boyer accent, you see a beautiful woman and you write her a note. I tried that once in America . . ."

He told of being taken by Harry to Ebbets Field to see his first baseball game. It had been a bewildering experience, further muddied by Harry's excited explanations of why men dressed in boy's knickers tried to beat each other over the head with a wooden club and then ran in circles. More comprehensible had been the behavior of his fellow spectators, who, having paid money, regretted the expenditure and cursed everyone on the playing field in terms he had never before heard expressed so openly.

Bored, his eyes had roamed the crowd, landing on Carmen, seated in the next section of seats. She cheered her matador not with a rose between her teeth, but with delicate nibbles on a hot dog, which she chewed gently before circling her orange lips with a long, curled tongue. He had to meet her. But how? She told him by raising her hand and signaling to the circulating hot dog vendor, a pimply faced teenager wearing a surgeon's white outfit. He wrote on the small notepad he always carried with him:

"Miss——. I do not know your name. But I do know you are the most beautiful woman I have ever seen. Where can we meet?" He signed it: *Your slave.*

He called the hot dog seller, bought one, then gave him the note with instructions to wait for a reply. The boy resisted until a nickel was dropped in his palm. She read the note and looked up. The boy pointed at him. He stood, swept an imaginary cape across his body, kicked the bull as it went by, and bowed. She passed the note to someone beside her and pointed. He congratulated himself on his conquest. Harry tugged at him to sit. He was obstructing the view of people who were now threatening him with the same mayhem they planned to visit on the players.

He watched an emissary from his beloved, a muscular teenager wearing an olive-colored T-shirt a shade deeper than his complexion, make his way toward him. The youth stopped at his row, reached past Harry, grabbed Aba's shirt, and pulled him erect. The Roman face bared its teeth and growled:

"You dirty old bum!"

Harry grabbed the assassin's arm with both hands.

"You leave him alone!" Harry shouted.

Around them, the spectators were calling for a good thrashing of "the shitty Giant fan."

His attacker turned to Harry.

"Whoever dat is to you, tell him to lay off my sister or I'll change his face."

He slapped Stolz. The force unhinged his jaw . The spectators cheered the gladiator as he strode back to his seat. Stolz ground his jaw back into place, thinking, *Olé*!

During the recitation, in which Stolz had acted all the roles, even slapping himself somewhat painfully, the woman's face had not strayed from her book. However, behind him there had been low laughter.

The woman said to the book:

"Serves you right. You know, I got a brother too."

Close to his left ear he heard the crack of a baseball struck by a bat followed by a high-pitched voice which rode words up the musical scale:

"Steeerike threeee. Yer out!"

He turned, almost rubbing noses with a Negro woman of about twenty-five. He remained close, examining her chubby face: luminous, black eyes, a jutting, aggressive chin under the canopy of round, glossy purple lips. Nesting behind her left ear, a white camellia highlighted the sheen of her straight black hair, pulled into a tight bun. Gold hoops dangled from her ears. Inside each was a die—four black dots on one, three on the other, Underneath her tan, belted raincoat, he glimpsed taffy décolletage.

"You a funny dude," she said.

"I'm glad someone thinks so." He tilted his head toward the reader. "May I join you, or would you prefer that I send a note?"

"Come ahead," she said, shifting herself.

Sitting beside her, he was seized with body-twitching shivers. Paradoxically, he began to sweat. He imprisoned his hands under his buttocks.

"You OK?" she asked.

He nodded.

"You all talked out?"

"No. No. I was just admiring your flower. Carmen would have done better with a camellia. It's the same message, only more exciting. The real Carmen, that is, not my brother-plagued one."

"You talk like those landlord Jewish cats in Harlem."

"Jewish cats?"

"Yeah."

"How can you tell a cat is Jewish? How can a cat own . . ."

She laughed.

"Oh man, we got us a real live square here. A cat is a person. A human-type being. That's what a cat is."

"Aha. And a dog?"

"A dog is a ugly mama."

His first days in America had been like this. He had learned English in school by studying Shakespeare. In America, Shakespeare was a greenhorn.

"A mama of what, who? *Oy*. Maybe we should tell names. I am Aba."

"I'm Leslie."

"*Oy*. Leslie is a boy's name. More code."

She straightened and pushed out her profile.

"Do I look like a boy?"

"Decidedly not."

"What do you do for bread. Oops! How do you make a buck?"

"I am a poet. It does not buy me much bread. And you?"

"I sing."

Of course, he thought. Her voice is a siren song.

"What do you sing?"

"What I feel."

At 42nd Street, the Dale Carnegie pupil rose. At the door, under a toothsome photograph of Miss Rheingold, she turned toward them and said:

"A perfect couple."

"I knew she was intelligent as soon as I laid eyes upon her," Stolz said. "She knows a perfect match when she sees one."

"Don't jive me."

"I won't, if you don't jive me."

"You know what jive mean!"

"No, but it can't be good."

"You one smart dude."

"I'm a cat and you a mama."

"That's what it is."

"When can I hear you sing?"

"Tonight. Right now if you want. I'm on my way to a gig."

Exiting the subway at Sheridan Square in Greenwich Village, they walked to a nightclub. Backstage, in a tiny room dedicated to a long, illuminated mirror, Leslie threw her raincoat to the floor, revealing a cluster of camellias pinned to her left hip. She stood facing him, back arched. Before he could embrace her, a Negro wearing a porkpie hat, burst in and pulled her to him. He tried to kiss her, but she dodged, saying:

"Got to go on soon. No smearing."

They separated.

"Willie," she said, "this is Aba. He a subway masher."

Willie's palm gyrated.

"Solid, man."

"Yes, solid."

Willie spoke to Leslie:

"You holdin', baby?"

"Uh, huh."

"Let's get down to it."

She held up her palm.

"Aba, Willie and me has a little music business to talk private. You go outside and ask for Barney. Tell 'em Leslie said to give you a table. OK?"

"Thank you," he said. "Nice to meet you, Willie."

"Solid."

Barney instructed a waiter to set up a small table near the stage.

"Ladies and gentlemen, Cafe Society proudly presents . . . Miss Leslie Jones!"

The spotlight caught her walking as if on an errand elsewhere, then, surprised at the setting, casually acquiescing to its requirement. Behind her a piano, guitar, bass and drums launched into a lively tempo. She sang:

Who do you think is comin' to town?
You'll never guess who—
Lovable, huggable, Emily Brown,
Miss Brown to you!

The only jazz he had heard was annoying noise from jukeboxes which hampered conversation. His foot began to keep time to be with her.

Leslie's voice was thin and scratchy like a worn record. It reminded him of a bat, swooping dangerously away from the notes and the beat, always recovering in time. She stood like an awkward schoolgirl, hardly moving her body, trying to hide her hands. She favored bending her neck slightly and singing upward. Between choruses she snapped her fingers and encouraged the musicians with "Yes, yes," or "Knock it down." She received vigorous applause.

For the next two songs the tempo slowed and her voice soared, until it was no longer earthbound. He heard what he desperately sought in his poetry: the soul's voice. The language was mundane. Yet her plaint that her lover was *as cold as ice* was to know ice as Rimbaud had known the color of vowels. And when she sang:

Tell her she's a fool—
She'll say I know, but
I love him so. And that's
the way it goes, when a
woman loves a man,

he knew he was in love. Their matchmaker, he later told her, had been a swinging Danish cat named Søren Kierkegaard, who had written:

"A poet is one who harbors a deep anguish, but whose lips are so fashioned that the moans and cries which pass over them are transformed into ravishing music."

At the conclusion of her performance, she sat with him. He did not wish to speak, only to hear her voice. She had another show to do. He offered to take her home. She said that was not possible.

"Why?" he asked.

"Life don't set up that easy."

"Even when a woman loves a man."

She laughed.

"Even."

After the second show, Willie claimed her.

"See ya, Aba," she said.

"When? Where?"

Willie thrust a large, reddish palm at him. "Hold it, Boss Charlie, we ain't on the plantation."

"Let's go, Willie," she said.

They turned and walked away. Behind her back she wiggled a finger dialing a telephone.

CHAPTER
15

OUT OF EARSHOT, MOSHE CATZKER WATCHED HIS WIFE LEAVE THE shivah after justifying flight for Lockerman and Mecklerberg by banging her palms against her temples in an evocation of pain and misery surely copied from the kvetch-ridden Yiddish King Lear, as overacted by Maurice Schwartz.

He told Harry, who was in the clawlike grip of the widow, that he was working the late shift at the paper, and that later on he and his mother would meet at the Cafe Royal. He offered Harry a dollar for supper, an apology for abandonment. The widow swatted away his hand.

"He eats here. He stays here tonight, mine Heshele."

On the street, he thought to invade the Half-Moon Hotel, then recalled a joke:

A man catches his wife in bed with another man. The wife screams at the husband: "Aha, loudmouth is here, now the whole neighborhood will know!"

Dr. Sigmund Freud, bent double at the waist, legs long-striding for a vigorous turn of eccentric dancing styled on Groucho Marx, gasped: "Jokes are serious things."

Catzker thrust his hands angrily into the pockets of his brown tweed overcoat, straining the threads. In the Norton's Point trolley, he imagined himself a tour guide extolling the simple but functional bungalow architecture and eruditely tracing the anthropological and cultural roots of quaint native customs such as wife beating and drunken pissing out windows. Transferring to the subway, he dozed and dreamed a Victorian scene: his wife and child, seated on a loveseat suspended from the ceiling by a heavy nautical rope, swayed back and forth by pumping their legs as if on a playground swing.

"You know," his wife said to his son, "you are not his child."

His son answered, "That explains my low IQ."

Catzker laughed, cheered and awoke.

Freud, a logger in high boots and plaid shirt, swung an ax at a tree, saying: "If a woman falls and no one hears, is her husband a cuckold?"

Manhattan, viewed from its namesake bridge, was a cemetery of giant tombstones. Near the Statue of Liberty an ocean liner, its enormity outlined by red and white running lights, moved slowly uptown.

On the side of a tenement building, he read once again, the comforting message that America had tamed its goyim: three-foot-high black letters which proclaimed: *Jesus Saves*.

In Kiev, Jesus had been a killer. A Capone ordering deaths. His pained face, demanding revenge, drove the goyim wild. They burst out of church doors like crazed bloodhounds.

One Easter the scent had led to his home. His father met them, offering himself, a Lot protecting God's angels from the Sodomites. They accepted, but dragged Catzker with them to witness Jesus' work.

His father was ordered to remove all his clothes, except for his shoes, and to walk into a lake. If he could walk on the water, he would be spared. He waded into the icy water, stopping when it reached his knees to turn and impassively watch his son struggling to free himself, and shouting: *"Tateh, Tateh!"* His father had placed his index finger to his lips, a familiar gesture of the studious man as always, requesting quiet, then continued slowly until the last strands of black hair floated like seaweed. Vanished, he gave his murderers no bubbles to savor.

In America, Jesus was downgraded to a slugger who broke a

few bones, a Polack or Irishman who spat a phlegm-filled "Christ killer," or a wise-guy college kid who sniggered a tag line to *Jesus Saves*—"*and Moses Invests.*"

From the Canal Street subway stop, he walked toward *The Morning Journal*, which occupied a five-story tenement at the foot of the Manhattan Bridge Plaza. The smells of Little Italy provoked a vision of the same murderous mayhem unleashed on Luigi Barbetta that had possessed him when, a year ago, he had overheard Velia on the phone arranging a tryst at the Half-Moon Hotel.

"Why can't I confront her?" he demanded of himself.

Freud, pouting, said: "Why don't you ask me?"

"OK, why?"

Freud shrugged: "Don't ask."

Pushcarts piled with mozzarella cheese, hard salami, olives, and finocchio lined Mott Street. Beside them, old men wearing long black overcoats and wide-brimmed black hats seemed mourners awaiting a funeral procession. He vowed to write a story transferring the scene to ancient Egypt, where anachronistic Italian entrepreneurs sold food for the tomb of a soon to be buried Pharaoh. Jewish pyramids, Italian catering and Egyptian mummies, he thought, *talk about tour de force!*

Attacking a slice of hot Sicilian dough, he burned the roof of his mouth. Did I, he asked Dr. Freud, do that on purpose? Freud, clad in Stalin's bemedaled finery, answered: "There are no mistakes, comrade."

At Bayard Street, he turned east, thinking: a rotation of a heel and Naples becomes Kiev. He stroked the sleeve of his coat, bought at one of the secondhand clothes cellar shops. He had told his wife that it came from Wanamaker's, because she insisted that all secondhand clothes were stripped from the recently dead. She knew this because she could smell death on them.

A bearded man wearing a yarmulke stood halfway up cellar steps, lightly flicking the sleeve of a gray suit that hung from the street level railing to announce the establishment below.

"*Fineh vayra,* ah sport," he said.

Catzker slid the lapel through his thumb and index finger.

"Pretty thin," he said. "Feels like from before the flood."

The man pushed his yarmulke forward until it covered the rim of his forehead.

"A regular Georgie Jessel," he said. "*Nu,* are you interested?"

"How do know it's my size?"

"If not, we got one that is. Come in, come in," he said, sweeping his arm toward the blackness below as if offering the delights of a pasha's harem.

"Maybe tomorrow," he told the entrepreneur.

"Tomorrow will be too late. Strike when the iron is hot, *boyaleh.*"

Freud, in session is his Vienna office, smiled, and said: "When your finger is cut, everything seems to touch it."

At Manhattan Bridge Plaza, he stopped to admire the arch which, modeled after the Piazza of St. Peter's in the Vatican, was monumental enough to announce heaven, but was forced to settle for the Manhattan Bridge.

Across the street from the newspaper, the display windows of the many jewelry stores were crisscrossed by metal security bars. The street, which during the day was crowded with pacing Jews selling diamonds out of their pockets, was deserted except for one tiny man who wore a built-up shoe for a clubfoot. His eyes followed Catzker, but he said nothing.

"How do you know I'm not a customer?" Catzker said.

The man dismissed him, picking his nose and shooting a piece of dried snot skyward.

"I know, *boychik,* I know."

A surge of anger broke sweat on Catzker's hands.

"I know better than you!" he shouted. " And you don't fool me with that clubfoot. Hiding, hiding, hiding. You think I don't know."

The man hopped and limped toward Canal Street. At a safe distance, he shouted: "*Meshuggener.*"

"Don't ask me for a second opinion," Dr. Freud said, writing out a prescription.

In the lobby of *The Morning Journal,* Fannie, the receptionist/switchboard operator, was deciding whether to answer the phone. She insisted that she could identify a legitimate call from a crank or anti-Semite by the sound of the ring. If she did plug in, she would answer in English or Yiddish, again depending on her reading of the ring: "So, what is it?"

Fannie regarded him quizzically, which meant that she was trying to remember a message for him. Writing down messages was out of the question, she said, because it was a job for a servant.

"Someone called, Fannie?"

"Yes."

"Who?"

"Not so fast. You don't say hello?"

"Hello Fannie. Who called?"

"Aha."

"Aha, who?"

"Aha, your wife."

"So?"

"So, she's in a movie, a long double feature. She won't be home till late."

"Did she leave a number?"

"Of what, the movie house?"

"I, too, am going to a movie."

"Pish, tush."

His fingers squeezed the brass knob of the entrance door but he could not alter its shape.

He walked quickly now, past dark shapes squatting or sprawled like beached manatees in the doorways of flophouses, pawnshops and restaurant equipment stores. An occasional grimy palm emerged as an emissary of nonsense sounds. Catzker did not turn his head. Just as he had written in the poem he had torn up years ago:

You passed him, the man on the street,
As he shouted: "Hey, Mac, hey, Mac."
Third Avenue walks have made you callous
But suppose pain lingered at your back.
Ah, he was just another bum;
You've been a sucker too many times.
Walk on with brisk steps of youth,
But remember how and where you're going.

He asked Dr. Freud: *Why do I remember that silly poem that was early proof that I was not a poet?* Freud, a dandy in a silk cutaway, minced out of an English drawing room, intoning: "Yet each man kills the thing he loves . . ."

Under the harsh light of a pawnshop window, a samovar spread its girth like a golden guardian over harmonicas, scout knives and dented trumpets. He pressed his nose against the glass attempting to read the Russian pedigrees etched in medallions around its base. The spigot shocked him by its resemblance to the gargoyles that had strained to fly off the largest church in Kiev and swoop down upon him. His cheeks flushed as he remembered his mother's chapped lips absorbing his tears.

"Hoo, hah," said Freud, clad in Gertrude Stein's tweed jacket and skirt, "unresolved oedipal is unresolved oedipal is unresolved oedipal."

At Grand Street, he jumped back as a cat leapt from a garbage can. A leftover *dybbuk*, he thought, recalling that he had seen that play at the Neighborhood Playhouse a few blocks away. Possession by a whining, platonic lover, he thought, *some dybbuk!*

Dr. Freud, propped up at a bar, said: "You also saw *Exiles* there."

"A bad play," Catzker said.

Freud, chewing on a long fat cigar, blew smoke rings that spelled *Poldy.*

On Stanton Street, a line waited in front of the Salvation Army. America, Catzker thought, has even made an assembly line of salvation: first kill the stomach pains with beef stew, and then on the belt to the Bowery Mission next door for conversion to the cap-

italist God, the giver of beef stew. He had no argument with it. Full
stomachs made drowsy, pogrom-hungry souls.

A stick figure walked toward him. A fingertipless woolen glove
removed a stained gray hat, uncovering brilliant, young red hair.
The hat, bottom up, brushed Catzker's stomach.

"I'm needin' a nickel, Mac."

"For what?"

"For food."

"Isn't it free?"

"I can get it for free. But if I have a nickel I won't be needin'
to beg. You know what I mean?"

Catzker did not. He considered dignity a capitalistic ruse that
kept people at killing jobs and then preached that starvation was
preferable to the indignity of accepting charity. They said his father
had died with dignity. How much more dead would he be without it?

"Cheap kike," the redhead shouted, "you'll be gettin' yours
soon." He turned, bent over and farted. The men on line shouted
and applauded.

I can grovel for my life before animals, he told Dr. Freud.
Dignity is never included in the lingua franca.

Freud, in professorial tweeds, pointed an instructive finger:
"when I was released by the Gestapo to go from Vienna to
England, they made one condition: that I sign a paper stating that
I had been treated well, which was, given the situation, true. I
agreed and the paper was brought to me. I read it and asked if
I could add a postscript. What would that be? they asked. Well, I
said, I would like to add this sentence: *I recommend the Gestapo to all
my friends*. They were delighted and I did it in my own hand."

"Are you telling me of the clever way you kept your dignity?"

"No," Freud conceded, "just that I was a wise-ass Jew."

Smiling in victory, Catzker walked through the skinny trees of
Roosevelt Park and onto Second Avenue.

On Fourth Street, a few people waited to buy tickets at the Public
Theater. Actors, he thought, have a peculiar talent that requires

no mind. Yet when they speak words, no matter how banal, they can temporarily fool you, like covering stink with strong perfume.

Two years ago the impresario of the Public Theater had called him and suggested that his serialized novel that had just concluded in *The Morning Journal* could, with a few alterations here and there, make a wonderful play. Catzker had been noncommittal because all his serialized novels were jellied in a common mold. He didn't know which one ran yesterday or three years ago.

He had gone to the paper to read *Fanneleh*. It was sad: after much misery in Poland and America, upright Fanneleh had found an upright husband and given birth to perhaps the next president of the United States. But because of her dark secret—her seduction by a goy postman in Warsaw and her enjoyment of subsequent trysts— she had to pay the moral price. Therefore she died in childbirth. It had seemed to him that many of his heroines died in childbirth. It was a clean way to get rid of them and finally end the story.

Initially, he had wondered why anyone would want to verbalize a tour de force of clichés. Then he had considered the possibility of being too hard on himself. Not Chekhov of course, but under the dross some light did seep through.

He had done the adaptation, inventing an ambiguous ending which the impresario suggested to provoke the audience to argue as to whether it was a moral or immoral play. Controversy brought crowds.

The first rehearsal had stunned him. The once scribbled sentences became beautiful, important. Shrieks of anguish were launched from Dostoyevskian raw souls; joy was a purifying thunderstorm. His respect for the actor's craft rose each day, especially when they congratulated him on providing them with beautiful prose.

Opening night revealed a flaw. The audience was not accustomed to ambiguity. At play's end, they remained silent, waiting for the next scene. When the curtain parted, presenting the entire cast ready for applause and bows, the audience was confused, especially at seeing the dead or near-dead Fanneleh, erect and glowingly healthy. When they understood, the reception was tepid.

The ending was rewritten to the original tragedy. The audience booed. By the time a happy ending had been set in place, there was no audience.

The impresario had summed it up: "I guess you are too artistic for my audience."

Catzker, now approaching the Cafe Royal, laughed out loud, remembering his vow that if he ever wrote another play, no matter what the subject, its title would be: *Too Artistic for My Public.*

He walked between the boxed hedges that in summer turned the Royal into a sidewalk cafe. The plate glass window was fogged. Catzker thought to identify by size and density whose unassailable theories had steamed each particular section.

He was about to enter when, like a cinder in his eye, the fifty-story Metropolitan Life Insurance Building on 23rd Street concentrated his consciousness on its flashing red lights and four clocks that, like a metaphysical lighthouse, warned New Yorkers, north, south, east or west, of the time, and of mortality by adding, every quarter hour, a chimed funereal measure by Handel. Presiding like a four-faced ogre over its troll neighbors, it paralleled the hegemony of the Half-Moon Hotel.

He turned and walked up 14th Street, passing Union Square Park where, despite the discouraging wind, euphoric orators on improvised platforms harangued bundles of clothes asleep or dead on the benches. He recalled another discarded poem, written while he was soaking himself in the new, bubbly bath of English and being flooded by Gerard Manley Hopkins. It was called *Union Square.* The only line he remembered was: "beards, bawds, blacks."

"Why blacks?" Freud, a white-sheeted Klansman, asked.

"Why not?" Catzker answered in Yiddish.

At Sixth Avenue he descended to the subway and boarded an uptown train.

"And I recommend Negro whorehouses to all my friends," he told a blushing Sigmund Freud.

CHAPTER

16

HARRY SAT ON THE FLOOR OF HIS GRANDPARENTS' BEDROOM. BAMA had insisted that he sleep in her bed, while she, who would not sleep anyway, would lie on the couch in the living room. After she had tucked him in, he had jumped from between the comforter and sheet, where death touched, itched and bit, put on his clothes, and slumped to the floor. Still death rode him piggyback, choking him with a leg scissors.

From the bedside table he lifted gingerly his grandfather's fat black Waterman fountain pen, and, gripping it as lightly as possible, wrote in Yiddish on the back of an unredeemed ticket for shirts from a Chinese laundry:

Dear Bama,

I remembered homework I had to do for tomorrow. Very important. I went out the window not to bother you. I will come after school tomorrow.

Love,

Heshele

He opened a window and eased himself into a narrow alley. His heavy corduroy jacket hung in the hallway. He wore only a light sweater. Yet, the exhilaration of disengaging from death broke sweat on his forehead. Halfway home he remembered that his house keys were in his jacket pocket.

The windows of his house he knew were securely locked against gangsters from every walk of crime who, his mother was certain, coveted entrance to the Catzker residence. He headed for the

Surf movie theater, hoping to arrive at break time, when it was possible to sneak in through the side exit door. On 33rd Street, he passed the Royal Pool Emporium, announced in one-foot-high black letters painted on a green background that covered a glass storefront. Through an unpainted chink at the top, he glimpsed Woody standing on a platform, similar to those used in performing dog acts, bent over a pool table and manipulating a cue stick. The residents of the freak house watched a match between Woody and Jo-Jo. All except Fifi.

Fifi had been on his mind, starring one night in a wet dream. Her uniqueness matched the promised uniqueness of "it." Because she was French (all the French thought about was screwing), her enormity was a hot bath of flesh. She had boldly invited him to enjoy her (what else would a Frenchwoman do?), and he remembered also the sweetness of her voice. Now he knew that she was alone.

He ran to the trolley and flattened himself at the back. The grinding friction of frequent braking became foreplay. He sprinted the six blocks from the terminus to the house and rang the bell.

"Entrez."

Fifi, wearing a blue dress dotted with pink shapes resembling flower petals, sat on a sofa, dragging strongly on a cigarette. Harry stopped in the middle of the room.

"Ah, it is 'Arry, *le gentil gosse,* but I have not any slips."

His face was hot. He knew he was blushing. The bulge in his knickers throbbed.

"Ah," Fifi said, nodding and smiling, "it is *peut-être* not ze slips zat bring you?"

Harry wanted to nod but could only stare.

"What can it be? Is puzzle to solve."

She motioned him beside her. She patted his head and ran her hand over his burning cheek.

"It gives *plaisir* zat I touch?"

He nodded.

"Perhaps we are solved. Ze little man wish become ze big man, *hein?*"

"Yes," Harry blurted out, dropping his face on her breast.

"But you must *regard* me. To make *amour*, must see each other." Harry looked up. He tried to imagine her without the fat that framed and subjugated her features and made of her body an example of logically extended human growth. Ugly or beautiful did not apply. She was described by other terms: consuming, enveloping, protecting, housing.

"Is good you choose me 'Arry. Is good to have woman of experience."

Age also did not apply. Her bulk was beyond time. He squeezed her breast.

"What you think you want, 'Arry?"

He squeezed harder.

"To stick you in me. Like hammer with nail."

Did it hurt women? It hurt cats. They cried.

"No, Fifi, I don't want to hurt you."

Fifi's finger traced the bulge.

"Is not hurt I talk of. Is ze feeling. A hammer and nail not have feeling."

"I have feeling for you, Fifi," he gasped, cursing her for delaying.

"*Bien, gosse.* We see." She extended her arms in front of her. "You must help."

He rose and gripped her hands. She rocked back and forth, almost pulling him on top of her, until, with a strenuous heave, she stood upright.

"Now let us see, what is what," she said.

She pulled his sweater over his head, unbuttoned his flannel shirt, undid the belt and buttons of his knickers, which fell to his ankles. She dropped his jockey shorts. His penis pointed at her, straining its root, threatening to detach from his body.

"*Bon.* You are, how we say, well prepared. Now, remove ze shoes and ze rest."

He pulled the wrong strands of his laces, knotting them. He sat on the floor, tugging angrily.

Fifi laughed.

"*Doucement*, we go nowhere. Now . . ." She undid the top button of her dress, and spread her arms.

His fingers slipped and fumbled with the remaining buttons. He wanted to rip the dress away. The dress parted. She motioned him behind her. He pulled off the dress. Her buttocks stunned him. Each was as large as the enormous globe in the Planetarium. He ran his fingers along the flesh, suddenly realizing that he was tracing a map of the United States. He felt giddy. He told Mrs. Gaitskill, his geography teacher: "I have done my homework."

Fifi sank to her knees and leaned forward, shifting her weight to the palms of her hands.

"Now, come in."

He had no idea of the interior of a woman's anatomy. All the dirty pictures he had seen were of a man on top of a woman. Somewhere in the tuft of hair between the woman's legs was where the penis went. In the cunt. But where was the cunt? His masturbatory visions had been short on precision.

He pressed his penis into the fissure between the mountains. The friction hurt.

"No, *gosse*, no." Fifi was breathing hard, snorting.

She tilted to one side, put a free hand between her legs, and guided his penis into flameless fire. He exploded lava.

The flow spent, he began to straighten. "No, no, 'Arry, " she gasped. Move in and out in me."

He rocked, surprised at his penis's numbness. Had he caught a disease? Suddenly, she filled the room with the sound of a speeding, mufflerless car, collapsed and lay prone on the floor.

"'Arry, please"

It took twenty minutes to raise and dress her. He sat beside her, embarrassed, as if they shared a disturbing secret. He wanted to leave.

"Well . . . ," he said, raising himself slightly.

She laid a heavy hand on his shoulder. "Zis is ze feeling for me," she said.

"I'll stay," he said.

"To be kind to ze freak."

"No, no, Fifi."

She dabbed her eyes with a gardenia-scented handkerchief, then reached into her purse and lifted delicately, between the tips of her thumb and forefinger, a small photograph. She handed it to him.

It had been bent and straightened, leaving lines. Age had yellowed the white and faded the black. A girl of about eight posed in front of a windmill. A row of domed trees formed the background. The girl was slight. She wore a dark jumper, same color knee socks, black shoes and a round light-colored brimmed hat. A dark ribbon circled the crown. Her hair hung down her back. Its length was not visible in the photo. Her hands held either side of the brim. It must have been a windy day.

"You like ze *petite*?"

"Yes. Is she an old friend of yours?"

She sighed. "A very close *amie*."

Fifi took the photo from him. She traced the outline of the girl with her finger and gave it back.

"Look at ze face, 'Arry. Perhaps you know her?"

Harry studied. The photographer had been more interested in capturing the entire windmill than in the girl.

"No," he said.

"'Arry . . . zat little girl is me."

Harry hoped surprise was not on his face. He kept his eyes on the photo to hide any expression and to confirm that the child was as skinny as he had thought. Yes. Bama would have force-fed her. He looked up at Fifi, who again was dabbing at her eyes.

"You will pardon me, 'Arry. Is time when ze memory make me sad."

Harry put his hand on hers. She sandwiched it.

"You see 'Arry, until I have twelve years, I like any child. I sing. I dance. I play piano. I good student at *l'école*. I have many friends. Zen when is my first bleeding, I begin to grow fat. Like ze

144

balloon zat never break, no matter how much air. My *mère* take me to doctor in Paris. He say stopping eat much. I say I do not eat much. Zey do not believe me. Zey stick needles in me. It make me sick, but still I blow up. My Papa say I make on purpose. Zat I can stop if I want.

"I love my Papa. At night in ze bed, I talk to God: '*Le Bon Dieu*, help me stop. Tell me what must do.' Nozing help. My parents must buy for me new clothes all ze time. At *l'école,* zey make fun on me. Zey stick zere fingers in my flesh. I tell my Mama and Papa I no go school. Zey say I must. *Finalement,* when I have zirteen, zey say not go."

She blew out a sustained chunk of air which unrounded her cheeks a bit. It was as if even now she was trying one more remedy.

"I miss *l'école*. I like read. Zat not stop. People say I full fat. No, 'Arry, I full books. You must read ze good books 'Arry."

He nodded.

"When I have sixteen, I am like today. I not go out house. I must eat so much my Papa say he has not ze money. My Mama cry all ze time. I hear my Papa say: 'What we do wiz her? How to feed her all her life? How we live? God curse us.' Zen zey both cry.

"One day I see in paper little words zat man look for, how you say, odd people, to be in show in America. I call ze number. 'Arry, you know ze one name Schnozz. It is he. I tell he of me. He come see me when Mama and Papa not home. He look on me all sides. He say good. You name Fifi and you come from *famille Louis quatorze.* I like zis Schnozz. He talk like book. He buy me ticket for ship to America. I no tell Mama, Papa. I leave note. I go America. I will write. I never do.

"Schnozz take me Coney. I sit in chair. People look, make fun, but is different. Zey pay to make foolish. I big hit. Newspapers ask how I am from *Louis quatorze*. I tell zem from books I read. Ze call me 'Queen Fifi,' who eat cake like say Marie Antoinette. I like zat."

She smiled, then sighed. She took the photo from Harry and held it in front of her.

"What you know of world, 'Arry?"

He shrugged.

"Is cruel."

He nodded.

"One time I walk sixteen street, where are ze Italians. Zey grab me, pull me into ze club down ze stairs, tear off ze clothes and say: Dance! Zen zey make pipi on me an' push me into street naked. Would zey do zat to zis girl?" she asked, shaking the photo back and forth.

It was a horrible story, but Harry reacted with shivers of pleasure. It was the first time anyone had opened up their life to him, asked him to share pain or joy. With his parents, Aba, Bama, Zadeh, he felt joined by an accident of fate which commanded them to love him. He never felt loved for himself. Had someone else been born, he would have received the same automatic love. But Fifi had chosen him! Something about him had caused her to confide, to share her suffering, to seek his understanding. She was telling him things which, he sensed, she never had been able to tell anyone else. He knew very well the loneliness that attached to such secrets.

He kissed her on the lips, then took her hand and spoke for the first time of a shame which often overrode his will, and paid unwelcome visits, sometimes invading his dreams.

He was nine. At Hebrew school he was given a cardboard box stamped with a Jewish star and told to collect money so that Jews could plant trees in barren Palestine. His teacher dropped in two pennies through the metal slit so that he could shake a message of generosity. The first two passersby responded with coins. Success created the Harry Ephraim Catzker forest of Palestine, through which he skipped. A boy his size suddenly blocked his path. He raised a hammer above Harry's head. Harry had visualized the claw marks it would make in his forehead, how it would splinter his teeth, enter his eye.

He fell to his knees and begged not to be ripped apart. The boy snatched the box from Harry's offering hand and said:

"You sing good. You should join the Jew choir."

Fifi smiled.

'Arry. Why feel shame? You do right. He have hammer. You have nozing. I do same zing."

"No, Fifi, I should have fought him. I should have tried to hurt him, to show him Jews can fight."

"'Arry, listen. When zose men push me down to cellar, I can scream for help. But I not, because if I do I have afraid zay stick me wiz knife or maybe worse. What sense?"

He nodded, but was unconvinced.

She smiled broadly. Her stretched lips dug deep dimples in her bloated cheeks. Her eyes caressed him. He hoped his eyes were as expressive.

"'Arry, you come see me again."

"Yes, Fifi,"

"We talk, yes. Like two people. You like I teach to you le français?

"Yes."

"*Bon. A tout à l'heure*. Zat is first *leçon*. It mean see you soon."

"Toot a loore, Fifi."

"You must kiss me on two cheeks. Zat is also France *leçon*."

Outside, he jumped straight up and clicked his heels together. He had done it! And in a French cunt! By the time his feet touched the ground, he felt shame for thinking of Fifi in that way.

CHAPTER
17

AFTER LEAVING FIFI, HARRY WALKED TOWARD HOME ALONG THE boardwalk. The strong wind off the Atlantic budged and chilled him. He isolated a gust and imagined its history: it had discomfited Ziegenbaum on the *Bremen,* eased along notes in bottles launched from every continent, slackened while passing over a lifeboat escaping a shipwreck, boiled white foam to artistically decorate buoys and beaches. In thrall of its journey, he did not see coming towards him Albert-Alberta and Otto. He would have collided with them had not Otto thrown a stiff arm against his chest, stopping him abruptly.

"Harry, old pal, I shall report you to the local constabulary for drunken walking," Albert-Alberta said.

Not ready to leave unresolved a perplexing thought, Harry asked: "When the wind dies down, does *that* wind die forever?"

"This chap needs a hot chocolate to sober him up," Albert-Alberta replied. "Look at you, you're dressed for the Fourth of July."

"Ach, is not cold," Otto said. He wore a light windbreaker over a T-shirt. "Get muscles," he instructed Harry, "muscles make you warm."

Albert-Alberta gripped Harry under the arm and led him to a diner on Surf Avenue. Seated in a rear booth, Albert-Alberta ordered a hot chocolate for Harry and a black coffee for himself. Otto asked for a glass of milk, telling Harry:

"Drink milk. Make strong."

Otto drained the glass in one gulp and went to the bathroom. Albert-Alberta smiled mischievously.

"Did you ever play secrets?" he asked.

"No."

"Well, we're about to."

Otto returned.

"Ah, Otto," Albert-Alberta said, "Harry and yours truly were discussing President Roosevelt and the disgusting trick he puts on."

"Trick?"

"You know, the wheelchair and all that."

"You mean, he not . . ."

"What better way to get sympathy?"

Otto thought.

"*Ach*," he said.

"*Ach*, indeed."

"How you know?" Otto challenged

"Think of the cigarette holder. Damn it man, it's all there."

Otto's brow plunged into deep thought.

Albert-Alberta threw up his arms in exasperation, saying: "God, man, don't you get it, the cigarette holder!"

Otto smiled, and said: "*Ach*, of course, the cigarette holder . . ."

He nodded and rose. "Have appointment, must go."

"He'll try and figure it out all night," Albert-Alberta said. "I give Otto many sleepless nights. He'll believe anything about Roosevelt. He hates him because of what he says about Hitler. He'll tell all his pals at the German American Bund. They'll believe him. Probably decipher something bizarre about the cigarette holder."

Albert-Alberta shot up his arm to a Nazi *heil Hitler*, then bent his elbow for a smart British salute.

"Were you in the army?" Harry asked.

"In a manner of speaking, sir."

"What does that mean?"

"I served, but did not serve."

"I don't understand."

"I dasn't explain until you are older," he said, cocking his head and fluttering his eyes.

"Hey, I'm old enough," Harry said, simulating shaving.

"Not for my army career, lovey."

"Soldier told me his."

"Soldier"—he sniffed derisively—"crawling on his belly in the mud. Some tale!"

"Were you in the war?"

"In a way. Yes, in a way. You could say that I was in the home guard."

"What's that?"

"It is men and women who . . ."

Albert-Alberta reached inside his sweater and pulled out a brassiere stuffed with rotting yellow sponges. He threw it to the ground. It bounced a bit. He swung his foot at it, like a football player attempting a drop kick.

"Damn it," he said, "I won't walk around like this anymore. I'm not a freak. I am not!"

His eyes became fixed, lifeless, as if painted. He spoke in a monotone without affect.

"My father was a general. He was a hero and he raised me to be a hero. I couldn't wait to be brave and collect medals. I was always dreaming about battles. My house was full of generals. They were big men with big mustaches who smelled of tobacco and whiskey. They would tell me about their famous battles and I would tell them that I was going to be a hero. They would laugh and pat me on the head.

"MacLaren was my favorite. He would come to my room at bedtime and tell me tales of India and the dreaded Dervishes. He took my breath away. He gave me a swagger stick. I was never without it. He liked to touch me when he spoke. His hands were firm, commanding. He pinched my cheeks till they hurt. He crushed my shoulders.

"He told me I must stand at attention in the nude in front of a mirror to see that my entire body was responding to military discipline. I did. I liked the sight of me.

"Then MacLaren said I had to stand inspection from him. First he corrected my posture with those strong hands. Then he said it would be more helpful to me if I learned by example. If I copied him.

"He took off his uniform and stood beside me in front of the mirror. He was a hairy man. Black hair was tangled all over him. He walked behind me and rubbed against me. His penis parted my cheeks. It was hot.

"He lifted me like a baby being carried to his bath and laid me on my stomach on my bed. That hot penis hurt me so much I screamed. He put a strong hand over my mouth and said pain was part of being a hero. That it hurt him too. But there would be pleasure too. Later, he brought me women's clothes and dressed and undressed me.

"One night my father couldn't sleep. He heard noises in my room and thought I was having a nightmare.

"McLaren was a bigger general than my father. I was sent to a faraway boarding school. I spent my vacations at an aunt's house. My father refused to come near me. He died in the war. I ran away to America and practiced the only trade I knew."

Albert-Alberta closed his eyes tightly. When they opened, his face was once again animated, mischievous. He smacked his lips.

"How do you like that, Harry?"

Harry shuffled his feet and looked down. .

"My dear," he said, "you fell for secrets. You didn't really believe me, did you? It's such a made-up tale. A *Canterbury Tale*. Next time I'll tell you about my mother the duchess, don't you know, and my father, the . . . oh that's too good to give away."

He picked up the brassiere and whirled it over his head.

"Whee, whirling teats!"

They parted in front of the diner. Albert-Alberta squared his shoulders and marched away, sounding the cadence with a briskly whistled *It's a Long Way to Tipperary.*

Harry watched him, seeing no sham in the precise rhythm of his step and the pride in the swinging shoulders. Or maybe it was just another layer of secrets? Truth, Aba said, was a lie you believe. Did that apply to his own version of secrets?

Hidden surveillance was the portal to Harry's one unassailable truth. Observing scenes in which only he knew the full truth because only he was aware that there was a secret watcher, created truth.

On hot summer nights, invisible in the shadows beneath the boardwalk, he waited for couples to collapse on the sand, breathing like spent runners and crying out like white men under torture by *Fu Man Chu.*

His favorite every-season spy place was a spot on the boardwalk overlooking the entrance to the Half-Moon Hotel. The big shots who wore ribbons across their chests in Coney parades, like the beautiful baby contest or the season closer on Labor Day, had lunch or dinner there, staggering out drunk, arms draped around supposed enemies and singing Irish sea shanties. During conventions, the whores from Rosie's marched into the hotel like soldiers in close order drill.

The entrance also hosted quick dramas: a man-woman screaming match, or a cop's car arriving for a payoff smoothly delivered by the uniformed doorman.

A year ago he had seen his mother enter the hotel alone. Surmising that she was buying a pack of cigarettes, he had planned to sneak up behind her and surprise her as she walked home. Three hours later she had emerged with a tall, well-dressed man who had brushed her cheek with a kiss and put her in a taxi. He had witnessed repeat performances by tailing her when she announced a trip to the movies to calm her nerves.

He wondered if his father knew. Or if his mother knew about the women in Harlem his father and Aba talked about while Harry eavesdropped beneath an open window. Both knew, he had decided, but didn't know, as in Bama's Yiddish dictum: *If you don't talk about it, and don't admit you see it, it doesn't exist.*" Anyway, whatever the state of awareness, it seemed a fair arrangement.

Harry returned to the boardwalk. The oxidized green hands of the round clock, set like a cyclopean eye in the tin sign identifying Silver's Baths, read nine-fifteen. His parents would not be home yet. He decided to wait until ten o'clock. If the house were still locked, he would sneak back into Bama's. To kill time, he put the Half-Moon Hotel under scrutiny.

Five minutes into his vigil, his mother and the man walked out. He looked like George Raft. Maybe he *was* George Raft. Everyone said his mother looked like a movie star. The man put her in a taxi.

When Harry pressed the bell at his front door, he braced himself for his mother's tirade for not having his keys, which would be delivered with an initial passion that would deflect his explanation.

"You mean," his mother said, "she put you in his bed!"

"Yes."

"A savage."

In the kitchen his mother resumed drinking her tea strained through a sugar cube, which she removed to drag on a cigarette. Harry poured himself a glass of milk and sat across from her.

"So what have you been doing? Walking the streets and catching pneumonia?"

"No, Mom, I sneaked into the Mermaid Theater."

She would not question the theater as refuge. When a thunderstorm threatened she ran there to escape the claps, which unnerved her. In Warsaw, a man walking in front of her had been shot and killed.

"What did you see?"

Luckily, he had noticed the marquee.

"Test Pilot."

"Any good?"

"I like Spencer Tracy."

"His face is too fat."

Her eyes wandered off. She looked sad, lost, helpless. He felt remorse for the displeasure she often stirred in him. She was an interloper, a barrier between him and his father. He stared at her face—his face—and thought: She is my mother, what does that mean?

He remembered his earliest memory. He lay in a straw basket watching her iron clothes. Suddenly he knew she would not always be with him. He had cried. The memory ended there. Too soon. It did not reveal what he meant to her. As that mysterious being known as mother, had she instinctively known what he was thinking? Had she picked him up to calm him?

He knew himself to be an embarrassment to her as a measure of her age. She told people: "He is my husband's child by his first marriage," which she triumphantly defended as the absolute truth.

He could not remember her praising him. Yet he had heard her boast to others that he brought home a straight A report card. And she worried about his health, demanding that he bundle up against pneumonia and barring him from swimming in Coney's polluted waters. These dictums were ignored, unenforceable because of her habitual absence. Perhaps, he concluded, motherhood is to be forced to care about someone you do not care about. And being a son, did that impose the same task?

Is that why, he wondered, when I read sadness in her face, as now, I pity her, wish to help her, and want to cry for my helplessness?

"Did you love Zadeh a lot?" he asked.

She sighed.

"No. Yes. I don't know. Love is a tricky word."

"What do you mean?"

"It's a word without meaning. Everyone supplies their own meaning—if they can."

"Will you miss him a lot?

She smiled at his persistence.

"Again, no, yes, I don't know. Will you?"

"Yes."

"Why?"

"Because he took my hand."

She put her chin in her palm and turned away from him.

"Do I take your hand?"

"You used too."

"When?"

"A long time ago. To cross the street."

"That's not exactly the same."

"I guess not."

"Would you like me to take your hand?

He shrugged.

"You answer like your father."

"Is that bad?"

"No. It just doesn't fit. Like that coat Lazar sent to you." She laughed. "That was my fault. I insisted you wear a coat for the funeral."

"Why?"

"Because it seemed right. Death makes more of a man than Bar Mitzvah does."

"I've had enough of death to last me."

"I suppose you have. When my sister died in Warsaw, I wondered why it wasn't me. I knew why: I was stronger. Esther was a mouse. But I still wondered. Maybe I still do."

Their eyes met.

Pity, Harry thought. We pity each other. Is that something that ties us together? Is that love?

CHAPTER
18

AT SEVEN THE NEXT MORNING, HARRY ANGRILY THREW OFF HIS blankets and groped his way to the phone. It was Saturday. An Orthodox Jew who read *The Morning Journal* was desecrating the Sabbath. Harry vowed to put a stop to this abomination, which threatened to rob him of his day of rest.

"He doesn't answer the phone on *Shabbos*," he growled into the speaker.

"Who doesn't?"

"The man you're calling."

"How do you know who I'm calling?" The pleasant voice seemed genuinely interested in an answer.

"Moshe Catzker, of course."

"Sorry, I don't know him. Do I? You know my memory is not what it used to be."

"Then why did you call his home?"

"Did I? Wait let me put on my glasses . . . Is this Esplanade two-six-seven-five-four?"

"Yes."

"Hmmm. Are you a boardinghouse?"

"No."

"Do you know a man called Aba Stolz?"

"Yes."

"Could you give me his phone number?"

"He lives here."

"Why didn't you say so in the first place?"

"You didn't ask me."

"Can I speak to Stolz?"

"He's asleep."

"How do you know?"

"He's always asleep at seven in the morning."

"Well, he'll want to get up and talk to me."

"Who is me?"

"I don't understand."

"Who are you?"

"Oh, didn't I tell you? You know, my memory is not what it used to be. Ben Druckman. Tell him Ben Druckman."

Harry knocked on Aba's door. Coughing signaled consciousness.

"Aba, there's a madman on the phone who wants to talk to you. His name is Ben Druckman. Should I hang up?"

"No!"

Aba flung open the door and ran past him. Ah, Harry figured, Druckman was a poetry lover, a patron. Aba hopped around his room, wriggling into the first piece of clothing that came to hand. Unwashed and disheveled, he disappeared into the street. Harry yawned. Maybe it was a dream. Yes or no, some sleep might bring clarity.

Aba moved in a combination fast walk and trot toward the entrance to Sea Gate. He was composing a poem: a paean to Druckman. He could not trot and think, therefore he alternated speeds.

Ancient warrior full of mercy, was that banal enough? *Jew, descendent from the house of David.* Good, good, he complimented himself, before recalling a newspaper article about a team of baseball players with beards who called themselves *The House of David.* Druckman would deny being a baseball player. Then a thought sent him into a full trot: *I'll do it in Yiddish. He won't understand. I'll recite one of my favorite poems and he'll listen. Compare it to Nick Kenney. If he asks for an explanation, I'll tell him story of Bar Kockva or some other heroic nonsense.*

At the gate, he was delayed. The guard asked for confirmation from the Druckman household, then, about to allow pass him, noted that Aba was wearing one black and one brown shoe, and called for reconfirmation.

The Negro opened the door.

"Thank you, Jerome," Aba said, testing his luck on a fifty-fifty proposition.

The man's puzzled expression signaled defeat.

"Sorry, James."

The man's eyes widened.

"Sorry, my memory is not what it used to be. What is your name?"

"Jesse, sir."

"Ah, the father of David."

"No, sir. I have a daughter named Franklina."

All hail Roosevelt, Aba thought, Moses to the black tribe.

"I'll remember, Jesse."

"Please follow me, sir."

Druckman, wrapped in a white terrycloth robe, blended into the white couch. He looked troubled. Why? On the phone he had intimated good news. Perhaps troubled to me is happy to him? Perhaps he can't remember how to look happy but remembers that he needs an expression?

"Hello Ben, I wrote a poem for you."

Druckman's eyes darted around the room.

"Want to hear it."

The eyes again. God, Aba thought, let him have destroyed the file already. He's going gaga fast.

"Yes, let's hear it?"

It was not Druckman's voice. Through a side door the chauffeur wheeled in a smiling Menter.

"Well, what the fuck are you waiting for? Give out with the monkey talk."

Aba recited the Kaddish, the Hebrew prayer for the dead.

"Now tell us what the fuck it means."

"It sings the praises of Ben Druckman. A fine man. A noble man. A friend to those in need."

Menter threw an Italian short-arm at Druckman.

"That ain't the kike I know. The sheeny I know has left the tracks. He jumps in where he shouldn't and if he doesn't stop, maybe gets himself killed."

Aba's demons danced. Each a Nijinsky.

CHAPTER

19

HARRY, HAVING TRIED UNSUCCESSFULLY TO SLEEP AFTER ABA'S BIZARRE exit, was on his way to the bathroom when his father lurched through the front door. In one motion he extracted Dr. Freud from the bookshelf and fell forward onto the couch. Harry applauded the balletic movement, but his father, nose already flattened against the spine of the book, was elsewhere, sniffing up wisdom. His father closed the book, smiled, drew his lips down at the corners, and slowly shook his head up and down. The usual tribute to Dr. Freud. Harry suspected that the purpose of the morning driving expeditions was to inject himself with a disease so that Freud could offer a cure, the way Paul Muni did as Louis Pasteur.

In the kitchen, Harry watched his father eye suspiciously the flame heating a kettle. His father trusted nothing in this room. It was stocked with spiteful instruments of doubtful purpose: cans that resisted opening, milk bottles bent on suicide leaps from the table, unwatched kettles boiling themselves dry, whose charred metal odor lingered long after the object had been dumped in the garbage.

A wisp of steam curled upward from the kettle's spigot. His father thrust his hand quickly to turn off the gas. He smiled in victory. On the table a tall glass holding a tea bag awaited the hot water. His father grabbed the kettle handle and quickly relinquished it, blowing on his palm. He covered the handle with a paper napkin, brought the kettle to the glass and began to tilt it forward. His forehead creased, searching for a memory.

"Hah," he said, leveling the kettle and holding it at his side while moving around the kitchen and opening drawers. In the third drawer he found a teaspoon which he put into the glass. He poured the water, watching the malevolent glass for signs of cracking despite his precaution. His concentration on disaster was complete. The glass overflowed. He leapt at the puddle, plunging the napkin down to wipe it up. The liberated kettle hit the floor. The water and steam reminded Harry of newsreels of Old Faithful geyser at Yellowstone Park. His father looked up from his wet shoes and spread his arms in helplessness. Harry got a mop. His father wrinkled his forehead and stared with blank eyes.

In consultation, Harry thought, as he made the tea and poured himself a glass of milk.

"Heshele, where did you learn to be so handy?"

"From you."

They laughed.

"What does Dr. Freud think?" Harry asked.

"Oh, he's very intolerant. He was a very neat man. He would have not allowed me to touch anything in his kitchen, like your mother."

Again they laughed. Harry loved to see his father laugh. His face was a combination of joy and wonder, as if in awe of the gift. Even his mother could not long resist the infectious invitation.

The front door banged open. Aba stumbled into the kitchen bringing with him the cold draft from the unclosed door.

"Goodness," his father said, "have I slept for three months and awakened at Purim? Aba, that is a most imaginative costume. Are you Haman or Madame Defarge?"

Aba stared at his father.

"Moishe, can I speak to you alone?"

"Sounds serious. I don't have five dollars to lend you. Three I might manage . . ."

"Please, Moishe . . ."

His father rose, saying:

"Lay on, MacStolz."

In his room, Aba laid his palm on the tan, fat eiderdown. The fluff rose between his fingers.

"It feels nice," he said. "I do that often to remember how good you have been to me."

"Aba, what's this all about? You know such compliments are not necessary."

"Maybe they should be?"

Aba was having trouble swallowing.

"Moishe, dear friend, I have something I must tell you . . ." His voice tailed off. "Moishe," he resumed, "why are we in Coney Island?"

"*Oy*, I feel a Stolz theory coming on. All right, I'll play semi-straight man. We are in Coney because it is cheap and the sea air reminds us of our beloved landlocked Ukraine."

"It is no accident that we are in Coney Island."

"True. I remember following a pillar of smoke from Ellis Island to Thirty-fifth Street."

"First, Moishe, think of the amusement rides."

"So, I'm dizzy."

"Where do they go?"

"Up, down, forward, backward, in, out. Who knows? Who cares?"

"Take the Cyclone, Moishe. It goes at great speed, but nowhere."

"Is it a metaphor for the human race? Aba, have you deteriorated to such banalities?"

Stolz assumed a classic John L. Sullivan boxing stance, left foot pointed toward the opponent, elbows bent, forearms extended fully, fists turned upward.

"Watch out, Moishe, I have been known to give punches."

"If you knocked me out now, it would be a mitzvah."

"Moishe, years ago, in Luna Park, people saw an elephant electrocuted."

"He was hit by lightning?"

"No, Moishe. He was electrocuted by his owners. Thomas Edison himself was involved in the preparation. The execution was advertised. It was an event. A show. Apparently the beast had outlived its usefulness. Thousands came to witness the execution and then dispersed to other enjoyments. It was considered a very successful promotion."

"You're inventing . . ."

"No, no, Moishe. I read it in a serious history of Coney Island. But what I can't get out of my mind is: How do you electrocute an elephant?"

"What does the book say?"

"It doesn't say how it was done, just that it *was* done.

"I imagine this: The elephant is brought out by his trainer. The beast, a seasoned performer, is overjoyed at the large crowd because applause brings food. Then six men carry out a gigantic electric chair and place it near the elephant. The trainer smiles to the beast. This is a signal that he is to be taught a new trick. The trainer shows the elephant how to sit in the chair. There is no need to strap him in because the beast is unaware of any danger. Electrical devices which will deliver massive current are attached to the elephant's body. The beast is happy. It is the first new trick he has learned in years. All is ready.

"A lottery is held. The lucky winner will pull the lever that will unleash the electricity. Before doing so, the winner clasps his hands over his head in a show of triumph. He pulls. The elephant's trunk lashes the air, creating a wind that sends people in the front rows reeling. Its mouth opens to a width no one thought possible. It trumpets a last desperate cry which fades to a mournful note that snakes through the Byzantine spires of Luna Park. The dead elephant rolls to the ground, coming to rest on its back, its four gigantic legs pointed heavenward. The crowd cheers. The trainer slices off an ear and gives it to the executioner. Parents instruct their children to remember what they witnessed today: *man, triumphant.*"

"You have been reading too much Céline."

"Wait, Moishe, wait. There is more. Years before this execution, when Coney Island was an elegant resort, men like Edgar Allan Poe and Walt Whitman spent time here. Whitman said that he loved the bathing and the loneliness. Especially, he said, *to race up and down the hard sand, and declaim Homer or Shakespeare to the surf and the seagulls.*"

"So now we have one dead elephant and one live poet. I am keeping count, Aba. You will be asked to bring them together."

"And so I shall. When Walt Whitman was in Coney Island there existed a hotel in the exact shape of an elephant. It was called The Colossus of Architecture, and indeed, it was, being 122 feet high, with legs 60 feet in circumference. In one leg there was a cigar store. The other contained various shops. The head faced the ocean, offering a wonderful view. Whitman must have stayed there. How could he resist? I see him in the elephant's head, reciting Homer and Shakespeare as the gulls settle on the elephant's ear, to better hear Walt."

"They were *gullible*. *Oy*, desperation has reduced me to punning. Is the end in sight?"

"Soon, Moishe, I promise. But one thing more you must know: Because of this elephant hotel, the elephant became the symbol of all American amusement parks that followed. No one really knows why. Some learned doctors say it was due to America's repressed sexuality."

"No wonder Freud hated America."

"Freud visited Coney in 1909."

"And stayed in the elephant?"

"No, the elephant was gone by then."

"Poor Siggy. Can you imagine the oedipal wisdom present in the belly of an elephant?"

"Now we come to Al Jolson."

"Aha, I've got it. The solution to this verbal charade is the elephant and the Jewish question."

Stolz shook a threatening fist.

"Now, what is Jolson's favorite phrase?"

"Get me a shiksa."

"It is: *You ain't heard nothin' yet*."

"He sounds like a man trapped in a room with Aba Stolz."

"Right. He has caught the essence of America."

"*Oy*."

"Moishe, isn't that what this country is always saying? Isn't it like a magician who performs the impossible and then makes it seem tame with his next trick? So, Coney Island, the trickiest, the most *you ain't heard or seen nothin' yet*, is the soul of America. And we inhabit and guard America's soul, even when it is dormant."

"A dormant soul. I like that, Aba. The rest you can dazzle Lockerman with."

"Moishe, have you ever been to Steeplechase?"

"Heshele keeps asking. Should I go with him?"

"At the very end of the rides, the last amusement on the ticket, there is something called an *Insanatorium*. You must pass through it to get out. And what it does is make performers out of the people who are leaving. They emerge onto a stage where a clown torments them. But what the spectators are waiting for is any good-looking girl who will be maneuvered to stand over a hidden grating, through which a sudden, strong updraft of air lifts her skirt above her thighs and reveals pink or white underthings."

"This is what my Heshele is yearning to see?"

"Moishe, I am in the audience waiting. Here comes this gum-chewing, five-and-ten-cent shopgirl. She is over the grate. There is her underwear. I am her human superior in every way. Her vocabulary is barely enough to make her primitive needs known. Her voice makes one wish for deafness. Yet, at that moment, I would do whatever she wants—give up all my rhymes, cluck like a chicken, bark like a dog—to see and hold what is between her legs. For me that screeching, embarrassed idiot, clumsily trying to pull down her dress, holds between her legs at that moment a mystery that gives me physical pain, because I need to solve it. And, in my mind, she torments me, saying: *You ain't seen nothin' yet!* How true. Millions hiding from me what is between their legs."

"Aba, at last we have arrived at your favorite subject, but was it necessary to get there by way of an elephant inhabited by Walt Whitman?"

"I thought the picture would appeal to you."

"It did. But why all this Cafe Royal banter? Especially here and now."

"I wanted to entertain you."

"Aba, I don't understand."

Aba sat heavily on the bed. He buried his head in his hands.

"I was putting off telling you the great harm I have done you."

"What harm?"

Stolz's hands fell between his thighs. He intertwined his fingers and staring at them, spoke:

"There is a cripple called Victor Menter, a gangster, an anti-Semite, whose useless legs bestride Coney Island like a parodic Colossus of Rhodes . . ."

When he had finished, he rose and stretched out his arms.

"Forgive me, dear friend, we are trapped."

They hugged, seeking each other's strength, and finding the odor of fear.

In the Cherry Tree: April 18, 1937

Aba: *Heshele, let us talk of Joseph Stalin and Leon Trotsky.*

Harry: *I know Stalin. My grandfather punches his face every time he sees his picture in* The Forward.

Aba: *And does he punch Trotsky also?*

Harry: *I don't know what Trotsky looks like, so I don't know if he punches him. But chances are that he does.*

Aba: *Trotsky was one of the leaders of the Russian Revolution.*

Harry: *Was he a great man?*

Aba: *Stalin does not think so. He exiled him to Mexico and now he says that Trotsky is conspiring with Germany and Japan to form an alliance against Russia.*

Harry: *For Mexico?*

Aba: *No, the Mexicans are disinterested in the quibbling of grumpy Russians. It is a personal charge against Trotsky.*

Harry: *So is Stalin saying that it will be Germany, Japan and Trotsky against Russia?*

Aba: *It appears so.*

Harry: *What does Trotsky say?*

Aba: *Comrade Trotsky says a new revolution is needed to overthrow Stalin. He says that Stalin should be eliminated, but not killed. Perhaps something was lost in the translation.*

Harry: *Aba, will your poems be translated?*

Aba: *Into which language, Heshele?*

Harry: *English.*

Aba: *To what purpose?*

Harry: *So everybody in America can read them.*

Aba: *American boy, Americans do not read poetry.*

Harry: *Yes they do. A man I know named Schnozz reads poems that are written every day in the* Daily Mirror.

Aba: *What does he say of this poetry?*

Harry: *He is amazed at how many words rhyme.*

Aba: *My poetry does not always rhyme.*

Harry: *Can you fix it?*

Aba: *As easily as Trotsky can fix Stalin.*

CHAPTER

20

WALKING ALONG WEST 40TH STREET ON HER LUNCH HOUR, VELIA Catzker shivered even as the bright March sun sucked hated sweat from her skin. A familiar coldness had invaded her, denying outer warmth. Why, after all these years, she wondered, has the dread retained its power to possess me?

The dread had entered her life at dusk on an icy side street in Warsaw, a month after her expulsion from the convent. She had been walking quickly to reach home before dark. Suddenly an explosion filled the street, surrounding her, vibrating in her ears as it ricocheted off solid rows of houses. Five feet in front of her a man floated forward as if executing a swan dive. He landed face down on the cobblestones and lay still. A finger-length fountain of blood spouted from a jagged hole in his black overcoat.

Velia, then Leah, breath held in, legs frozen in midstride, created a mannequin of imminent or just completed motion. Behind her pounding boots echoed through the twilight.

Two peasant policemen had questioned her, pawing at the tiny swellings on her chest, slobbering over the heat of this twelve-year-old Jewess, conjecturing as to growth of pubic hair. Only the arrival of her mother, screaming that Leah had brought everything upon herself by being on that particular street at that time, had prevented a vaginal probe.

The next day a presence had followed her. She heard footsteps. Strong fingers tried to capture her shoulders. She told her mother, who warned that fantasies provoked pogroms.

She could not face the street where constricting arms waited to crush her. She begged friends to walk with her even if it was out of their way. She refused shopping errands. Thrown bodily from the house by her mother, she would flatten herself against an outside wall, waiting for a friend. If no one came by, she returned empty-handed, rushing into the bathroom feigning or experiencing cramps.

Her pursuer's intentions were clear: to rip off her nipples and pull out her few pubic hairs. Six months passed before she could venture out alone, but only in daylight and never without the dread.

Three years later, during her five-week journey to America, seasickness and vigilance against men who pressed against her and tried to drag her to dark, isolated places denied her sleep. At Ellis Island she collapsed during the medical examination to determine her admissibility to the United States. In a private room she was poked at by slobbering men who claimed to be doctors. She knew better.

At fifteen, to thwart her pursuers, she shaved her triangle of fine blond hair, bloodying herself and her father's straightedge razor. He commanded her to discard the untouchable object far from the house.

He barred her from contact with boys. She obeyed gladly. Closeness to a boy nauseated her. She ran, sweating, from their touch. They called her *sweatstink*, holding their noses. Approaching sixteen and yearning to be invisible, she was the opposite: a fully developed woman who drew whistles and propositions. She tried to flatten her breasts by knotting brassieres tightly, but her flesh overflowed and bounced.

She felt physically dirty. At every class break she ran to the bathroom to wash. At home she took long baths though the water was barely heated. She feared crawling things entering her. She scratched at her vaginal lips until they bled.

One day she found, in the school bathroom, a movie fan magazine. Her parents had barred her from the movies, which taught filthy ideas. The magazine told of a life as clean and orderly as the regimen in the convent. Theda Bara's sparkling dark eyes reminded her of the Mother Superior. No wonder she made men her slaves. She and the nun shared the mystical power to bend others to their will. She stole movie magazines from candy stores, hiding them under her mattress and awakening at first light to enter their world.

Late one hot summer night, unable to sleep, she put on a robe and sat on the stoop of the tenement, reading by the light of a street lamp. A gang of hoodlums grabbed her, stuffed a dirty handkerchief in her mouth, and were carrying her to a roof for a gang rape when a cop happened by. During the ordeal, she had remembered stories of girls raped and thrown off roofs to their deaths. She was not frightened. Death would end her torment and return her to the convent.

Suicide enticed her. However, she decided on resurrection. Leah committed suicide, and Velia, the enslaver, was born. Leah had been dirty, mired in the shit of the tenements. Velia was as clean as a blond, gentile nurse. Leah had shut her eyes to escape from reality to darkness. Velia needed only a blink to enter a wish life.

When her initial flight from Leah through Schrafft's was halted by her father, she knew that she must escape her parents. The where was not important. She choose the most accessible path: Moshe Catzker.

Catzker, a twenty-year-old deliverer of beds and mattresses for Kaplan's Bedding on Stanton Street, who called himself a poet, had been pestering her for almost a year. He would wait for her outside school and walk beside her reciting poems in Yiddish. When she ran, he dared not pursue.

The next time he appeared, they shared a chocolate soda in a candy store. Catzker promised that her beauty would inspire thousands of lyrical poems. She had found her first slave.

A week later, on a lumpy bed in a room that smelled of feet, she stayed her nausea while Catzker hurt her terribly. Her blood

stained the sheet and caked on her buttocks. He called it the nec-
tar. She ran to the bathroom and threw up.

It became less painful. Her body was numb, floating like an
angel on serene Polish clouds. Catzker, pumping, sweating, stinking, breathing like a mad dog, was a comedy seen from afar.

Soon it would be time to talk of marriage, escape. But then
her nipples hardened and she awoke to nausea. She wanted an
abortion, but Catzker would not hear of it. He was in delirium. The
child would be the most beautiful the world had ever seen; her all
over again. He wanted to ask her parents for permission to marry.
She replied that her father would call the police.

They were married at City Hall with a five-cent ring from
Woolworth's. When they told her parents, her mother made a
semicircle over her belly and spat. Her father ripped a patch of hair
from his head. Six months later, two days after her seventeenth
birthday, Harry Ephraim, named after a dead grandfather and
dead uncle, was born.

Velia passed Bryant Park, turned left onto Fifth Avenue, and
blew a kiss to the regal lions who sat like two snobbish doormen on
the steps of the 42nd Street Library. Such lions would guard the
entrance to her villa in Italy, next to Greta Garbo's.

A large, square car stopped at the curb alongside her. Vince,
the chauffeur, blocked her path.

"Get in the car," he commanded.

She tried to dodge him. He grabbed her wrists.

"I'll scream," she threatened.

"There's nothing to be afraid of. My boss just wants to talk
to you."

"Let go of me this minute!"

"OK."

His grip lightened. She relaxed. Suddenly she was shoved violently and tumbled into the backseat of the car. Her head fell onto
a lap. She looked up at the cripple. The car moved forward. There
were black shades on the windows. Menter smirked down at her.

"Wanna give me a blow job?"

She sat up and moved as far from him as possible.

"Look at me!" he commanded.

She did not turn her head.

She saw his palm coming. She braced, feeding rigidity into her neck, pressuring out her jawbone to create a solid wall on which he would break his fingers. She willed herself to become marble. She swallowed sticky blood. He rubbed his palm. She smiled. She had hurt.

"Luigi told me you were a tough cunt."

"Luigi! What has he to do with this?"

"Everything."

She sagged forward like an old woman overtaken by sleep.

"Yeah. Luigi liked your hot Jewish pussy. But he's had enough of it. A kike is a kike, man or woman."

"Why does not Luigi tell me this himself?"

"That's none of your fucking business. You're talking to me now, and if you want to keep that sheeny nose of yours breathing, you'll listen and listen good."

He sent a murderer, she thought. Murderers murder. No more problem for the workingman's friend.

"What happens now?" she asked.

"That's better. Luigi is a soft guy. Personally, I would have thrown you out on your fat Jew ass. But Luigi got you a job with Sam Rolfe of the Fur Union. You can start spreadin' your legs for him."

Yes, like a whore, she thought, *passed on.*

"And you never speak to Luigi again."

"That should not be too difficult."

"Don't be such an uppity cunt, it ain't healthy."

"Where are we going?" she asked.

"Coney. Cab service. I think you should suck Vince's uncircumcised prick for a tip."

"I must get back to work."

"No, cunt. You never go back. All your shit will be sent to Rolfe's office."

They stopped in front of her house. The chauffeur opened the door. He unzipped his fly. She ran past him, but knew she could never outdistance their laughter.

CHAPTER

21

HARRY WALKED INTO THE FREAKS' HOUSE FOR A SOCIAL VISIT. THERE would be few betting slips to collect. Saved summer wages had dwindled. Some residents temporarily had left Coney. Lohu and Mohu had joined a carnival that meandered through the South. Olga was in Leningrad with a Russian circus. She had sent Harry a picture of her feeding bears ice cream.

Those whose appearance permitted had found normal jobs. Otto was a bouncer in a Yorkville bar owned by a cousin. Albert-Alberta, all male and very British, was an elegant host at a Child's restaurant on Broadway. Jamie, his second mouth bandaged, washed dishes at a Queens diner.

Jo-Jo had been employed as a shipping clerk at a Garment Center dress house. The boss called him *Bow-wow*. One day he brought his five-year-old grandson to see his discovery. The child laughed and petted Jo-Jo. He asked his grandfather to make Jo-Jo bark. Jo-Jo refused. The child threw a tantrum. Jo-Jo was fired.

The story, told him by Jo-Jo, was part of a ritual that had developed over the winter months. Harry, provided with hot chocolate and cake, listened to tales resembling a musical round. The meshing lyrics told of the torment and humiliation endured at the hands of so-called normal human beings, who treated freaks as a permanent sideshow put on earth to provide endless amusement. As common property, freaks could be commanded to perform by anyone—especially drunks—for the pleasure of everyone.

Jo-Jo told of being forced to put his palms against a bathroom wall and hump a urinal. In a bar, Blue Man's shirt had been ripped off and the crowd, given pens and pencils by the proprietor, drew blood while covering his chest and back with dirty words. In Jersey City, Olga had been pinned into a barber's chair and shaved while grimy fingers confirmed that she was a woman. And poor Fifi, pissed on.

Exempted from the freaks' condemnation and disgust, Harry felt close, familial. Harry, too, felt at odds with the world, weighted down by layers of weltschmerz and anomie pressed upon him with love by loved ones ignorant of its toxicity on the young. He had been taught a controlling world. which preached capitalistic hypocrisy as God-commanded values and punished heresy by exile, enisling as freaks all who refused to believe.

In his house, society was the criminal. Lockerman asked: *What is a greater crime—to rob a bank or to open one?* John Dillinger was a victim, robbing banks before they robbed him. His betrayer, the lady in red, had been duped by the capitalists. At school the bubble gum trading card of G-man Melvin Purvis, who had tracked down and killed Dillinger, invoked hero worship among Harry's classmates and disgust in him. And above all, Jews, history's permanent underdog, could find friends only among the oppressed. If not for a less than total disbelief in Bama's warning of the evil eye, he would have openly proclaimed brotherhood with the freaks.

Fifi sat on a couch reading. Delicate pince-nez spectacles on her massive face shrank them to a child's scaled-down replica. She laid down the open book, placed the spectacles on the spine and offered her cheeks for kisses. The soft, heavily powdered flesh smelled sweet but tasted bitter.

The dining room table had been moved aside. Otto, wearing only shorts, was bent over a heavily weighted barbell. Trickles of sweat navigated his muscles.

The strongman had appointed himself Harry's mentor in

matters of physical well-being, insisting on a program of weight lifting. The first lesson had been a show of Otto pressing, snatching
and curling hundreds of pounds while Harry gasped in admiration. There had been no further instruction, but much talk of the
upcoming wondrous transformation of Harry's body, while Otto
kneaded Harry's nonexistent muscles like a Dust Bowl farmer sift-
ing spent soil. Sometimes Harry's released flesh bore bruise marks
for which the strong man apologized, while stifling a grin:

"I no know mine strength."

The hurt, Harry knew, was Otto's crazy way of expressing friendship and a pat on the back for Harry's tolerance to pain, a stoicism
Otto revered.

"Hello Harry," Otto said, grabbing the barbell and thrusting
it over his head, while simultaneously executing a skip that placed
his left leg in front of his right before drawing them even. Harry
applauded.

"Now you try it," Otto said, laughing and pointing to the bar
that had shaken the house upon striking the floor.

Harry grabbed an imaginary barbell and imitated Otto, tottering and groaning. Fifi laughed. Otto forced a smile.

"I ever tell about 1936 Olympics. Hitler shake my hand."

Harry knew that Otto revered Hitler and Nazism, but forgave
it as one of Otto's mental tics—an opinion that passed for thinking
and assured the strongman that his brain was not void. Harry was
certain that Otto liked him. Even so, his expression soured at the
pride in Otto's voice.

"Harry," Otto said, creasing his brow, no doubt imitating a
German American Bund deep thinker, "Hitler have nossing against
you or you people. He want to send dem to homeland in Palestine
or Africa."

"Otto . . ." Fifi began, but she might as well have tried to brake
a speeding train.

"It is healsy t'ing to send Jews from Germany. De Germans be
healsier and also Jews. Both pure. Is in de Bible, God say to Noah:

get two animals of same breed—*same breed*—to start new, pure world. We obey God, *yah* Harry?"

Harry refused to meet Otto's eyes, but nodded slightly to end the subject. Fifi's face was impassive, but her body gave off odors. Anger made her sweat. She was furious.

"Is not time for nap, Otto?" she snapped.

"Yes," Otto answered, oblivious to anyone but himself. "Harry, be sure take many naps. Is very healsy."

He clamped Harry's shoulder, tilting him.

Harry sat next to Fifi. They had not repeated sex. Tacitly, instinctively, they had agreed to lift that moment out of the normal flow of life and to forever share it in Harry's favorite country: limbo.

She took his hand and patted it.

"Otto is crazy like he is strong. But I like him. How you hate ze baby for making *kaka* in pants?"

Harry smiled. Because of her appearance, it had taken him some time to realize that she was very smart. She spent the winter reading, and writing notes in the margins of books, like Zadeh.

She had given him French lessons, using texts far beyond his novice status. After being told the plots, he closed his eyes as she read to him from *Nana* or *Madame Bovary*. The soft French voice sang of the heroine doomed by a cruel world. Yet another version of the freak message.

"'Arry, you have perhaps read this *livre*. It is called Of Ze Mice and Ze Men."

"No, Fifi."

"You should read. It is about ze cruel heart. Zis *Americain*, Steinbeck, know life like ze French peoples."

She handed him the book.

"It's a funny title," he said, "it sounds like a fairy tale, maybe where a mouse becomes a prince."

She patted his head.

"You have ze imagination. Not let anyone to take it away. No. I not understand myself. Maybe you help."

She opened the book and showed him the frontispiece: *The best laid schemes o' mice and men gang aft a-gley.*

"What mean that? Is English? Only find *gang* in ze dictionary. Not make sense."

"Maybe it's about a gang of mice . . ."

"No, 'Arry is not one mice in book."

"What's it about?"

She cocked her head and pointed to Otto's barbell.

"Is about man like Otto, but not like also. Otto big, strong, but inside is baby. In book is same, but big difference. In Otto is cranky baby. Strongman in book is baby full of love. World hate so much love. Make angry."

"Why?"

"Because zey cannot love. Zey forget how. Because is easier to hate."

"I don't hate, Fifi, but I don't think I love."

Fifi's head bolted backward as if struck.

"Not say that, *gosse*. Is terrible and not truse. I see love in you. Most certain you love Mama, Papa."

"I know I'm supposed to love them."

"What you feel for zem?"

"I'd like to make my mother happy. But I can't. I don't think anyone can. I don't want her to be sad."

"And ze Papa?"

"I like to be with him. I'd miss him if he went away. There is also a friend of his I'd miss and my grandmother. They would miss me too. But it's not easy to explain. It's like it has nothing to do with them or me. It's like we don't attach ourselves to things about a person, but because the person is always there. It could be anyone else."

Fifi lifted his chin which had dropped as he spoke. She stroked his cheek.

"*Pauvre*. Is your age of all confusion. Not worry."

She lifted her hand. He grabbed at it and returned it to his cheek.

179

"Sank you," she said.

The front door opened. Albert-Alberta strode snappily into the room, swinging a black walking stick whose silver handle bore a coat of arms. He swatted at Otto's barbell.

"I slave all day at Child's abatoir and come home to this outrage. Where is that muscle-bound moron? And look at you two: Has the photographer left without informing you?"

Fifi shook her head.

"Ah, Albert-Alberta. You make happy. Is good."

"Yes, jolly old me. Except I was fired today. Can you imagine? One of the customers recognized the half-man et cetera and told the manager, who didn't believe I had a twin brother-sister."

"*Merde!*"

"No, Fifi. It shows I am a star. Recognizable. I shall demand a large raise this summer. In any case, the best laid plans of mice and men et cetera."

Fifi and Harry straightened and stared.

Albert-Alberta brandished his stick.

"Not one step closer. This opens to a sword, usually reserved for unruly Bulgarians. What's got into you two?"

"Albert-Alberta, what you say of mice and ze men? You know ze rest about ze gang?"

"Blimey, I've stumbled into the Robert Burns society."

She handed him the book

"What it mean, *Gang aft a-gley*?"

"It means that the best plans made by mice and men often don't turn out as planned. They get screwed up. It's Scottish, as I am on my maternal side."

"But why ze mice and ze man?"

"Well, old Bobby Burns didn't mean exactly mice. It's a contrast, you see. From the weakest to the strongest, the biggest to the smallest, the same applies: What you aim for is not necessarily what you get even if you figure it out real well. *Capeesh*?"

"Ze disappointment," Fifi said, nodding.

"Yes, Fifi my love, but more than that. It's that the cards are stacked against you from the start. Deal them out anytime, any way, and you're a loser."

Fifi looked at Harry and shook her head.

"Is not true. No, is not true."

Albert-Alberta shook his head.

"Fifi love, you sound like Otto when he decides that night is day and would rather walk around like a blind man than admit there is no light. Look at me, you and the rest. Do we have anything to look forward to except being shat upon?"

Fifi's fingers curled into fists. She tapped the knuckles against her forehead. The sound was like footsteps.

"Yes, you right, but for we freaks." She opened her hands and let them fall onto Harry's lap. "But not for zis *petit*. He will do anyzing he want. He will have much love and happy and make for ozer people happy."

"I hope so Fifi, but . . ."

Harry had put his hands on top of Fifi's. He intertwined their fingers and squeezed. He inhaled her odor, trying to deposit it in some part of himself where he could reproduce it at will. He wanted her never to leave him.

22

HARRY WATCHED BAMA STUFF INTO AN IRON GRINDER CLEANED CARP destined to become gefilte fish. She stepped aside to allow him to tamp down the fish with a heavy wooden block, then grasp the grinder's handle and turn it to the crunching sound of flesh and cartilage being ripped apart. Wormlike squiggles oozing through the grinder's tiny holes, falling into a tan ceramic mixing bowl while he breathed as infrequently as possible the released fumes, were the staples of his Friday afternoons.

Bama was uncharacteristically silent. He thought she might be ill. A few times he had caught her looking at him with sad eyes. Perhaps it was his slight resemblance to Zadeh.

"I saw the Polar Bears running into the ocean last Sunday," he said, trying to cheer her. "How come you weren't there?"

She did not answer immediately. Instead, she was opening and closing kitchen cabinets to no purpose.

"I don't do that anymore. Never again," she replied.

"Why?"

"Never mind, Heshele."

She laid her palms on his cheeks. Her movement was jerky as though choreographed by an incompetent puppeteer. Her fingers mashed his nostrils, forcing him to breath through his mouth. He looked into eyes blind to external sight. He felt his breathing threatened by an unearthly force.

"Bama!" he yelled

"What? What? What?"

Her eyes focused. She looked at her hands. Terror spread across her face.

"*Oy*, I hurt you. I hurt my precious Heshele."

"No, Bama. No!"

"Forgive me. Please forgive me. I don't know what I do. If I do, I chop my hands off."

He flung his arms around her neck and drew her to him. It is, he realized, the first time I pulled her or anyone to me. They pull me. I wonder if I'm doing it right. She kissed his neck.

"Forgive me, my precious."

He pushed her to arm's length and flexing his biceps in imitation of Otto's showmanship, said: "You didn't hurt me. You made me strong . . ." He smiled. "Like a Polar Bear."

Something overtook her again.

"Heshele, maybe you should go home now. I'll see you later with the Mama and Papa. I want to rest. Yes."

"Bama, are you sick?"

She shook her head.

"No, no, Heshele. Don't worry about me. I just must think about something." She jabbed her index finger at her forehead. "I'm not as smart as my Heshele. I go slow."

On his bike, pedaling distractedly, he thought: *Is she dying?* He chased away the idea. Bama was indestructible. She could chase death as easily as the evil eye.

In a few hours his parents and he would make their obligatory monthly pilgrimage to Bama's *Erev Shabbes* meal. The other three Fridays, Harry alone represented the Catzkers. With some time to kill, he pedaled toward one of his favorite Coney attractions: Lazar, the tailor.

Lazar was a man in perpetual motion. He ran and jumped around his tiny shop as if competing in a decathlon. He was a magician extracting endless pins from his mouth to design a road map of alterations on a dress or suit, an explorer hunting through

hanging clothes for a garment promised that day, or an angel surrounded by clouds released by his pressing machine. Seated, his pace
did not slacken. His foot pumped as he guided cloth through an
ancient Singer or he rapidly sewed by hand, biting off excess thread.
His face dripped sweat as his long, curly black hair bounced to the
rhythm of his decisive movements.

Harry entered the store. Lazar spit out some thread.

"Hello Heshele," he said, elevating a button on an overcoat by
winding black thread beneath it. "You didn't visit me last week. I
missed you. You weren't mad on me?"

"No," Harry lied.

His eyes led Lazar to the pressing machine, which measured
about five feet long and two feet wide. To operate it, Lazar would
smooth a garment onto the waist-high, stationary bottom slab which
was covered with tan cloth. The matching top, an arm's length
above, was pulled down by its protruding wooden handle until it
snugly sandwiched the material. Simultaneously, Lazar depressed a
pianolike pedal which shot wrinkle-smoothing steam through the
jacket, trousers or dress.

The last time Harry had visited, Lazar had not used the
machine. He had teased Harry with false starts. After an hour
Harry had left without saying good-bye.

Lazar smiled. "OK *boychik*, here I go. How can I resist such
a boy."

He rummaged through a pile of clothes and pulled out a dark-
blue double breasted suit.

"Mr. Menter. Fine material. In hell may his deformed bones
rot for the money he takes from me."

Lazar approached the machine. Harry stood behind him.

After positioning and steadying the suit jacket, the tailor stood
on tiptoes to tug at the handle. The top and bottom came together
with an explosive hiss. Harry closed his eyes for an instant. When
he opened them Lazar was a man in the clouds. A man in hell. A
man entering heaven.

Lazar repositioned the jacket. Louder hisses. Thicker steam. Harry saw only unrecognizable shapes. It was the Creation. It was *In the beginning*. It was more magic than on ten Bowerys. And it was his alone!

Lazar neatly placed the suit on a hanger, handling the material with crisp familiarity. He turned to Harry, who stood, head bowed to fulfill his part of the bargain. Lazar tousled his hair and pinched his cheek. Harry didn't like his cheek pinched, but it would have been worth it even if Lazar were a violent flesh grabber, which the tailor was not.

The expected flow from Lazar's eyes slowly made of the tailor's cheeks a riverbed surrounding an island of thin nose. Lazar's wife and two children had been suffocated to death by thick smoke from a Nazi incendiary bomb rising into the family's Berlin apartment from the tailor shop below.

At home his father was seated on the couch in the living room reading a large, thick book that rested in his lap. His mother had not yet arrived.

"Hello, Heshele," his father said, smiling and rubbing the tip of his nose. "I am a clairvoyant. I see in by my crystal nose that you have just come from a gefilte fish factory."

"Twenty silver dollars for the gentleman in the balcony," Harry replied, imitating the voice of Dr. I.Q., host of a popular radio quiz show.

He sat beside his father.

"What does Dr. Freud say about gefilte fish?"

"It's not Freud," his father said, pointing to the title at the top left-hand corner of the page.

"Hey," Harry said, "*Hamlet*. We read that in school last week. Some of the kids call it 'Omelet.'"

"You think that's funny, Heshele?"

"Not really, Pop."

"Good. How did you like it?"

"Pretty good. I could see Errol Flynn playing Hamlet, especially that last dueling scene. And Boris Karloff as his father's ghost. Although you might have to change the ending. Errol Flynn never dies."

His father laughed.

"How about the language?"

"There was a lot I didn't really get. But some of it was like when Aba recites his poetry or when I hear Fats Waller play the piano. It puts a rhythm in your body."

His father's eyes widened. He looked surprised. But Harry recognized an expression of admiration. He drank the sweetness.

"What about Polonius?" his father asked.

"Who?"

"Polonius, Ophelia's father."

"Oh, yeah. Hamlet kills him, right?"

"Right."

"What about him, Pop?

"He's the best-drawn character in the play. In fact, one of the greatest of literary creations."

"Why, Pop? I hardly remember him."

"One day you will, Heshele. He is not for your age."

"What's so great about him?"

"He's a bore. A boring old fool."

"And that makes him great?"

"Yes, Heshele. Because Shakespeare puts this dullard's thoughts into language so exquisite, so beautiful to the ear, that banality is transformed into wisdom and the most unoriginal man imaginable seems a creative sage."

His father turned the thin pages, creasing them with heavy fingers. His excitement when discussing literature changed a phlegmatic man of slow movement into a frenetic enthusiast, eager to share his ardor.

"See, see here!" His father's nicotine-stained finger ran over the small print: *This above all: to thine own self be true,/And it must fol-*

low, as the night follows day,/Thou canst not then be false to any man."

His father patted Harry on the lips with the tips of his fingers, a habit he had learned from his own father, a scholar who thus readied pupils to ingest wisdom.

"Not a comma of originality. Pure bourgeois homily taken from the book of common banal prayer. But Shakespeare, the miraculous tailor, wraps it in Joseph's glittering coat. You understand, Heshele?"

"Well . . ."

"Wait," his father interrupted. "See here: *Neither a borrower, nor a lender be; For loan oft . . .*"

Harry heard the front door open. His father obviously did not. His mother stopped at the threshold of the room and listened.

"Hah," she snapped, "I'd like to see the day that you became a lender, Mr. Rothschild."

His father shrugged.

"Velia, you have an intensity of focus that I envy. I am surprised that you are not rich."

She jabbed an index finger at him.

"*We* are not . . . Well, are we going to our monthly poisoning? It is time."

"Velia . . ." his father began.

"Moishe, I don't care if the world and Mars are about to blow up, you are coming."

The narrow entrance to Bama's bungalow home framed actors walking onto a stage. Harry strode in, confident of his reception. Velia took short, tentative steps, like a bather testing the ocean's temperature, as she tried to read Bama's mood. The final entrant lacked correct wardrobe: bedroom slippers and trousers slit up the leg, the uniform of prisoners walking *the last mile* to the electric chair. Catzker shuffled in, tripping over the raised threshold and stealing center stage with a tottering star turn.

Bama, wrapped in a soiled apron, kissed Harry, nodded to her daughter and shouted to her son-in-law not to fall on the porcelain knickknacks that infested the room. She walked to a table on which four place settings of thick ironstone dishes, Woolworth wine and water glasses and gleaming silver cutlery were laid out on a damask tablecloth whose edges almost touched the floor. A challa, a bottle of kosher wine and an ornate pewter kiddush cup were lined up in front of one setting.

When each stood behind a chair, she lit the white Shabbes candles dwarfed by their thick silver candleholders, while sing-songing a prayer welcoming the Sabbath.

She nodded to Catzker who overfilled the narrow kiddush cup with wine, marking the cloth.

"Klutz," Velia said.

He recited the kiddush, sipped, then tore off a piece of challa, raced through the blessing of the bread and sought Bama's permission for all to be seated.

Bama retreated to the kitchen to fetch the first course: gefilte fish.

"Go help her," Velia said to Harry.

"She always tells me she doesn't need help."

"So. Let her say it. You understand nothing."

In the kitchen, he was turned away but allowed to accompany her and the fish. She doled out the lumps which resembled giant amoebae. Harry watched his father inundate his portion with powerful white horseradish to kill the taste.

"So," Velia said to her mother, "what's new?,"—bending back to her food while awaiting a perfunctory answer.

Bama was silent.

Velia raised her head.

"I am going back to Warsaw," Bama said, her eyes seemingly already there.

"You are what!" Velia shouted. "You take a trip now, with everybody talking about war?"

"Not a trip. Forever. And I am going to be married."

The Catzkers stared open-mouthed as if directed to register simultaneous shock.

Bama laid an envelope on the table.

"My sisters arranged everything. They sent the boat ticket. I leave next Wednesday. I will marry Salik Rabinowitz, the husband of my dear childhood friend Manya Persky, may she rest in peace. We will live in Warsaw in his apartment. He is a wealthy man and an Orthodox Jew. He would never think of coming to godless America, so I will be safe."

Velia's mouth moved but fashioned only strangulated sounds, like a Hollywood Indian repeating *ugh*. Catzker stared at Bama, blinking periodically, as if to confirm a shaky reality by its reappearance. Harry, feeling a need to break the ominous silence, chose the automatic response to an announcement of marriage:

"*Mazel tov,* Bama."

His mother uttered a short shriek which unlocked her verbal capacity.

"*Mazel tov! Mazel tov!* A monster I have brought into this world."

She turned to Bama.

"Mama, are you crazy? Europe is on the brink of war. One war in Warsaw was not enough for you?"

Bama waved off the words.

"All my nine sisters say there will be no war in Poland They are in Warsaw. They know better than you."

She reached into the envelope and extracted a passport-size photo, which she handed to Harry.

"This is Salik Rabinowitz."

The man's features were hardly distinct. The certainties were baldness, ears attached his head at not much less than a ninety-degree angle and a large, round nose. Harry immediately thought of a turtle he had seen recently in an animated cartoon.

He smiled, nodded his head and offered the photo to his mother, who pushed it away. The photo fluttered to the floor. He bent down to retrieve it. Bama's arm restrained him.

"Let her do it."

"Tell her!" Velia screamed at Moishe.

His father, who, absentmindedly, or inadvertently, had been spooning pure horseradish into his mouth, began to cough violently. He grabbed for a pitcher of water and knocked it over. The water ran off the table. His mother jumped back and up. Bama snatched the wet photo and ran for a mop. Harry followed her to the kitchen, filled a glass with water and put it in his father's hand. He gulped greedily. The coughing stopped. Tears covered his face.

"Tell her," his mother commanded, standing away from the table where Bama vigorously swished the mop.

"Mrs. Fishman," he said, asking for her attention which remained with the mop. He shrugged and continued:

"Things are not good for Jews in Europe today . . ."

"And they were good yesterday," Bama interrupted. She straightened, returned the mop to the kitchen and emerged wiping the photo with a kitchen towel.

"No," his father agreed, "things were not wonderful before, but now there is Hitler, who is pledged to expel all Jews from Europe, if not kill them. You see what he has done in Germany."

"Germany is Germany and Poland is Poland."

"I cannot argue that point, but all the experts expect Germany to make war on Poland."

"Experts! Hunchbacks and cripples! Catzker, shall I live out my life alone in this hovel?"

His father was silent. Even his mother seemed swayed.

"What will you do with all your things?" she asked.

"The silver, the kiddush cup and the candleholders, I will take. The rest you can give to that goy god army that plays trumpets."

"I would like Zadeh's Bible," Harry said, because he felt it was somehow wrong that it fall into the hands of the Salvation Army.

Bama pulled him against her.

"Of course, Heshele. Of course you shall have it. And the chess set too, so you can remember all the tears he drained from you. The big philosopher. Bigger than God."

She kissed the top of his head.

"You will visit me in Warsaw. *Oy,* my sisters will love you."

"Sure, Bama. I'd like that."

"Mama," his mother said, "promise me that if there is danger, you will come back."

"Go shit in the ocean, Leah. Unless you come to Warsaw, you have seen the last of me."

CHAPTER

23

THE NEXT WEDNESDAY, AT EIGHT IN THE MORNING, THE CATZKERS and Stolz pulled up in a cab at Bama's house. She was transporting more than silver. Stolz and Catzker could barely lift a metal steamer trunk the size of a chest of drawers, which did not fit in the cab's trunk. The driver refused to help because of a hernia which he described in great detail as Stolz and Catzker courted the affliction. He agreed to tie down the top of his trunk on condition of an immediate one dollar tip and verbal indemnification against flat tires, chassis damage and a ticket for a driving violation.

Bama looked on imperiously at the grunting men, refusing to relinquish Harry's hand so that he might help.

"They need the exercise," she proclaimed, smoothing her unbuttoned black Persian lamb coat which, parting, revealed a tight-fitting green suit and askew silk stocking, bunched into high-heeled, pointed black shoes.

Harry never had seen Bama other than in the kitchen or in mourning uniform. Her face, under a black lace veil suspended from a green, plumed hat surely copied from Errol Flynn's Robin Hood attire, seemed remote, unavailable. She was dressed for the world, no longer exclusively his property. Betrayal awakened a baby voice angrily complaining: "Bama go way!"

Stolz sat up front with the driver who quizzed him on hernia symptoms. In the rear, Harry and his father crouched on jump seats. Mother and daughter shouldered themselves into opposite corners, like boxers between rounds.

"So," Velia said to no one, "the weather seems calm. It should be a smooth departure."

Bama also spoke to the air.

"If it were a hurricane, it would be a pleasure to leave this godless country."

"When did you become so Orthodox?" Velia asked.

"When I live with big philosophers who know nothing with nothing. My luck. All my sisters tell me don't marry that apostate, but I know better."

"Mrs. Fishman," Catzker said, trying to head off a mother-daughter brawl, "your late husband was a freethinker, not an apostate. He never renounced being a Jew."

"Another big philosopher heard from. Shit in the ocean."

Tacit agreement sealed the rest of the trip in silence.

At the foot of West 38th Street, the driver inspected his cab for damage while two porters wrestled Bama's trunk onto a cart. Bama and Veila followed him. Catzker and Stolz feigned negotiation with the cabby until the women were of sight. Harry stayed with them.

The three walked onto the vast covered pier. Bright sunlight revealed the pigeon droppings and other filth on the angled glass roof. On the left, a gigantic red-and-black swastika flag hoisted between the two squat funnels of the *Bremen* was whipped by the stiff March sea breeze. Snatches of *Deutchland Uber Alles* drifted in and faded as if transmitted from an underpowered radio station.

"My God," Catzker said, grimacing at the flag, "don't her sisters live in this world?"

"Bama said Hamburg is the closest port to Warsaw," Harry explained.

"Heshele, if one can skirt Hell, it is best to take a little longer," his father said, staring at the flag, which had frozen his attention.

"Moishe," Stolz said, "did you know that this ship was once owned by Jews, as was the whole North German Lloyd Line? And as Heshele the expert can tell you, it once held the record for the fastest crossing from Europe to America. A Jewish record."

"Is that true, Heshele?" his father asked. "Your friend Aba tends to convert his imagination to facts. Good for poetry, but not so good for unimportant things like building ships or making a living."

"Aba is right about the record," Harry affirmed, "and *that* record was broken by its sister ship, *Europa*."

They were stopped at the gangplank by a sailor wearing a swastika armband.

"Is needed visitor pass," he said.

Catzker showed his *Morning Journal* police pass and Stolz flashed credentials from the long-interred Polish newspaper. The sailor pretended to read, then nodded his head.

"Yah, but what about *das* boy?"

"He is the son of my publisher," Stolz replied, "a powerful man, who has interviewed Chancellor Hitler."

The man stiffened. His right arm shot up a bit then subsided. "*Yah*, you can go."

Stolz extended his arm toward the gangplank in deference to the powerful son, who preceded the two somber journalists.

Onboard, they followed the sound of music to a brass band, including a tuba, playing in the main ballroom, which struck up a Latin American medley of *Brazil, Frenesi* and *South of the Border*. The heroic attempt at a Latin American beat was thwarted by individual instrumentalists who lapsed into the traditional *oom pah pah*, creating a musical war. They concluded by transporting *Ding Dong, The Witch Is Dead* to a Bavarian beer hall.

Harry watched a peculiar change come over Stolz and his father. When they had approached the *Bremen*, the men had been nervous, fearful. But as it became clear that those wearing swastika armbands were, in effect, their servants, they had turned into mischievous children given control of the household staff.

Stolz inspected a ten-foot-high fountain spouting water colored by revolving hidden lights, which was planted dead center of the immense dance floor.

"Swim and dance at the same time, German efficiency at work," he said, thrusting his hand into the fountain and then signaling for a steward. He showed his hand to the bemedaled man.

"The water is green and my hand is not. This is some sort of trick!"

The man stiffened.

"Not at all, sir. We never claimed our water was green. It is the lights that are green." The man's English was clipped British Public School.

"Then you should hang a sign on the fountain stating that, so people will not be fooled. German honesty must be beyond reproach. Will you see to that?"

"I shall speak to my superior," the man said, offering the Nazi salute and a brisk *Heil Hitler* before marching off.

"Well, Aba, you lost that one," Catzker laughed. "He shoved Hitler in the face of the troublemaker Jew."

Stolz shook his head.

"Not in the least. You must never underestimate the German lack of humor. We had a perfectly normal, logical exchange. He and his superior will arrive at a logical conclusion. As for Hitler, he sealed our serious discourse. Made it kosher, so to speak. *Oy*, from such a people anything is possible."

"What do you think, Heshele," his father asked, "was the man polite or insolent?"

Harry had paid little attention to the exchange. The hated swastika, symbol of pure evil, till now a black-and-white photo in a newspaper, swam all around him like intersecting bent eels. The angels of death who wore them were benign, obsequious. Instead of barbed wire there was highly polished rosewood, ebony and brass. He felt trapped in a bizarre nightmare.

"Don't you want to kill all these Nazis?" he said.

"Yes, Heshele," his father answered, "but how? We must settle, as Jews have done since the killing days of the Bible ended, for gaining a moral or intellectual victory. It satisfies our souls as we are being murdered by our inferiors."

Along the narrow gangways they delighted in forcing swastikas to give way. In the Hall of Shops, Stolz sniffed and said: "I think so, but I don't believe it. Not even the Germans . . ." He rushed toward a small mother-of-pearl fountain and bent over it. "Yes! It is. It's real perfume."

Harry sniffed. He sneezed, sending perfume flying. From somewhere a swastika appeared with a mop. Harry started to apologize. Stolz pulled him away.

"Heshele, never . . . Listen, I have an idea. Do you know anything about this ship that is not so good? I mean that is not one hundred percent German?"

"Yes. I think so."

"OK."

He stopped a swastika.

"What is the name of the captain of this vessel?"

The man snapped to attention.

"Captain Ziegenbaum!"

"No, first name."

"I do not know it."

Stolz showed his press credentials and signaled to Catzker to do the same.

"We are journalists. We would like to talk to Captain Ziegenbaum about his most important post. We are most impressed with his ship."

"Wait," the swastika said, "I telephone."

He disappeared into a cabin.

"Aba, you are going to get us arrested," Catzker said, "but I don't mind. Do you, Heshele?"

"Nah," he answered, preoccupied with the thought of meeting his wily adversary of the boardwalk races.

The swastika reappeared.

"Follow me."

They were escorted to the bridge. Ziegenbaum was a beefy man, not dissimilar in build and even facial appearance to Max Schmeling, the boxer who had beaten Joe Louis and then had been destroyed in one round in a rematch. Harry was disappointed by the absence of the arrogant white scarf which injected adrenaline into his pedaling.

He only wears it at sea, he told himself, guarding personal enmity.

"Gentlemen," Ziegenbaum said, his voice substituting for a heel click, "I am at your service."

"Just a few questions," Stolz said. "We have been interviewing passengers and they seem delighted with the *Bremen* . . ."

"As well they should be," Ziegenbaum interrupted. "We take great pains with every detail. Nothing is left to chance."

"Of course," Stolz said, "how could one doubt German efficiency. But my colleague and I were wondering: Are the racial policies of Chancellor Hitler affecting your passenger volume?"

Ziegenbaum set his jaw firmly.

"We are at capacity."

"Are there many Jews?"

Ziegenbaum grimaced.

"We do not inquire into the racial background of our passengers. Now, if you will excuse me, I . . ."

"Just a few moments more," Stolz said. "This young man, who is the son of my publisher, has a great interest in transatlantic liners and particularly, he has told his father, in this ship, which is why he is accompanying us. I wonder if he could ask you a question?"

Ziegenbaum beamed at Harry.

"Of course."

Harry spoke rapidly. He had formed the question and had practiced it silently.

"Is it true, as I read in a book, that originally the *Bremen's* funnels were so low that cinders and oil fell onto the deck and onto passengers and subsequently some height had to be added?"

Ziegenbaum pursed his lips. It seemed as if he were about to spit at Harry.

"Design of the ship was not and is not part of my duties. The passengers are more comfortable on the *Bremen* than on any other ship."

He turned his back to them.

"But I will add this as to design, I remind you that on our maiden voyage we captured the *Blue Ribband* emblematic of the fastest time for crossing the Atlantic: four days and seventeen hours."

"And forty-two minutes," Harry added as they were hurried off the bridge.

Stolz and his father sandwiched Harry in a squeezing, pinching embrace.

"Hero of the Jewish people," Stolz cried.

"Descendent of the Maccabees," his father said, then relinquished Harry to give full force to a laughing fit, stoked by *and forty-two minutes, and fortly-two minutes, oy, Heshele.*

The bell signaling visitors ashore sobered them. In Bama's cabin, Velia and Bama sat stone-faced Bama leapt at Harry, crushing him to her.

"*Oy*, Heshele where were you? I was so worried I would not see you before the ship goes."

"We saw the captain," Harry said.

"The captain?" Velia said. "Did you give him good instructions on how to sail the boat?"

A swastika stuck his head inside the door.

"Visitors ashore, please."

Harry tried to break away from Bama. She clutched him more tightly.

"You will visit me, Heshele." Her voice skidded through sobs. "You promise."

"Yes."

She wet his face with kisses.

He walked toward the door. His mother stood up. She faced Bama. The two stared at each other, similar jaws clamped. Velia stepped toward her mother. Bama rocked forward like a Jew at prayer. They fell into each other, sobbing.

"You, too, Leah. You could visit."

"Yes, Mama."

Harry, his parents and Aba stood on the dock amid the point-ing, waving crowd. Harry scanned the hundreds on the decks but could not find Bama. Was she in her cabin, crying? How lonely she must be. He chastised himself for having fun while she wanted to share her last moments in America with him. He had wanted that also. But the call to adventure by the two men he tried to emulate had outweighed all else.

"They're all going back like good Germans to defend *das Vaterland* from attack by Belgians and Martians," Stolz said.

For the first time he could remember Harry resented Aba's cynical eye. The moment was too sad. His mother gripped his father's sleeve, resting her head on his shoulder, as if unable to stand on her own.

"What will happen to her, Moishe?" she asked, her voice slip-ping into childhood conundrums only a parent could solve.

"I don't know, Velia. It can't be good. But if anyone can land on their feet, she can. That woman has guts. Crazy as it is, what she is doing is somehow right. She won't accept the space on the shelf reserved for her."

Harry silently thanked his father for his mother and himself. He felt like a member of a family.

The four walked to the Times Square subway stop, where Stolz left to pursue facts in the 42nd Street Library. On the trip home, his mother clung to his father, finally falling asleep.

"So, Heshele," his father said, "how do you feel?"

"I feel as if Aba, you and me shouldn't have had a good time."

"No, no, Heshele. One can laugh at a funeral before crying."

"Was it her funeral?"

"Haven't you yet learned metaphor in school?" His father smiled, but his eyes remained sad.

"What was my grandfather, your father, like? You never talk to me about him?"

His father looked down at his sleeping wife. He beckoned Harry to bend forward, so that he could whisper.

"Perhaps this is the right moment. I don't know. I just know the joys of fatherhood. There is no manual on the responsibilities . . ."

He whispered the story of the pogrom and murder. Long before he finished, both cried.

"God, Pop. How did you . . . what did you . . . feel?"

"I don't know, Heshele. I think I turned it into a nightmare. That it really wasn't happening. That when I woke up he and I would hold hands and walk back to the house. For months, maybe years afterward, every time I saw a goy, I had to restrain myself from leaping on him."

"Should I never trust goyim. Should I hate them?"

"Do you know many?"

"Yes."

"Who?"

"A soldier who was gassed in the World War. A dwarf who runs a bike shop. Freaks like the fat lady, the world's ugliest woman, the dog-faced boy . . ."

"They all sound like honorary Jews," his father interrupted.

He closed his eyes, rubbed and pressured them with the backs of his index fingers, then opened then and shook his head.

"I don't know what to tell you about goyim. Europe was easy: Stay away. Don't be where they can reach out for you. But America confuses me. There is anti-Semitism, but a kind I don't understand. They don't like the Jews, rather than hate them. They don't want to go near them, rather than kill them. It seems to be live and let live, but separate lives."

He sighed and smiled.

"But as you could have guessed there is *on the other hand*. A few days ago, I covered a German American Bund rally in Madison Square Garden. There were twenty-two thousand people there and I don't know how many were turned away. I saw a crowd of *pogromchiks*. I saw men who killed my father. Are they what America is becoming?

"On the third hand, there is the American national anthem—
Don't push me around—and that seems to go for pushing your neighbor
around. So Heshele, I have given you, what else, a Talmudic answer.
As the sages in the Gemara, after arguing a point for one hundred
pages, proclaimed: *pilpul,* which means *no conclusion* . . . who knows?"

"It was a good answer, Pop."

"It certainly was, Moishe," his mother said, opening her eyes.
She lifted her head, smiled, and in a perfect imitation of Bama's
Yiddish, snapped:

"Shit in the ocean!"

CHAPTER
24

FOR HARRY, AS FOR CONEY, THE HERALD OF SPRING DID NOT RIDE nature's zephyrs, but rather entered on the crashing sounds of hammers and the whine of saw teeth ripping through lumber and releasing the perfume of sawdust. Hearing that message, Harry pedaled toward it, anticipating the source: a concession owner repairing damage inflicted on hibernating wood, rubber and metal by the salt-breathing, insomniac Atlantic.

These men always were eager to interrupt their labor to compare the ravages of winters past with the most immediate, and to boast that, while listening to weather reports in Miami and other warm climes, that they had been able to calculate precisely the effect of nature on their enterprise. Harry listened closely to these recitals, excited at the idea of truth distilled at long range. It was magic, like a blindfolded mind reader stationed in limbo.

A flash of black fur changed Harry's itinerary. Not since early February had he checked on the wild dogs. Fifi, the world of freaks and Woody had claimed most of his out of school time.

Calling himself a traitor, an abandoner of the abandoned, he hunched over the handlebars and sprinted to a spot overlooking mounds of garbage waiting for collection. Here the pack would emerge to feed.

The dogs would be cautious. Early spring was a time of danger. A collarless dog was considered a carrier of rabies. ASPCA wagons patrolled. Cops and concession owners shot. As the days warmed, the pack turned increasingly furtive, traveling not bunched up, but in a shifting single file, as if to deny any friendship or connection. By summer, they had disappeared.

During their first summer of absence, Harry had thought them captured or killed. But during the subsequent late autumns a few veterans always had reappeared, joined by the newly abandoned, who would from time to time detach themselves from the pack and race up a street, only to return moments later. These dashes went on for about a week—the time it took, Harry figured, to erase the memory of having once been a pet.

Bear's head eased across the shadow of the boardwalk. She sniffed, moving tentatively, ready to retreat. Assured, she walked onto the Midway.

Harry was startled. Her teats were rounded and drooping. She had given birth. The pack followed. Another surprise: WK, the cowardly Weasel King, pranced behind her like a proud racehorse. Was he the father? Did he, like Douglas Fairbanks, now travel on the queen's business?

Lindy, hopping and tilting on his three legs like a drunk looking for a bathroom, and Curly, half covered with fur and halfbald, as if groomed by a lunatic, had survived the winter. Rabbi, mostly white, mostly terrier, with a black marking that smeared a beard across his square jaw, was gone. There were no new members. Winter was not a time of abandonment.

Bear's snout poked gingerly into a garbage pile, while WK burrowed in until his great head had disappeared among the paint cans, rags, paper and residue of hot dogs and hamburgers.

Where were the pups? Harry wondered. Had they survived? Was Bear still nursing? Perhaps Rabbi was alive—baby-sitting? WK's head snapped back into view, a decapitated mouse in his jaws. He dropped it before Bear. Bear hunched forward. The sun glinted off the spittle on her teeth.

Thunder. Bear's head exploded, becoming part of the garbage heap. Blood flowed. Confettilike innards grew out of her headless body. She lay beside the mouse, two corpses seemingly decapitated by the same executioner.

At the sound of the gunshots WK had leapt high in the air and run toward the beach, his front left leg elevated, waving like an erratic metronome.

Two cops walked toward the garbage pile. The silver buttons on their blue jackets reflected pinpoints of sun, reminding Harry of the magical light that announced fairy godmothers in the movies.

Harry recognized them. They were the *twinnies*, so named because one was rarely seen without the other. Rumor had them father and illegitimate son. They did resemble each other, but, Harry had concluded, no more than any other two Irish cops. Tim, the older one, strode swaybacked, a domed stomach forming a blue hill. His face lived in the shadow of a Jimmy Durante nose, on which swollen veins meandered. Walking hip to hip with Kevin, whose nose already was lightly tinged, he presaged his thinner partner in twenty years.

They were the designated bagmen for the precinct. Harry had seen them in the bike store, joking with Woody, shoving him playfully, but always with an undercurrent of menace. After Woody had handed over the Friday envelope, he would stand stone-faced as Tim's hands kneaded his hair, a prelude to the unvarying parting words:

"That gives us another week of luck."

The two cops looked down at the corpses. Kevin held his revolver barrel up to his lips. He blew into it.

"Hey Kevin," Tim said, lighting a cigarette, "you got a mouse."

"The fuck I did. I got that dirty mutt. Blew his head clean off."

Tim dragged and exhaled. A comic strip balloon of white smoke hung over his mouth.

"You sayin' *I* shot the mouse?"

"I ain't sayin, nothin'. Look at this."

Kevin pointed to dark spots on the ground leading to the beach.

"One of us got the big one. Let's go finish 'em off."

"Nah," Tim said, holstering his gun, "let 'em bleed to death. He threw his lit butt at Bear and spat:

"I hate dogs. They're asshole smellers."

"So are a lot of freaks and homos around here."

"Oughtta shoot them too."

Tim removed his black-peaked hat, fished out a white hand-kerchief from the lining and wiped his face and the back of his neck. He tilted his head toward the sun and spotted Harry.

"Hey, kid, some show, huh? Couldya tell which one of us got the mutt?"

Harry brushed the sleeve of his corduroy jacket across his wet cheeks. The ridges in the material hurt like a cut.

"Her name was Bear."

Tim replaced the handkerchief. He put on his hat, gripping the peak, pulling it down, then lifting it slightly.

"Was he your dog?"

"Sort of."

Kevin jabbed his index finger at Harry.

"Whaddya mean, sort of? If he was yours, he shouldda had a collar and a leash. He coulda bit somebody."

"She wouldn't do that."

"The fuck he wouldn't."

Kevin pulled out a pad from his back pocket.

"Now suppose I write you a ticket for lettin' him run loose."

Yes, Harry thought. *Yes, I want that!*

Tim put his hand on Kevin's shoulder. He whispered into his ear. Kevin shrugged and put away the pad. He wrist-snapped his finger at Harry.

"I'll let you off this time. But if you ever get another dog, leash him. Understand?"

Harry did not answer.

"Did you hear what I said!"

Harry nodded.

"That's better."

The cops turned and walked toward their patrol car. Harry heard, as he knew he was supposed to: *kikes, kids who work for dwarfs.*"

Harry descended to Bear. He flailed off the feasting flies while collecting paint-stiffened rags to wrap her in. The material gave only enough to form a stretcher. He laid it on the seat of his bike and pushed it toward the beach. He wished the cop had given him a ticket so he could have buried it with Bear, as her owner.

Under the boardwalk, Harry knelt and dug. Grains of wet sand tore the flesh under his fingernails.

He pushed the rags to the rim of the hole and tipped in Bear. He looked down on four rigid paws. He covered her up, thinking, Shouldn't I say something? In the movies someone always says something. Jean Hersholt's face appeared. Harry said:

"Good-bye, Mama."

Drained of energy, Harry sat on a bench on the boardwalk. On the horizon, he saw the *Mauritania*, not much larger than a ship target at the rifle shoot concession, glide as if on ice. He was glad it was not the *Bremen*. Captain Ziegenbaum would have sped up to take advantage of his fatigue.

The *Mauritania* was a ship to be watched, not raced.

It was an old liner, the sister ship of the *Lusitania*, the liner that had been sunk by a German submarine in 1917, killing more than a thousand people. An act so barbaric, according to his history teacher, Mr. Simon, that it had convinced the United States to enter the World War against Germany.

One fall day Harry had seen the *Mauritania* playing hide-and-seek in a fog, and he knew the truth: it was really its sister, turned ghost ship, appearing on the horizon but never arriving anywhere. She was an occupant of limbo. Aboard were the souls of her drowned passengers demanding revenge, as they did on the *Inner Sanctum* radio story about a ghost ship. Also on board were the undead spirits of the crew, slaughtered by Dracula on his voyage to England. Now Bear's soul had migrated there.

He forced his protesting body onto his bike, scanning the beach for WK. At 27th Street he spotted a familiar stooped back. He ran onto the beach, shouting:

"Soldier, Soldier."

Soldier turned. He held something against his chest.

"Damn, look, Harry."

Soldier held out to him a pup no more than six inches long—a miniature Bear.

Harry took it. It was as warm as boiled corn. It nuzzled Harry's palm.

"Where'd you find 'em, Soldier?"

Soldier took off his wool hat and scratched his head.

"Damn, it was the craziest thing that ever did happen to me. I was walkin' along the beach to go to some meetin' Woody told me about. All of a sudden this big dog comes runnin' to me from under the boardwalk. She's hurt, limpin', carryin' this here pup in her mouth. She comes up to me, drops the pup and runs back under the boardwalk. I picked up the pup and went after her, but she was gone. Craziest thing."

"Can I have him, Soldier?"

Soldier tugged at his ear and then put the tips of his fingers on his lips.

"Damn, I'm sorry Harry. But he was sorta left to me. That mother dog picked me out. You know what I mean? I gotta take care of him. Ain't that right, Harry?"

Harry handed the pup back.

"Damn, Harry, don't cry. I really gotta."

Soldier brought down the corners of his lips. He looked like a gasping fish.

"Damn, I guess you're right, Harry. I ain't fit to take care of it."

He held out the pup to Harry.

Harry jumped backward.

"No, Soldier. No!"

He lifted his bike over his head and ran.

IN THE CHERRY TREE: JULY 4, 1936

Aba: *Today we celebrate freedom, American boy.*

Harry: *There will be great fireworks tonight.*

Aba: *Stefan Lux will not see them.*

Harry: *Who is Stefan Lux?*

Aba: *A man who celebrated freedom yesterday.*

Harry: *How?*

Aba: *He shot himself.*

Harry: *Why?*

Aba: *It seems he wanted the world to take notice of what Hitler is doing to the Jews in Germany.*

Harry: *Will the world notice?*

Aba: *It is a civilized courtesy to grant a man his dying wish, especially if it is no bother to do so. Already the newspapers have recorded the event.*

Harry: *What do they say?*

Aba: *That Stefan Lux, a Jewish journalist employed by a Prague newspaper, killed himself in Geneva at a meeting of the League of Nations.*

Harry: *What is the League of Nations?*

Aba: *It is where all the countries of the world meet to make the world better.*

Harry: *What do they do?*

Aba: *Talk. For example, they told Hitler's friend Mussolini not to conquer Ethiopia.*

Harry: *And what did he do?*

Aba: *He conquered Ethiopia.*

Harry: *Did they punish him?*

Aba: *Yes. They allowed people to say very mean things about him, especially the emperor of Ethiopia, Haile Selassie.*

Harry: *Aba, I have heard of Haile Selassie, but I didn't know he was an emperor.*

Aba: *Who did you think he was?*

Harry: *He was a mystery. He is in a song: "A Shanty in Old Shanty Town". They sing, "I'd be just as sassy as Haile Selassie." I thought maybe it was just something that rhymed.*

Aba: *Heshele, wonderful American boy, do you think now they will sing, "I'd be just as sassy as Stefan Lux?"*

Harry: *It doesn't rhyme.*

Aba: *Then the world will not notice.*

CHAPTER
25

VICTOR MENTER HAD MADE ELABORATE PREPARATIONS. BY OBTAINING from an official at the Board of Education a large blackboard, chalks of various colors, a rubber-tipped pointer, standard blackboard erasers and individual, backless classroom seats which sprouted on their right sides palette-shaped writing surfaces, his living room had been converted into a classroom. Woody wore a blue-and-silver arm badge inscribed: *Monitor.*

In the lobby of the Half-Moon Hotel, Joe Baker paraded, encased in a sandwich-board sign, its front a collage of Coney's freak attractions, the back announcing: *Victor Menter's Annual Freak Party. Elevator to the Penthouse.*

The meeting had been called for noon. Menter smiled at the seated freaks, who reminded him of an *ungraded* high school class of incorrigibles, put under the eye of a muscular educator instructed to keep them quiet by any means, including fists.

He regretted the absence of Fifi, who he had decided could not be a practical participant in the arson. He had imagined insisting that she could fit into a tiny seat, stuffed there by Otto as human derrick and aided by Woody with a shoehorn or Soldier coating her ass with petroleum jelly.

Only Otto had balked at sitting in *a baby chair,* a reticence quickly overcome by a flash of meaningful eye contact. Mohu and Lohu, in abutting chairs, were chattering happily in Japanese. Olga had squeezed in by swishing a hilarious sitting shimmy. Albert-

Alberta and Jo-Jo were in a spirited spitball fight with Jamie, who had started it. Everyone was bunched together except for Soldier, who had arrived carrying a tiny pup, which appeared to be dead. He sat on a radiator at the back of the room petting the motionless animal. Menter had not planned to separate Soldier from the rest, but bowed to the logic of chance: *crazy was not a freak*.

"OK, monitor," Menter said.

Woody handed out black-and-white-speckled three by five notebooks and freshly sharpened yellow pencils.

"Very good, monitor," Menter said, "give yourself a gold star."

He put a cigarette in his holder, lit it, dragged, blew a perfect smoke ring, through which he jabbed his middle finger, and said:

"Just so's we understand each other, huh?"

His eyes slowly moved from face to face.

"Now I want everyone to take notes, because there's goin' to be homework. And this is a subject nobody fails."

He tapped a pointer against the blackboard, which was covered by a bedsheet.

"We'll get to this a little later. Now we learn current events. We begin with a history lesson."

The last sentence was delivered in an appreciably louder voice, while turning slightly toward an ajar door to his right.

"Students, today we're goin' to learn about Jewish lightnin'. Jews are so good at burnin' down buildin's that they got their name on the insurance scam. It's what kikes do best: screw everybody and walk away with all the dough. Now class, can you answer this question: What does a Jew hate more than pork?"

"Jesus Christ," Otto shouted.

"Very good, Otto. Monitor, put him down for a gold star. But that ain't today's answer. What a Jew hates more than pork is . . . asbestos."

Menter laughed. Woody, hee-heeing, scooted among the seats, calling for response and receiving mechanical *ha-has*. Menter slapped his forehead.

"Don't you dummies know what asbestos is? Or are you all kike lovers? A Jew'll burn down anythin'—even his mother's house with her in it—to make a buck. Look at their names: Blazeski, Burnheimer, Flameski."

He paused again, waiting for laughter.

"Oh God," he moaned, "they think they're real names."

He aimed a pointer at the freaks.

"You are goin' to make some Jewish lightnin'. Right Woody?"

"Right!" the dwarf shouted.

"Now, first I want to tell you about this kike torch I knew personal. His name was Izzy Stein. We called him Izzy the painter, on account of he said he was a painter so he could buy lots of kerosene, which is used for mixin' paints. He mixed the kerosene with naphtha so when you lit it, it went boom and spread fast. We'll use that. What was good enough for Izzy the kike is plenty good for this gang. You know, Izzy set the world record. Set maybe five hundred fires before one of his kike buddies squealed on him. Izzy, of course, squealed back. Got off light. I saw him in the street the other day. He's a rabbi. Kikes respect people like Izzy."

Menter uncovered the blackboard, revealing an architect's drawing of the buildings on the Bowery, also known as the Midway, a small street of food and game concessions and freak shows that ran about one hundred yards between the boardwalk and Surf Avenue from Steeplechase to West 10th Street.

"Ain't that beautiful?" Menter said. "Ain't I a artist?"

Menter tapped the blackboard.

"There are thirty wood buildin's bunched together here. We hit four or five and the fire jumps to all of 'em. There ain't no alarms or watchmen. I've got copies of this drawing I'll give you. Each of these shacks has a side or back entrance. That's how you're goin' to get in and out. In Coney, nobody will think twice about freaks on the Bowery. I want every one of you to know the entrance to every shack. So you can do it in the dark with your eyes shut. So anyone can substitute for anyone else. Next time you'll be assigned one of the buildin's. We got some time. We started early because you ain't the brightest, so we give ya plenty of time to learn. Next time I'm goin' to ask questions. And I better get the right answers. Get me?"

Menter tried to flip the pointer to Woody, but it slipped from his hand and knocked the cigarette holder from his mouth. Albert-Alberta laughed. Menter rolled toward him, stopping the wheels when they indented his shoes.

"You think that's funny? You homo limey scumbag."

Albert-Alberta shrugged.

"Woody, whaddaya got on this turd?"

Woody took from his back pocket a pad, flipped the pages and read:

Wanted in Philadelphia for sucking a kid's lollipop in a Market Street toilet. Jumped bail. In San Antonio the cops would like to know what happened to money a widow lady gave him to invest.

Menter gripped Albert-Alberta's cheeks between his thumb and forefinger. He pressed inward, forcing open his mouth.

"It's not funny anymore, is it, cocksucker?"

Albert-Alberta shook *no*.

Menter retrieved the pointer and thrust it at the freaks as if it were a dueling sword.

"Remember," he said, "Woody's got the same or worse on all of you, in case you was thinkin' of finkin' out."

Soldier stood up. He cradled the stiff pup.

"Damn, you're goin' to hurt and kill people."

Menter waved him down.

"Nobody gets hurt. Nobody dies. We ain't a bunch of scumbag kikes."

Aba Stolz and Moses Catzker heard to the shuffling sounds of the freaks' departure. The small room in which they sat contained a cot covered with a khaki army blanket and a tall, bulky Philco radio on which a silver-bordered glass picture frame, usually seen in Woolworth's caressing Joan Crawford, displayed a uniformed

Adolf Hitler, extending his arm in the Nazi salute. Below his gleaming boots, which marked him as somewhat splayfooted, an inscription in blue ink read: *To my good friend Vic.* It was signed: *"Adolph."*

Vince wheeled in Menter. Woody followed

"I hope you heard my lecture good," Menter said.

The two men nodded.

"Do you know why you are here?"

"No," Catzker said.

"See Woody, there are some things a smart kike don't know. Well, I'll tell ya. You two are part of this deal. The dumb freaks may fuck up, but two smart kikes won't. Woody, give 'em sketches."

Woody handed each a sheet of paper.

"Now, like I said out there, you study and walk till you know it like the tips of your circumcised dicks. I'll reserve a good buildin' for my kike team to torch"

"What if we refuse?" Catzker asked.

Menter laughed, then wheeled himself close to Catzker.

"Listen, kike, you're already in so much trouble that arson is a parkin' ticket. The immigration boys are dyin' to hear about your buddy. Aside from that, Vince here, you know Vince, he's big, strong and mean, he doesn't take kindly to people who say *no* to me."

Catzker, the little boy, had screamed to deaf ears. They had held him so he could not break away to help his father. No one held him now. He jumped up.

"I'll take my chances with the immigration!" he shouted.

Vince shoved Catzker back into the chair.

"Now you listen good," Menter said. "You got a wife, you got a kid. I got no use for them, *capeesh?*"

Catzker buried his face in his palms. Stolz put his hand on his friend's shoulder.

"Ain't that pretty," Menter said. "I guess we understand each other now. And if we don't, there's one more thing. I get anymore lip from you, I make your son part of the deal. Father and son torchin' together, a kike thing if there ever was one."

THE BIKE STORE WAS LOCKED. HARRY WALKED TO THE ROYAL POOL Emporium, which was run by Woody, to give the dwarf the few slips. The place was empty except for Sam, the manager, and his brother, Sidney, a victim of Down's syndrome, who was the rack boy.

"Where is everyone, Sam?" he asked the manager, who was known as *the fresh air fiend* because he had never been seen without a cigarette between his lips. Fat and lethargic, he often dozed off with the ever-present weed implanted. Startled awake by fire singeing his lip, he would light a new cigarette with the sparks of the minuscule butt.

Sam shrugged.

At that moment the door opened and Woody led in all the residents of the freak house except Fifi. They were a state of high excitement.

"What's up?" Harry asked Jo-Jo.

"Woody challenged Otto to a game. He spots Otto, his fifty to the Kraut's fifteen."

Otto didn't stand a chance. Woody was a shark who could easily run fifty straight balls. Otto knew that, but backing down to a dwarf, Harry figured, was intolerable to his Aryan pride.

Woody directed Sidney, whose right cheek was a red boil, as to where to set up a one-foot-high platform. As the dwarf mounted, he said to Harry:

"Did you know that Sidney is Otto's English teacher?"

Otto spat.

Sam approached Woody.

"Can I go out for a few minutes? Got something to do."

"Sure, Sam. But don't be too long, because the game won't be."

"Stop talk," Otto said, "start game, freak."

"You'll pay for callin' me that. And not only on this pool table. We're playin' for five bucks, right?"

"*Yah, yah.* Shoot."

Woody broke the rack, leaving Otto no shot. The strongman tried to follow suit, but left an opening. Woody seized it. The cue ball clicked against a ball with a purple stripe, which, rolling, became a purple-and-white magic lantern before disappearing into a hole in the corner of the table. Woody dismounted and pointed Sidney to the new location.

Woody ran forty-two balls. As Sidney set up a new rack, the dwarf gave Otto the finger.

"Eight more, Otto, and your five bucks are mine."

"Shoot, don't talk, freak."

Woody swung his cue stick above his head and brought it down against the table's wooden rail.

"You don't call me that! You hear, you no-balled, muscle-bound, pansy kraut? One more time and there'll be a cop knockin' on your door."

Otto's eyes murdered, then acquiesced.

"*Yah, yah.*"

"Now watch me sink this shot, Otto, but more important, watch the beautiful position of the cue ball for the next shot. Position is everythin' in life. Ain't that right, Kraut? Ain't that what you tell little boys?"

Otto, who wore a chest-hugging white turtleneck sweater and a wide Sam Browne belt that pinched his waist, hardened his pectorals and drew his forearm back against his biceps, bulging them.

"Vat vould you giff for a body like dis von, Voody?"

Woody spread his legs and cupped his crotch.

"I'll take what I got, Kraut. How would you like to suck my petunia, which is man-size?"

He turned to Harry.

"You know what the kraut wears for a jockstrap? A rubber band and a peanut shell. Ain't that right, strong-ass?"

Otto threw his cue stick onto the table scattering the balls, and bellowed:

"I am all around me der sick bodies I vomit to see."

Woody picked up a ball from the table and gripped it behind his right ear.

"Kraut, you owe me five bucks for the game. Some shit screwin' up the table when I need eight to win. The dough now, or I bounce this off your kraut skull."

"Ven ve finish game."

"How the fuck can we finish when you screwed up the table!"

"Not my fault!"

Otto strode toward the door. Woody jumped off his platform, hit the ground and somersaulted into Otto's path. They froze about a foot apart. Woody's outstretched arms suggested a comic book Christ. Otto pawed the ground like a skittish stallion.

"You don't leave without payin' the dough."

Otto threw a crumpled bill at Woody's feet.

"On der floor, vere you belong."

Woody signaled to Sidney to pick up the bill.

Otto slammed the door. A few seconds later the pane glass facade was shattered from the outside by a seven ball, which then ricocheted off the wall about two feet above the seated Blue Man. Jamie, standing closest to the front, was pelted with glass, He put his hands to his cheeks. Blood rose through his fingers. .

The freaks stampeded for the door. Albert-Alberta, hands on unstable breasts, ran past Harry, yelling:

"On your horse, boy! You don't want to be here when the constables arrive."

A smell of shit as palpable as taste and a breath-starved wail focused Harry on Sidney, who stood next to Woody. His tiny pink eyes teared. Woody, holding his nose, pushed him away. He began to whoop like a police siren.

Woody ran to a back room, returning with two empty cartons marked *Wheaties* and *Butterfingers*.

"Kid, help me break these down."

They flattened out the cartons. Harry held them against the shattered pane while Woody, on his platform, secured them on the unbroken glass with surgical adhesive tape which he ripped into strips with his teeth. The wind pushed the cartons, but they held.

Woody remained on the platform, surveying the street.

"Now what the fuck do I do with Sidney? Sam ain't in sight. He was supposed to be back by now. Shit, I can't go near that moron. Fuck it! We'll lock it up with Sidney inside. Sam shouldda come on time. It's his brother. Right, kid?"

Harry wondered: What does that terrified thing feel? Maybe nothing. Maybe that's the way God made up for the way he was. There was already so much pain that God said: *Let there be no more pain.* But Sidney was crying because . . . because ...

Harry's stomach cramped violently. He burst through the swinging bathroom door and pulled down his knickers and underwear just in time.

When he came out Woody had put on his blue serge double-breasted overcoat and a wide-brimmed Stetson hat. The dwarf was swinging a silver key chain with two keys attached, wrapping it around his index finger and then unwinding it.

"I know how it is, kid. That moron's stink almost got to me. Now you go outside. I'll do the rest."

Harry, chills passing through his upper body, while his bowels burned, walked past the howling Sidney without looking at him. He watched Woody shove Sidney onto a bench. The dwarf smelled his fingers, spat on them, and bent over to rub them on the patch of trousers that showed beneath his coat. Woody locked the door.

"What a fuckin' mess. That lousy kraut will get his. Don't worry."

"Did you call the police?"

"Police, hell. We got better ways. Victor Menter owns this place. The kraut would be lucky if all he had after him was the cops."

Harry heard a faint whimper from the pool room.

"What about Sidney? Won't Sam be mad you left him like that?"

"Fuck Sam. He was supposed to be here."

"Sidney could walk right through the cardboard. Maybe we should fix him up or something?"

"Nah, kid. Sidney stays where he's put. Don't feel bad. He ain't got no feelings. He's just another freak. You goin' home?"

"Yeah"

"Come on into the candy store, I'll buy you a milkshake."

"OK."

They sat at a back table. Harry sucked the thick liquid through a straw. Woody sipped a coke.

"Ever think of goin' on the road?" Woody asked.

"What do you mean?"

"Just takin' off. Ridin' the rails, hitchin', like that."

"Never thought of it."

Woody jabbed his finger at him.

"You should. Good experience. Teach you about life. I did it for about five years. I could give you great addresses of friends of mine everywhere."

"Yeah. But what about school?"

"I meant after school lets out. That'll give you from July till past Labor Day. Good weather for bummin'"

"I'll think about it."

"I'd do it if I was you. Even be good for your health."

The dwarf's face was firm, serious. Woody was willing him to go.

In the Cherry Tree: December 11, 1937

Aba: *Heshele, today we celebrate a birthday.*

Harry: *Whose?*

Aba: *Ours. Mankind. Great men in Washington, at a place called the Carnegie Institution, have closely examined some bones found on the Island of Java and decided that they belonged to the first human being, One million years ago. Previously they had thought we were a mere half million years old.*

Harry: *What did the man look like?*

Aba: *An ape.*

Harry: *How do they know it was a man?*

Aba: *From the teeth. Apparently they can tell the difference between the teeth of apes and men. There are no secrets from these scientists.*

Harry: *What about Adam and Eve?*

Aba: *What about them?*

Harry: *Wasn't Adam the first man?*

Aba: *Perhaps the man on Java is Adam.*

Harry: *Then the Garden of Eden was on Java.*

Aba: *Why not?*

Harry: *I thought it was in Palestine.*

Aba: *Perhaps they will find bones in Palestine that will prove you correct.*

Harry: *Why are there no apes before men in the Bible?*

Aba: *Because the Bible does not believe in evolution.*

Harry: *That one day an ape became a man.*

Aba: *As you say. But there is more. Once an ape became a man, his brain developed rapidly, so that he could think complicated and beautiful thoughts, as indeed did the scientists who examined the bones of the Java man.*

Harry: *What thoughts were those?*

Aba: *Well, it seems they could not put together the skull because it was badly cracked and the reason for this, they all agreed, based on their knowledge of man, was that it had been bashed in by a headhunting enemy so that he could eat the brain, which, they assure us, is a headhunter's delicacy.*

CHAPTER
27

WALKING HOME, HARRY WONDERED AT WOODY'S SUGGESTION. EVERYONE swore that the dwarf always had an ulterior motive, but what could Woody gain by sending him cross-country? Perhaps to visit the friends he had mentioned, who were fellow bookmakers or worse. Would it be a dangerous mission that defied even the FBI? The idea appealed to him, but he needed to be wary of being set up as a fall guy. He must outfox Woody, the fox.

Entering his house, he was surprised to see his father, mother and Aba. Usually by early Saturday evening they were on Second Avenue, having a drink before seeing a play or sitting with friends in a cafe.

"Ah, Heshele," his father said, "I'm glad we caught you. Put on your best clothes, you are coming with us to witness history."

"*Ils ne passeront pas!*" Aba shouted, raising a fist over his head.

Something French, Harry thought, maybe Fifi should know.

"Lafayette, we are here," he said, fitting in.

Aba and his father laughed.

"Not Lafayette, Heshele," his father said, "Asch."

"What is Asch?"

"Indeed, what is it?" Aba answered. "It is an apostate, with the talent of a flea, who has chosen to lick the boots of the goyim for profit."

"Huh?"

His father beckoned Harry onto the couch beside him.

"There is a Yiddish writer named Sholem Asch, who has written a book called *The Nazarene,* in which he paints a glowing portrait of one Jesus Christ. The book is a best-seller. He is making a fortune."

"Blood money, Jewish blood," Aba interrupted.

"Yes," his father continued. "Tonight, as is Sholem's habit, he will dine at the Cafe Royal. But tonight he will not dine, because when he tries to enter, the Yiddish writers and actors will stand in front of the Royal, hands joined, barring the apostate from their presence. And you will see it. No, better, you will lock hands between Aba and me."

"That is just right," his mother said, "a child for child's play. A big moral statement, hah! You're all jealous of the money."

During the subway ride, his parents became embroiled in a squabble over whether his father should take a second job as a teacher of Yiddish. Harry and Aba moved away to allow them vitriolic privacy.

"*Nu*, American boy," Aba said, waving an imaginary flag, what have you been up to?."

"Aba, am I too young to write?"

"Of course not. Rimbaud had written much excellent poetry at your age. What did you have in mind?"

"I'm not sure. I have an idea for a story about a boy, maybe about my age, who is asked to become involved with bad people, maybe even gangsters, like Lucky Luciano."

Aba's green eyes widened.

"Interesting. What does the boy decide?"

"I'm not sure. See, he doesn't know exactly what they want him to do. He wonders whether he even may be asked to kill people."

"And could he kill?"

"Oh, no."

"Then he must say no to these people."

"But he doesn't know if he will be asked to kill. He doesn't know what he must do until he does it."

"And how does the story end?"

"I don't know, Aba. The job would let the boy travel all over the country, and he would like that, but . . ."

Aba's palm rested on Harry's knee.

"Things are difficult to write, if you have not lived them. And since I am certain that all this is foreign to you, why don't you choose another subject. But do write, Heshele, do write."

In the Cafe Royal a low cloud bank of tobacco smoke lay over tables at which women sat silent while men shouted, gyrated their arms and leapt up to deliver important words directly into a recipient's ear. The language was Yiddish, compressed into a mighty singsong noise; a bastard echo off the crumbling Walls of Jericho.

"Hello Milton," his father greeted a waiter wearing a tuxedo dotted with a menu of stains. "What do you recommend tonight for the first dish?" Milton, who studied and imitated the expansiveness of the actor patrons, put the tips of his fingers to his lips and kissed them loudly.

"The sweet herring swam in the Garden of Eden. It is my personal favorite. But if you prefer something more substantial, than take the chopped liver with fried onions and *schmaltz*. It is also a personal favorite, but forbidden to me by my stomach."

"I'll take the chopped liver," his mother said.

Aba and his father ordered the same.

"And the young Mr. Catzker?"

Harry was pleased that Milton recognized him. In the last two years he had no longer been occasionally invited to accompany his parents to the Royal. His height and general appearance set people to reevaluating his mother's version of her age. She was in a battle with Stella Adler for reigning beauty of Second Avenue. Harry and motherhood were hardly the attributes she wished to project.

As an infant he had been brought often and allowed to crawl on the floor, sheltering under tables.

"Heshele," Aba had told him, "one day you can boast that you saw the most famous Yiddish feet in America."

"Milton," Harry answered. impersonating Edward G. Robinson, a man who knew what was what, "I will also have the chopped liver."

Milton placed on the table a plate with four round scoops of chopped liver. Each smeared some on a slice of black pumpernickel bread and chewed while Milton hovered, eager for the verdict.

"Excellent." his father assured. "Such chopped liver my enemies should never taste."

"Thank you, Moishe."

"*Nu,* Milton, what for a main dish?" Aba asked.

"Everything is wonderful. The goulash, the schnitzel à la Holstein"—he kissed his fingers again—"but for gentlemen and a lady of your taste it must be the roast goose and a good bottle of Magyar wine."

"Done!" Aba said.

The others nodded. Milton retreated.

"Heshele," Aba said, "you see all these people here? They write plays and poems. You think that's just noise you hear. No. It's plays and poems. Maybe we could write one, hah?"

He winked, called Milton and, pointing to a distant table, asked: "Isn't that Feibush Steinberg, the impresario?"

"Yes."

"Please ask him to join us. Tell him I have a theatrical proposition that could prove mutually beneficial."

Milton spoke to a man considerably older than the three other men who shared the table. The man looked toward Aba, shrugged to his companions and approached.

Steinberg wore a tan cashmere suit, black shirt and red ascot. His large face lay under a domed, shining, bald pate. His features were aggressive: hyperthyroid, black, bloodshot eyes, a wise nose, which sprouted hair from the nostrils, and a gray Vandyke beard that pointed almost straight out, as if to jab.

"Feibush Steinberg," he said, waving three fingers at the table.

"Won't you join us in a glass of wine?" Aba asked.

"Thank you."

He sat down.

"Milton said you had a proposition you wished to lay before me. I know you as a poet, Stolz. Have you turned playwright? In any case, I ask, as Diaghilev was wont to: *Amaze me!*"

"Most apt. You see I have this idea for a play . . ."

"My dear Stolz, I do not wish to be rude, but you must be aware of how many ideas for plays are brought to me each day. I need plays, not ideas."

"Of course, Steinberg. But as you have noted, I am new at this. A little background will help. I am to be married to the daughter of Druckman, the rich ex-bootlegger. Some call him a gangster, but I think they go too far. My father-in-law-to-be has confessed to me that it has always been his ambition to be involved in the theater. He added that if I would set myself to writing a play, it would be his pleasure to ensure that it was produced."

"Your father-in-law . . ."

"To-be . . ."

"Wishes to invest?"

"Without a doubt."

"Tell me your idea."

Aba looked first at Harry and then directly into Steinberg's half-closed eyes.

"I thought it should be a subject that interested Druckman. So I conceived of a young Jew hired by Italian gangsters to do their killing for them. Perhaps it even touches Druckman's own history. The youth travels the country and becomes a sort of traveling salesman of death. A catchy title: *Traveling Salesmen of Death*, don't you think?"

Steinberg stroked his beard

"Jews hired by Italians to do killing is an interesting twist, reminiscent of Babel and even Bialik. But why should Italian gangsters have need of anyone to do such deeds for them?"

"A good question. The answer is relationship. If one Italian gangster is killed, all Italian gangsters in the immediate vicinity are suspected. Here, the killer does not know his victim, and besides, he is a Jew, and as such is known as a member of a law-abiding people. No connection. No suspicion. The perfect crime!"

Harry stared at Aba. Now, he thought, I really know how amazing is a poet's mind. His father was having a difficult time suppressing laughter, while his mother absented herself by vamping any eye that wandered her way.

Steinberg pulled strongly at his Vandyke as if to test its reality.

"But the fact that this killer is Jewish, is that the only Jewish component? This is the Yiddish stage."

"Of course, Steinberg, but I thought you would see the analogy with the Maccabees and the Romans. Perhaps not a perfect match, but I will work on it."

Steinberg's bulging eyes seemed in danger of tipping out of their sockets.

"Yes, well, hmnn . . . your father-in-law . . ."

"To-be . . ."

"I would like to meet him. Here is my card. If he would call me."

"And I can tell him you are interested in my idea."

"Yes."

They watched Steinberg return to his three disciples.

His father, Aba and even his mother, who obviously could flirt and listen, burst into laughter.

"Where," his father, now thrown into hiccups, gasped, "did you get that marvelous *bubbe-mayse*?"

Aba looked around furtively.

"I had a collaborator, who shall remain nameless."

"In what lunatic asylum does he reside?"

"In what lunatic asylum do we reside?" Aba replied.

Harry saw Aba's eyes meet his father's. Something passed between them which dampened joviality. Both sighed.

"He is coming! He is coming!" Mishkin, the ex-Berlin soccer player, who had been assigned to spot Asch and race to sound the alarm, shouted if the Nazarene himself were at hand.

Harry, between Aba and his father, turned left and right, scanning the line which began at the Royal and stretched far beyond. It was a picture that would be in history books! Even his mother, after vowing to remain aloof, had joined, saying:

"How many times does one get to see Yiddish writers agree on anything?"

Excited whispers flew from ear to ear:

"There he is . . . I see him . . . Does he see us . . . ?"

It reminded Harry of the movie in which the FBI waited outside the theater for Dillinger.

Across Second Avenue a small figure, huddled in an overcoat, waited through the changing of two red traffic lights, trying to make sense of what he saw. Finally, he crossed the street.

"Apostate!" a voice shouted

He nodded his head, shrugged and turned to recross the street. Feet shuffled. It had been too quick. The culprit had denied them mortified flesh. Then a female voice began to sing the *Hatikvah*. Immediately, everyone joined at the top of their lungs. Locked hands swung back and forth. His father interrupted his monotone screaming to shout to Harry:

"Make a joyous noise!"

Pedestrians stopped. A crowd formed. The choir freed their hands to point at the small, bent overcoat taking tiny steps away. The crowd, ready to play, pointed also. Some sang. One shouted:

"There he is: *M*!"

The song over, everyone filed back into the Royal, congratulating each other. At the table, Aba said:

"We showed discipline under fire. No one broke ranks."

His father laughed.

"Suppose he comes back tomorrow or the next day," Harry asked, "how will you know? How will you keep him out?"

"We will not keep him out," his father said. "We have told him what we think of what he has done. It is sufficient."

"I thought you hated him."

"Perhaps we do," Aba said, "but blood is thicker than walking on water."

"Harry," his mother said, her hand designating Aba, her husband and then sweeping the room, "with them, nothing is ever serious. Just jokes."

CHAPTER

28

THE SWEATING MAN'S SKEPTICAL EYE'S NARROWED TO A SQUINT, HONING his gaze to pierce Harry's forehead and read the truth. He removed a white triangular cloth hat, revealing a bald head sprinkled with brown age spots and laid it next to a stack of sugar cones. Cocking his head left, he said:

"You sure you're not one of them rich kids from Sea Gate, just here for the summer? I've had too many of you pulled outta here by the ears. And their parents cursing at me."

Harry spoke rapidly: "I live on 35th street. I go to Lincoln High. I know Schnozz and the big talker who runs the kiddie rides, and . . ."

The man smiled and held up a believing palm.

"OK, OK, the pay is fifteen cents an hour. On Monday, Tuesday, Wednesday and Thursday you work from six at night to midnight. On weekends you start at noon and maybe go a little later. It depends on the weather. Any problems?"

"No."

"What's your name?

"Harry."

"Mine's Morey," he said, lifting a sugar cone out of the stack. Turning toward the two cylindrical white vats which resembled cement mixers, he asked: "Chocolate or vanilla?"

"Chocolate."

He pulled down a gearstick-shaped handle. Cocoa colored frozen custard filled the cone, growing thinner as it rose, like the decreasing drips on a sand castle. The last drop angled off, resembling the floppy top of a stocking cap. He handed the cone to Harry and laughed.

"Right now you're thinking: *Boy oh boy, all the custard I can eat.* In three days you'll hate it. Believe me."

Harry licked the smooth sweetness. He didn't believe him.

A customer rested his girth on the metal counter.

"Gimme a vanilla, and fill it!"

"Always," Morey said. "Best nickel buy on the Island."

He built a white spiral taller than Harry's. In one slurp, the customer decapitated the custard to the rim of the cone and left. Morey pointed an instructive finger:

"Give fat guys more. Fat guys have fat friends looking for cheap things to fill their bellies. He'll tell his buddies."

Harry nodded.

Morey winked.

"You just watch me, kid. You'll learn a helluva of lot more'n pullin' custard."

Harry smiled a thank-you.

"Listen, Harry, can you come back around five? It's the beginning of the July Fourth weekend and the other kid quit on me with no warning."

"Sure."

Harry walked his bike onto the boardwalk. He watched clean-up crews, wearing yellow-billed caps and matching oversized gloves sweep the residue of last night's joy into small mounds: pink strands of cotton candy which clung to sticks like the last feathers of a sick bird, impaled brown apple cores, teeth-gouged corncobs, buns, meat scraps and grease, mustard, and ketchup-stained paper. Other cleaning men stood on the runningboards of small dump trucks, jumping off to shovel the garbage into the truck bed. They moved slowly, screwing up their faces in displeasure while shouting, "Fucking, filthy animals!"

It was midmorning. The beach was a patchwork quilt of bathing costumes and beach umbrellas. At the ocean's edge, nude toddlers raced toward the water, their parents in lifesaving pursuit. Older children built sand castles. Muscle men fought mock battles, wrestling each other to the ground, checking if any female had eyed their flexed biceps. Sometimes four or five would carry a struggling victim to the water's edge, where after swinging him back and forth like a hammock while counting to three they would fling him into the water. If a girl was in their grasp, they swung her higher and longer, encouraging her screams and wriggling.

Most of the beach people lay prone, tilting their faces toward the sun, coaxing a handsome tan. Beach umbrellas protected only the aged and babies.

Boys Harry's age, harnessed to heavy metal containers filled with dry ice and ice-cream pops, tottered though the sand, wary of cops who, under orders from merchants, would confiscate their inventory. Hawking ice cream was one of the jobs Harry had considered after he had lied to Woody, saying he would no longer pick up betting slips because he had been offered a better-paying summer job. The truth was that when he had proudly told Aba of his criminal activity, the response had been an order to stop:

"You are putting yourself in bad company. I am not against breaking the law for pleasure or even principle. But to do it for profit is to join hands with people like the Rockefellers. Very bad company. Not fit for a good American boy."

Woody had cursed him. His normally dead-white face gone purple, he had shouted:

"And to think I felt sorry for ya! That's the thanks I get for tryin' to save your ass . . . to help ya out."

"Huh," Harry puzzled, thinking Woody's rage had unhinged him.

"What about the fucking bike!" Woody shouted.

"What about it?"

"The deal for that piece of shit I took off your hands. You owe me payments."

"You said it was an even trade."

"Shit, I did . . . Soldier!"

Soldier appeared.

"Damn, hello Harry. How are you?"

"Never mind that shit, you nut case. Listen to me good. Didn't I say to you just yesterday that maybe it's time this little shit starts payin' off the bike I give him?"

Soldier's fingers masked his eyes.

"Well?" Woody screamed.

"Damn, I'm thinking."

"What the fuck is there to think about, you gassed-up cripple? You remember damn well."

Soldier removed his hands from his face. He did not look at Harry.

"Damn," he whispered, "seems like I do remember something like that."

"Damn right!" Woody said.

He shook a fist at Harry.

"Now, what the fuck are you going to do about that?"

"I'll pay you."

"You bet you will. With interest too. Two bucks a week for ten weeks. Got it!"

"Yes."

"And if you miss one payment . . . bye-bye bike."

"I understand."

"Get the fuck outta here, before I take the bike now."

Riding home, Harry had heard the sound of running behind him. He stopped and turned. Soldier ran into him. They fell to the ground. Harry jumped to his feet and pedaled away. Soldier shouted:

"Damn, Harry, don't hate me."

Harry stopped at a safe distance.

"You came to take my bike."

"Damn, no! No! I'd never do that. Never!"

Soldier came toward him body bent forward, nose parallel to the ground. He laid his hand on the back fender. Harry pulled the bike away. Tears ran down Soldier's cheeks, wandering through the stubble. A lump formed in Harry's throat. He pushed the bike within Soldier's reach. Soldier stroked it.

"Damn, it's a nice bike, Harry. And you're a nice boy."

"Thanks, Soldier."

"Damn, Harry, it wouldna made any difference what I said, except for me."

Harry shrugged.

"Damn, if I woulda said Woody was lying, he woulda said I was crazy and don't remember nothing. But he woulda got even. Woody always gets even. So I said what he wanted. I shouldn't, I know. But Harry, I can't fight . . . even if I think to. Damn, I smell mustard and my head is like to break."

Harry grazed a playful slap past Soldier's cheek.

"Soldier, I know we're pals."

Soldier straightened his body.

"Damn, Harry, can I hug you?"

"Sure."

Soldier put his arms around Harry's waist. Their cheeks touched. Harry heard the sound of a kiss but felt only Soldier's beard, first on one cheek and then the other.

"Damn, I learned that from the frogs in France. They do it all the time. It's nice. They even did it when they gave me a medal. This big general. He smelled like a whore at Rosie's. You ain't mad at me, are you, Harry?"

"Never, Soldier."

"Damn, if you need dough to pay off Woody, just ask me. I got no use for money."

Soldier backed away.

"Damn. Please Harry, I can't stand to see nobody cry."

"I can't help it Soldier. It's not bad. It's not about anything. It's just crying."

Soldier sniffed loudly.

"Damn mustard."

He turned and ran. After a few steps he jumped, then skipped, then ran to begin a new cycle. Harry thought of the montage of athletic events that introduced the Movietone sports.

Harry looked at his watch: two o'clock. Three hours to kill. He decided to take a secret lesson from his employer.

From the other side of Surf Avenue he watched Morey entertain customers, serving the cones with elaborate hand flourishes, like Mayor La Guardia conducting a symphony orchestra. Sometimes he would whirl around and present the cone from behind his back to a child sitting on a parent's shoulder.

Suddenly the scantily clad clientele was joined by a group of eight kids, ranging in age from about eight to sixteen, dressed in identical dark blue blazers stamped with a gold coat of arms topped by a cross, matching shorts, white, Buster Brown–collar shirts, black knee socks and patent leather black shoes. They marched behind a man whose flour-white face and lampblack brush mustache recalled a silent movie. A swagger stick was tucked under his arm.

Harry crossed the street and edged closer until he could read the lettering on their coats of arms: *New York Rectory Orphanage.*

Harry thought: *I used to be an orphan.* It was a time of much screaming in the house. One day his mother had snatched him up and taken him on a thing that had moved and made a terrible noise, which he later realized was the subway. Soon after, Zadeh had come and taken him. He hadn't seen his mother or father for a long time. When they reappeared, he was surprised. He wasn't expecting them.

Harry felt a chill. Aba said you felt cold when someone walked over your grave. It also applied to your parents' graves. He mounted his bike and pedaled furiously, escaping from the orphan curse.

On the Midway, stymied by a wall of bodies that refused to part, he skidded into a narrow dirt alley between the House of Horrors and the Penny Pitch concession.

Two figures wearing oversized sombrero hats tilted forward to obscure their faces ran toward him from the end of the alley. They seemed hostile, perhaps members of one of the gangs from tough sections of Brooklyn who invaded Coney to rob holiday visitors or take pleasure in beating them. He ducked his head into his arms, preparing to cushion the blows.

"Hey, it's Harry," a familiar voice said.

"Yah, yah."

Harry raised his eyes. Before him stood Jo-Jo and Blue Man.

Two more orphans, Harry thought. But maybe not. It seemed important to know.

"Did you guys have parents?

Jo-Jo shook his head slowly from side to side and said:

"Harry, we thought you were our friend. Not like the rest."

Blue Man looked down at his feet.

"Yah, yah, eventually zey are all ze same. Why don't you be wise like everyone else and ask: *Did your parents have any children zat lived?* Don't you think zat is funny?"

Harry blurted out an explanation. The two smiled.

"Hey," Harry said, "I don't even know your real names."

Blue Man straightened, clicked his heels and bowed slightly from the waist:

"Herr Doctor Yanos Musil, at your service."

Jo-Jo, attempting an imitation, tangled his feet and grabbed Harry to keep from falling:

"Herr, Mr. Stanislaus Pruyzenski. How's that for a mouthful?"

They laughed.

"Are you really a doctor?" Harry asked Blue Man.

"Yes. No. I mean not like you mean it. I not cure ze sick. But I am doctor of a university. On my degree it say *doctor juris,* a lawyer. In Prague all important men are called doctor."

"Did you defend murderers?"

"No, Harry. I went to ze university only because Mama and Papa say I must. No, I do it for Mama. For Papa I do nozing. My Mama, she is very nice. I wonder what she did after I left?"

"Left for where?"

The Blue Man shrugged.

"I never want be lawyer. To say you did wrong, he did right. You good. He bad. Who knows zis? Nobody. People make believe zey know. Zey are liars. But because I am Herr Doctor, I get good job in Prague in bureau where people who hurt zemselves at work come ask for money. All day I see people who are missing parts: hand, fingers, toe, eye, ear, even nose. Some take off zere clothes to show what is missing or broken.

"I make friends wiz anozer Herr Doctor from my university, who also not want be lawyer. We give away ze most money we can. He do things like zis: one day a man come to him because he is very sad. My friend says the man has lost his soul at work. He give him ze most money and write on record: *Zis man lost his soul at work. Until God is found to provide one, he is our responsibility.* We laugh about our boss with a briefcase full papers looking for God to give him bill.

"One day a circus from Germany comes to Prague. I go wiz my friend. Is ze first time I ever see circus. My Papa say it waste of money. He never take me. When I walk in, I see men and women way up swinging like shooting stars. I see elephants made into kings and queens by jewels. I see women wiz heads of white fezers standing like statues on running white horses. I know zat all my life I looking for zis. A life full of magic.

"I tell my friend I will go with ze circus. He say he would like be up on ze trapeze and never come down. He always saying crazy zings like zat.

"I tell ze man who runs circus I want go wiz him. He show me somezing look like salt. He say is silver nitrate and if I swallow some every day my face turn blue. Zen he will put me in uniform of red and gold and I will stand in front of ze circus and point people to ze way in. He tell me it will not hurt me. Doctor's use for medicine.

"I turn all blue. But is no good. Ze children afraid of blue face and hands. Zey cry.

"Owner say zere is one zing left to do. I must sit almost naked

in a cage and let people look at ze blue man. I say: no, I not animal. The owner say: OK, leave circus. What can I do? I so tired. My
head hurt most of ze time. I go into cage zat has on it sign: *Blue man
from ze moon*. People yell at me, srow zings for to make me jump.
Want me to eat peanuts like elephant. Zey shake fists. Zey say I
from ze devil, dirty freak.

"One day we come back to Prague. My friend come up to cage.
I cry.

"He say: 'why you cry? You are in ze circus. You have what you
want. Zat is important.' I point to blue body. I hit myself. He say:
'what you showing me, Yanos? I not understand.' I yell: 'I blue. I
freak!' He say: 'I jealous of you. If I could be anyzing in world it
would be red Indian.' Zen he take out a notebook write someting,
tear out ze page and give it."

Blue Man handed Harry a picture frame the size of a pocket
mirror. The glass pressed a square of cracked, yellow paper on
which black ink swept like hairpin turns through a mountain road.
He translated:

Zere is a coming and a going.
A parting and often—no returning.

"I wonder where he is. He not healzy man. Maybe dead.
Funny, we about same age, but I zink of him as fazer. See Harry, I
was like you when Mama, Papa disappear. I was orphan. But zen I
find fazer."

During the Blue Man's tale Jo-Jo had sat down on the dirt, his
back against a wooden exterior wall. With a piece of straw he absentmindedly drew stick figures in the powdery earth. Now, he spoke
to them:

"I never had a father or found one. My mother said my father
died before I was born. What's the difference . . . My mother is
beautiful."

"Do you have a picture of her?" Harry asked.

A growl from deep inside Jo-Jo's throat became a barked
word: "Whore!"

Blue Man sat down next to him.

Jo-Jo bared his teeth.

"She's a whore. She always was. I probably cost my father a half a buck."

"Is not so," Blue Man said.

"Oh yeah, whaddaya expect for half a buck? A dog, that's what."

"But you tell me your Mama is nice. She always wiz you."

"I lied. The only time she was nice to me was when there was a chance she could get me into Ripley's *Believe It or Not* for money. Then she hit me when he turned me down."

Jo-Jo spit on the figures he had drawn, obliterating heads, arms, legs. He covered his hands and mumbled:

"You told the priest I was from God . . . for your sins. I love you so much. All those hands on you. Coal-black fingers grabbing, pulling. And you wouldn't even hold my hand."

His voice disintegrated into babble. Blue Man put his arm around Jo-Jo's shoulders. Harry slowly backed out of the alley on tiptoes. It seemed important not to make a sound. At the end of the alley, he stopped. Had he not known them, he would have guessed that they were father and son enjoying a moment of intimacy.

On the boardwalk, near Steeplechase Amusement Park, a perimeter of space segregated a knot of people, a configuration which usually meant a fistfight. He edged closer to see the action. It was not a fight. A group of men in suits and ties flanked a man in a white linen suit and ivory-colored Panama hat who was talking and waving his hands toward the beach and then at Steeplechase. He swept his right hand over the beach as if to smooth it out. The other men nodded. Two cops, front and back, cleared a path. Passersby gawked and shrugged. Such treatment usually was accorded to a movie star, but the crowd could not find one.

The man was a mystery Harry needed to solve. Intent on hearing some words that might provide a clue, Harry got his feet tangled up with his bike. He fell, creating a roadblock in front of the group. They stopped. A cop muttered, "Dumb kid" and pulled him to his feet. He was about to shove Harry aside when the mystery extended his hand and settled it on Harry's shoulder.

"Are you all right, son?"

"Sure. I'm sorry I got in the way."

Harry began to move away but the hand restrained him. He was sure he was in trouble.

"I said I'm sorry, mister. I gotta meet my folks."

One of the group pointed to Harry's captor and asked:

"Do you know who this is?"

"I said I'm sorry."

"This is Robert Moses."

The tone demanded recognition.

"Oh," Harry said, trying to remember him in a movie.

"He is a Commissioner," the man said.

It became clear. He was the Fire Commissioner looking over Coney, where fires were a way of life. Maybe, he thought, Mayor La Guardia is here in his fire hat.

The Commissioner bent down to Harry's level.

"Have you ever been to Orchard Beach?" he asked.

His breath smelled like violets.

"No," Harry answered.

"Why?"

"I like Coney."

The Commissioner swept the beach with his arm.

"You like this filth? Nothing green. All these people rubbing together like guppies in a fishbowl. Wouldn't it be better if all these shacks were gone and there would be space? The eye could breathe."

The answer was no, but Harry was in no position to be honest. Yet he couldn't desert Coney. He shrugged.

"How many times a year do you come to Coney Island, son?"

"I live here."

The Commissioner's fingers recoiled from his shoulder. He barked at the cop:

"Let's move on. Why the hell are we standing here!"

Harry jumped out of the way. As the Commissioner passed, Harry saw him take a handkerchief from his lapel pocket and wipe his hands.

In the Cherry Tree: February 29, 1936

Harry: *Aba, today is Leap Year.*

Aba: *What does that mean?*

Harry: *It means we have an extra day in the year.*

Aba: *What happens to that extra day when there is no leap year?*

Harry: *It is not needed because the earth is spinning correctly and does not need another day to correct its mistake?*

Aba: *And what would happen if we did not correct the earth's mistake?*

Harry: *I don't know.*

Aba: *I will tell you. All the calendars in the world would be of no use. For example, we all know that King George of England died last month, precisely on January twenty-eighth. But if we had not made up all our leap years, there would be many different calendars, subject to the whims of many calendar makers, and there would be great confusion as to the day George died. Because of this some people might believe that for a day or more England was ruled by a dead king. Even worse, some could conclude that England had both a live king, Edward the Eighth, and a dead king, George the Fifth, and would not know whom to bow down to.*

Harry: *How does someone get to be a king?*

Aba: *He is born a king.*

Harry: *King David was not born a king. He was born a shepherd.*

Aba: *Correct, Heshele. Sometimes the people make a person their king.*

Harry: *How do they know whom to choose?*

Aba: *They choose a man most unlike themselves.*

Harry: *Why?*

Aba: *Because they know they are not kings.*

Harry: *Suppose they make a mistake. Can they tell the king to stop being king?*

Aba: *Yes. But first they must find a day that has disappeared when there is no leap year, and do it then.*

CHAPTER
29

"Well, Harry," Morey said, stowing his white hat under the counter, "looks like it's time to knock off."

Harry put his hat beside Morey's. He looked across garbage-coated Surf Avenue at the smoky, darkened bulbs in the marquees of the Loew's Coney Island and RKO Tilyou. An occasional car dragged a carton under its chassis or sent refuse soaring like spiraling footballs. A cat scooted from under a parked police cruiser which appeared empty, but where, front and back, cops were stretched out.

A magician had performed a wondrous disappearing act. The bumping, chewing, licking, smooching crowd had evaporated in the time it had taken Harry to look up from filling his last cone. Even next door at Nathan's, where through the night people had covered the sidewalk and cars had triple-parked, only two customers remained, one a bum promoting a handout.

Harry's legs tingled. He shifted his weight, lifting each foot and rotating it. Morey laughed.

"Feel it in the legs. Sure. A couple of days and you'll get used to it. But don't try to go to sleep right away. You've got to unwind. You lie down now and you'll feel like your legs are exploding."

Harry nodded.

"You didn't do bad, kid. A little sloppy, but that's to be expected. But you got to remember equal portions. Nothing make 'em madder than seeing someone get more. They like to kill."

"Yeah, one guy said to me: *How come you gave that broad more than me? You got a thing for her?*"

"I heard that. He was a fat guy. Fat guys always think they're getting the short end of the stick. Well, let's go."

Harry, leaning on his bike, watched Morey pull down the rolling metal door onto the sidewalk, then turn a handle which passed a bolt through a wicket sunk into the concrete. He inserted a key in the handle, turned, tested, flipped the key and caught it behind his back.

"Kid, you want me to drive you home?"

"No thanks. I'll walk awhile. Maybe it'll help my feet."

"Good idea. Well, seeya tomorrow."

Morey walked toward a parking lot. After a few steps, he stopped, turned, and pleaded:

"Harry, don't screw me. Come back tomorrow. You're really very good."

"I will. I swear."

Harry walked his bike along a deserted side street toward the boardwalk, where he intended to pedal away the agitation in his legs. The heavy air lay on his head like a wet sponge. A rat crossed a few yards in front of him heading for the garbage on the Midway. He wondered where the pack was and if any had died.

The wind picked up. Lightning lit up black clouds. He counted seconds: one thousand and one, one thousand and two . . . A deep rumble like a diving roller-coaster began at one thousand and five. *Five miles away, nothing to worry about.* He was being scientific. He would not allow his mother to pass on to him her irrational fear of lightning.

Suddenly the boardwalk glowed silver and white. An almost simultaneous crack of thunder mixed with the ripping sound of a sheared tree. Raindrops the size of blood-bloated bugs fell. *Not near the ocean. Not under a tree. Don't be the tallest object.*

He flattened himself under the eaves of the rifle shoot. Rain flooded the Midway, launching an armada of garbage.

As in a mercurial dream, a white bolt with a tail like tree roots hit the thirty-foot-tall *High Striker,* a test of strength in which a blow from a sledge hammer sent a metal disk, grooved on two pieces of wire, careering upward past sections marked *powder puff, pen pusher, muscle man, champ* and finally against a golden gong which rang and vibrated for *superman*. The lightning severed the gong, which spun away like a Hercules-thrown discus, while the wood splintered. Embers generating heat as strong as the midday sun whizzed by him.

The rain was now a waterfall; its source, heaven. Ankle deep in water, he awaited death riding the electricity through a puddle, into his wet socks, up his legs and finally severing his head as it did the gong. He imagined his decapitated body, crackling like a shorted wire, floating down the Midway, a feast for the rats.

He called on God. He was willing to strike a bargain: *Spare me and I'll do anything you want.* He often made the same offer in return for a victory by the Brooklyn Dodgers. As payment, God imposed tasks such as being extra nice to Joe Baker, or giving a little kid a speedy ride on the handlebars of his bike.

God was unavailable, absorbed in playing a game of lightning hopscotch up and down the Midway. Across from Harry, under a sign that promised *The greatest variety of freaks and living monstrosities from all parts of the world,* renderings of Jo-Jo, Moho and Loho and Fifi glowed like sepulchral pop-outs in the House of Horrors ride.

He conceded that he should have expected annihilation because the people in his two lives—his father and Aba on one planet, and the freaks on the other—had somehow merged through common furtive eyes and whispers meant to exclude him. According to his science teacher, the fusion of matter and antimatter would blow up the world. What was more matter and antimatter than writers and freaks?

Science brought salvation. He remembered the same teacher saying that the safest place in an electrical storm was inside a car because the rubber tires served as a ground. He didn't know what that meant, but his bike had rubber tires. He laid his legs across the handlebars. Safe, he laughed hysterically at a self-portrait: a Sholom Aleichem schlemiel sent to buy a boat and talked into a bike.

God, somewhat spent, previewed his next appearance by showcasing his bag of horrors: dinosaur tails scalding the ocean, thunder too loud for mere ears, clouds weighted by water tumbling to the ground. But he knew he had escaped God's enema, as he had Zadeh's.

The wind went limp. The cool air smelled of shelled creatures sprinkled with a pinch of salt. It pricked the nostrils. A languid, reassuring three-quarter moon popped into the sky like a quickly hung prop. Only the ocean disturbed the silence, still crashing like a child unable to end a tantrum.

Harry pumped the bike pedal lightly, creating whirlpools. Water rippled outward, just like ocean liners pushing out monster waves.

As he turned a corner, he saw, three yards in front of him, the backs of Otto and Albert-Alberta. Otto, his torso bare, crushed water from his undershirt. As he walked, rolling left and right, hills of muscles wiggled. Albert-Alberta's purple blouse clung to his almost shoulderless shape, a sapling to Otto's giant redwood. Harry decided to play private eye, tailing them and eavesdropping. It was not difficult.

They were yelling at each other.

"Ach," Otto spat, "you are de disgusting homo."

Albert-Alberta threw out his arms in disbelief.

"You can say that to me, who has welcomed you with open rectum? You can deny being a homo?"

"Yah."

"How, pray tell, does that come about?"

"Only de one on de bottom is de homo."

"Why is that?"

"Because dat is de woman's position."

Otto slid one palm quickly over the other, signaling an irrefutable fact.

"I think you really believe that," Albert-Alberta said.

Otto stopped walking and twisted his body to flex the maximum amount of muscles.

"Yah. Could dis body be homo?"

Albert-Alberta mimicked the pose.

"Charles Atlas is a homo."

"Liar."

"I have a fifty percent chance of being right."

"*Yah. Yah*. Fifty percent, dat is you. Fifty percent and fifty percent add to nothing."

Albert-Alberta executed a bump and grind.

"I've also had women," he said, squeezing imaginary breasts. "There was a German fräulein, a maid in my cousin's house in London. Big, fat, stinking, the way I like them. Would fart while fucking. A rare talent."

"Englander pig, you make it up."

"Otto, I make up everything. Just as you do. And then we believe. And that makes it true. Like your Mr. Hitler and my Mr. Chamberlain."

"You crazy. Hitler is de great man. He not make up nossing."

"Who's pumping on top, Hitler or Chamberlain?"

Otto's bent fingers clamped onto Albert-Alberta's shoulders and lifted him straight up, like a picture about to be hung on a high hook.

"Englander, I no bluff. You say like dat about Hitler, I kill you. No bluff. Trow you in ocean."

He swiveled Albert-Alberta to show him his grave. They saw Harry. Otto dropped Albert-Alberta, who called to Harry:

"Have you got a ticket? The ride is open."

"Is that an exercise?" Harry said to Otto, smiling at the strongman. Otto did not offer Harry his usual smile of greeting, but rather the menacing stare that threatened audiences as a prelude to running amok.

"You haff followed us, *yah?*"

"Followed you? Oh yeah. Up the . . ."

"What you see?"

"I see . . . saw you walking."

"What you hear?"

"Something about Hitler. Otto, what . . . ?"

"In alley, what you see!"

"What alley?"

Albert-Alberta splashed water on Otto, who spat and wiped his lips.

"Englander pig! You trow dirty water in my mouth. You make me sick. I kill you."

"Otto, leave the kid be. Harry, how come you were out here in the rain?"

Harry explained. Otto shook his head, squeezed a bruise into Harry's arm, and said:

"Come, ve valk togedder. Get on bike. I help."

Otto grabbed the handlebars with one hand, tilted the bike and Harry until the front wheel barely touched the water and ran. Harry screamed:

"Faster Otto, faster."

Suddenly the bike gained weight. Albert-Alberta lay on his stomach, holding on precariously to the back of the seat and kicking his legs.

"What an act!" he shouted, before his lips went under water.

Otto turned right on the corner of Surf Avenue. A car traveling in the opposite direction made a skidding U-turn and mounted the sidewalk in front of Otto. A back window rolled down halfway. A gun pointed at Otto's forehead.

"Drop the bike," a voice commanded.

Otto froze, still holding the bike.

"I said drop it!"

Albert-Alberta stood up. Otto let go. As the wheels hit the ground, Harry leaped off and spoke to the presence behind the gun:

"He wasn't hurting me, Mr. Policeman." He pointed to Otto and Albert-Alberta. "We were just having some fun."

"Don't I know you, kid?" the voice said.

Probably a cop from Woody's, Harry thought.

"I don't know," Harry answered.

"What's your name?"

"Harry Catzker."

"Catzker, of course, you should be home. We'll drive you." He spoke to the driver.

"Vince, load the bike in the trunk."

"You, bullet head," he said to Otto, "take your freak buddy and move on,"

Otto began to protest. Vince stepped out of the car, gun in hand.

"Get lost," he said, waving the pistol toward Nathan's.

"Don't do anything to Harry," Albert-Alberta pleaded. "He's only a kid."

"Get lost!"

Albert-Alberta grabbed Otto's hand and tugged. As they ran, their heads swiveled sideways to catch what was happening behind them. In front of Morey's custard stand, Otto stopped and shook a fist.

"I kill you!"

Harry got into the backseat.

"Now I remember you," he said.

The man frowned.

"Being a cripple is a great identification."

"I didn't mean it that way. Before, I couldn't see your face."

"Oh, sure."

The car pulled up in front of Harry's house.

"How'd you know where I live?"

"I know plenty."

Vince unloaded the bike and leaned it against the car.

Harry opened the car door. Menter put his hand on his shoulder, restraining him.

"I just remembered, Harry. You can deliver a message to your father for me. Tell him that you are now part of the enterprise."

"Huh? You know my father?"

"Sure do. Just tell him exactly what I said." Menter put his hand on Harry's chin and turned his face so that their eyes met. "*Victor Menter says that you,* Harry, *are now part of the enterprise.* He'll understand."

CHAPTER

30

ABA AWOKE FROM A DEEP, DREAMLESS SLEEP, SNIFFING THE SEASIDE odor of female sex fluids. He extended his left arm and squeezed gently the nude woman's warm, ice-smooth breast, popping the nipple between his middle and index fingers. She hissed like an angry cat.

The woman was a creator of sounds. Sometimes the sound was an imitation, identifiable. More often her mysterious vocal cords whispered echoes of the familiar, pleasing the ear but teasing the brain, like an elusive word. He named them: *Love Song of a Dinosaur, God's Sigh, Thunder Squelched*. Each challenged him to a poem. He failed, piling up cosmic litter, dumping garbage on the moon.

He turned his head and lightly kissed her shoulder. Even in this sunless room, her brown flesh shone. He finger-walked through her coarse pubic hair. She yawned, slowly diminishing the sound, like the fading notes of *Taps*. It was a familiar message. She did not wish to make love. Last night's pleasure was still in her.

Stolz had tried to convert her to his way: however intense the pleasure, it can be exceeded. She answered with the humming sound of her own orgasm. Pressed for more precise explanation, she said:

"When I had enough, I had enough. Ain't no sense in lookin' fo' mo' than enough."

He named the sound: *The Fo' Mo' Than Enough Blues*.

She curled into a fetal position, firming her buttocks into beckoning mounds. His palm read their contours. His brain, however, stunned him by recalling a newspaper account of a first-century city unearthed outside of Tel Aviv. Quick realization that *Tel* in Hebrew meant hill or mound made suspect his claim of being a pure sensualist.

The Marquis de Sade you are not, he conceded, followed by a mental picture of Nietzsche as a lion tamer, instructing: *When you go to woman, do not forget the whip,* which segued into: *Is it perfume from her ass, that makes me so digrass?"* The literary free association stiffened him. He thanked his friends for their labor of love, but asked: What now? They were silent. He smirked in superiority and quoth himself: *I am a memory come alive,* the title of a poem in which memory is an ever-replenishing corporeal organ of pleasure.

The woman's fame had embarrassed him. When he had called the day following their first meeting, he had apologized for his ignorance. She had answered:

"That's the good part, honey. Ain't many dudes don't want Leslie Jones. But you put eyes on Hannah Brown."

Over the next two weeks, seated at a table three feet from Leslie and Willie, he had watched them make love as the notes of his tenor saxophone penetrated her welcoming wet voice. After each performance, Willie claimed her. Finally, Willie took an out-of- town booking.

On a Sunday morning in early fall, he had walked from the subway stop to 143rd Street and Lenox Avenue. Negro men and boys in dark suits, ties and felt hats and women and girls in colorful dresses and hats, jabbering happy sounds, left their churches, locked hands and strutted in celebration of their own beauty. They were not threatening, but he could not suppress memories of isolated nakedness in Polish streets. His breath came hard. He walked sideways, trying to diminish his visibility, trailing his fingernails along the buildings like a blind man.

Wearing only a white slip, she framed herself in the doorway, her chocolate flesh an opaque feast. She encircled his waist and pulled him inside. They kissed. He closed his eyes, inhaled her scent and imagined her tongue fed him camellia petals.

He cleared his throat to speak. She placed her index finger on his lips. She led him to the bedroom and stood rigid before him. He bent down, pulled the slip over her head, kissed it and threw it on the floor.

He undressed. She pulled him onto a lumpy bed. She lay on her back, eyes closed. His hands smoothed and clutched her heat. She did not touch him, or move until she pulled up her knees and spread her legs. He mounted and penetrated.

Suddenly, the inert body bumped and ground like a burlesque queen in her final turn. Camellia scent carried by a continual *wheeeee* broke against his face. The savage surprise pulled from him a long orgasm, drained of pleasure by his panic to retard it. Desperately he returned vicious thrusts, pleading for her satisfaction before he lost his erection. Five minutes later, when she announced her orgasm with a low, deep hum and bumps that nearly lifted them off the bed, he also flowed. He collapsed off her, thinking of Gide's boast of having had fourteen Arab boys in one night.

"I love you," he said.

"I love you," she answered, "but let's not get too personal."

He became one of her lovers. She never deceived him about that. There was Willie and perhaps others, whether long or short term he did not know. When he asked, the reply was a blues lyric sung over laughing lips: *"She's yours, she's mine, she's somebody else's too."*

As a teenager, she had been a prostitute, or close to it. Men had given her money. She insisted that payment was not the object. She needed to be in their arms. He stopped asking about other men.

At her performances, he was awed by her ability to layer words with sounds of sadness or joy independent of their banal meaning, creating an emotional Esperanto. She was, he concluded, in a trancelike state of ecstasy which stunned her parishioners.

She took him to after-hours clubs in Harlem that opened at four AM, the mandatory closing hour for establishments that sold liquor, where famous Negro and white musicians played jazz and celebrities danced or listened. There, he had secured Joe Louis's autograph for Harry, watched the British heiress Nancy Cunard dance with her hand on her black partner's penis, talked briefly with an intelligent but insane actor who wanted to put on an all-Negro cast production of *Macbeth*, and was asked by Tallulah Bankhead: *Do you still enjoy fucking?*

He smoked marijuana with Leslie, but refused heroin. Pointing to her collapsed veins, he told her she was killing herself. She shrugged:

"It make me happy."

"But I love you. I want to help you."

"Don't need no help. Didn't ask."

The only other irritation between them was the secret of her voice. His intellect would not allow such art to go unexplained or be explained as a dumb vessel carrying a treasure.

"When you sing, what do you feel?"

"I feel."

"When you sing about a lynching, do you see a corpse on fire?"

"I'd puke."

"What do you see?"

"I can't see nothing. The spotlight blinds me."

"You know people commit suicide after hearing *Gloomy Sunday*."

"So."

"You do that to them. Do you realize your power?"

"I don't mean to make them do that. But the song does remind me of a funeral in a way."

"Aha, you see a hearse."

"Aba, I don't see no fucking hearse. I had it. Now cut this crap or get lost. I sing what's in my heart and that ain't the same two nights in a row or two songs in a row."

Eventually, he admitted that his supposed comfort at sharing her was a lie. I must, he concluded, marry her, immediately laughing at his Jewish cure for infidelity. He imagined the dialogue:

"Leslie, now that we've been married by a rabbi, you can't have any other men."

"You Jews have heavy laws."

"Yes."

"I guess I'll pass on bein' Jewish."

The words *She's yours she's mine, she's somebody else's too* gave him no rest. Once they sprang whole and audible into his reading of a Yiddish poem. Afterward, his host, a manufacturer of corsets, congratulated him on mixing in a touch of English. Aba was, he said, in step with the American product of the future.

Desperate for exclusivity, he suggested they have a child. She laughed, then suddenly began to cry.

In her teens she had contracted gonorrhea. A local Negro doctor in Baltimore said he could cure her for fifty dollars. He had performed a hysterectomy.

"I wish that doctor was still alive so's I could kill him."

She had sobbed like a child. He had cradled her in his arms and whispered to her the soothing words of assurance that there was nothing to worry about, with which his mother had calmed him:

"Zorg zuch nischt."

The Yiddish escaped his lips, chasing away the reverie and presenting a nagging present. He looked at his watch: five after nine. At ten he was due in Sea Gate for a reading. He jumped out of bed, noting mournfully his creased, crumpled clothes.

On the subway he spit on his palms and smoothed his clothes. *Correct dress,* he thought. *They expect a bum. Who else would come begging so early in the morning—and late yet?*

Running from the Norton's Point terminus toward Sea Gate, he saw a familiar back moving unsteadily, as if hurt.

"Moishe," he yelled.

Catzker turned. He extended his arms to Stolz, keening:

"Oy, oy, oy."

Stolz embraced him.

"What Moishe, what?"

"Oy, oy, oy."

"Moishe, who died!"

"No one, Aba."

"Then what?

Catzker told of Harry's message from Menter.

"No! No, Moishe! With Heshele's life he does not play."

"But how?"

"The police."

"Yes, let us go."

"Just me, Moishe."

"Why?"

"Think of it dramatically: one murderer turns in another. It satisfies the audience's deep yearning for retribution."

"You are not a murderer, Aba. Stop talking nonsense."

"Ah, but I am, Moishe. It can't be expunged. Even self-defense is no defense against dreams that come in the night. And besides, if something goes wrong, what do I have to lose? What lies ahead? Mourning Jews murdered in Germany? I have no readers. I have no family. A few friends may cry before telling jokes. Heshele will say Kaddish. What more could I ask?"

"No, Aba, together."

"Insane man, does it require two to talk to the police? You must not be involved in this. Walk with me to the station, but wait outside."

Inside the precinct house, Stolz told a uniformed policeman that he wished to see the head man. He refused to explain, except that it was very important and he was not crazy. He was shown to a small room, where was a man who resembled W.C. Fields was seated behind a desk. The man stood up. His body was lean and wiry, completely at odds with his head. He offered his hand:

"I am Detective Shay."

"Aba Stolz."

"You have some information for me?" The detective spoke slowly, precisely, as if brackets constrained each word.

"Yes."

"Well?"

Aba coughed.

"Do you have some water?"

Shay left the room and brought back a paper cup filled with water. Aba gulped, spilling some on his shirt. He patted it dry, thinking, *Good-bye four wrinkles.*

"Arson," he blurted.

"What?"

"Arson. Planned by a man named Victor Menter."

"How do you know?"

"I was to commit it."

"Who else?"

Aba told of the freaks, aware that he would probably be taken for a madman. But the detective listened intently.

"Have you told this to anyone else?" he asked.

"No."

Shay stood and pointed his index finger at Stolz.

"Don't. You never know who's listening. Menter is a powerful man. You're a brave man and you're lucky you came to me. Keep it that way. Now go about your business like nothing happened. Leave everything to me. On your way out, give your name and address to the cop behind the desk, just like it was a run-of-the-mill thing. And remember, it's just between us for now."

Aba asked Moishe to accompany him to the house where they awaited the great poet. At the entrance, they embraced.

"I love you, Moishe."

"And I you."

"Life is strange, but in the end there is clarity."

"*Oy,* a Stolz theory. You don't have time."

"Let Heshele grow straight and tall," Aba said.

"That is your job, too."

Catzker watched his friend mount the cement steps of the red brick house. There was a slight tear in the back of Aba's shirt. Tomorrow, he commanded himself, you will buy him a new one.

Stolz pressed the white bell button. The perforated golden metal beside it challenged: "Who dat?"

"Aba Stolz."

"Say again."

"Aba Stolz."

"Yeah."

He was buzzed in. A tall Negro women holding a sponge in one hand and an envelope in the other bore down on him. She handed him the envelope and stood, hands on hips, while he read its contents.

Dear Mr. Stolz,

We waited for you for two hours then decided to go for a sail on the bay in my boat which we had planned anyway after your reading. There were very important Jewish people here. They are influential in business and other places. They were anxious to hear your poetry. They were disappointed and, it hurts me to say, insulted.

If an accident befell you, you could have called. Being a poet does not mean you can't act like a mensch. Jews as good as you were here. Make no mistake about that.

I was embarrassed. My wife ran to the bathroom to hide her tears for being made a fool in front of important people.

I will no longer gather fine Jews to hear you read. I still appreciate your ability but I have lost respect for you. If I recall correctly our arrangement it was for $5. I give you $10 to show you I am not angry, just disappointed that one Jew can treat another Jew like this."

Stolz waved the bill in front of his eyes, thinking, *Five dollars for reading, ten for not. I am on my way to becoming a rich man.*

The woman whistled, and said:

"Iffin I had dat, I'd get me some real Sunday dresses."

"I think that's what I'll do," Stolz replied.

He watched her face consult with her ears as to what she had heard. She was worried. She had been instructed to hand over an envelope and had already overstepped her boundaries with a personal comment to a crazy man who was worth ten dollars to her employers. That made him important. He could report her for sass, which would mean her job.

Her eyes pleaded with him to forget she existed. God, he remembered praying when he saw hooligans on a Warsaw street, make me invisible. God had not heard his prayers, which was as it should be, because he probably did not exist. But if he did, Aba Stolz would show Him something about answered prayers.

"Just jivin', Mama. Rest easy."

His Negro slang, lying like bacon grease on his *schmaltz*-coated tongue, produced the buffoon accent of a low Jewish comic. Leslie could imitate perfectly. Yet, Yiddish in her mouth sounded anti-Semitic. Authenticity, he had concluded, does not give license to shout *Jew* in a crowded world of anti-Semites.

The maid, he realized, was now sure of dismissal, since his words, meant to soothe, were in her ears anti-Negro. *From your mouth to God's ears* was the eternal Yiddish plea. He left quickly, getting out of the God business.

He walked out of the gate and onto Surf Avenue. He heard the ocean and children's shrieks. *Not my world,* he thought, closing his eyes and experiencing blindness. An arm doubled over his, crushing his flesh. Vince was beside him.

"Don't say nothin'. Just walk."

What about screaming, he thought, is that OK? How did he know it was me? He knows. He knows. I know. I knew. An eye for an eye. A murder for a murderer. He heard Ronald Colman's words on the way to the guillotine: *It is a far, far better thing that I do, than I have ever done. . . .* Strange, he thought, a perfect English accent. Inside me is a polished goy.

Vince shoved him into the passenger seat, locked the door and slid behind the wheel. He turned toward Stolz and smiled. Were his eyes more zealous than usual? Yes. Yes. It is in anticipation of killing. He probably gets an erection. He looked for a bulge, but saw none. Maybe I'm not his type.

The car moved slowly up Surf Avenue.

"Where are we going?" Stolz asked.

"Just for a ride."

"You're taking me for a ride."

"You seen too much gangster movies."

"How's Menter?"

Vince's right arm swung off the wheel. The back of his hand crushed Stolz's nose. It spurted blood on his shirt and pants. Vince wiped his hand on Stolz's shirtsleeve. Stolz held a handkerchief to his nose. The sight of his own blood, as usual, brought him to the edge of passing out. Pins and needles danced on his scalp. His head became weightless, floating. He closed his eyes to avert a blackout. He felt giddy.

"The Polish *pogromchiks* hit harder," he said derisively.

"Don't gimme dat kike shit."

"Where is Menter locked up?"

"Locked up, my ass! You t'ink a shitass like you can get Vic? Don't make me laugh. You'll see soon. We goin' to see him. So be a good boy and maybe he'll be good to you."

"No!" Stolz screamed.

"You t'ought you could get Vic. What a jerk."

Indeed a jerk, Stolz thought. A dead jerk, who saved no one, nothing.

They were on a highway, passing signs to Canarsie.

"We going to Canarsie, Vince?"

"Yeah. Somethin' to do before we see Vic."

"How are you going to kill me?"

"You jerk! If I was goin' to, I wouldda done it long ago. I do what I gotta, den we go see Vic."

He tries to keep me calm, not to make trouble, not to try to jump out of the car, Stolz thought. Or maybe . . .

Life, a wriggling worm, itched his testicles. He scratched. Life felt good. Vince grabbed his arm.

"No moves, get it."

"Just an itch, Vince," he said. "Life."

On the way to the gallows, Stolz pondered, what should one think. Will it hurt? Is there a God? Can I escape? No. Death is the only subject. Proximity provides light. A once-in-a-lifetime privilege not to be squandered.

The country from which no traveler has returned, Stolz lectured to a fascinated bust of Shakespeare, *is not a country at all. It is the last thing we see on earth. What did you see, dear William? A nurse's hand? A cup of broth? Your second best bed? A horse bearing down on you? That's your view of eternity. No vast landscape. A cup. A horse. A finger. Furthermore, sirrah, we do not travel. Eternity is brought to us. Mine will be a gun or a knife.*

"Vince," he said, " did you ever think of putting notches in your hands?"

"What?"

"You know, like the cowboys. Every time they killed a man they notched the handle of their gun."

"Ha-ha."

"I'm serious. As a matter of fact, if you lend me your knife, I'd like to put two notches in mine."

"You tryin'a scare me?"

"I *have* killed two people. One of them was my mother."

"I don' like dose kinda jokes."

"No joke, Vince. When they broke down the door, I hid under the bed. When I got out, they had split her head open."

"Who the fuck you talkin' about?"

"*Pogromchiks.* Polish killers, who kill Jews because Jesus tells them to. One *pogromchik* kills more than you ever will."

"Did dey really kill your mudder?"

"Yes."

"And you let 'em?"

"Yes."

"An' did nottin'?"

"I killed the one who killed her."

"So it's OK."

"What about my mother?"

"Her time was up."

"She was forty-five."

"Her time was up. I know guys younger, dere time was up."

"So if you kill someone, their time is up."

"Right."

"You know, Vince, this is the first time I ever told anyone about hiding under the bed when my mother was killed. It's like a confession and you're a priest. Forgive me, Father Vince."

"Cut dat kike shit."

The car left the highway, bumping along a dirt road, past hills of junked cars. They stopped on a stretch of weeds and withered grass.

"Walk wit' me," Vince said.

Is eternity also sound? Stolz thought. Will it be this voice forever?

He thought to run. No, he told himself, not like an animal. With dignity. He laughed out loud.

"Don't go crazy now," Vince said, gripping him under the arm.

Stolz looked for a gun. They walked. A burning entered his back. He coughed. The burning went in and come out, faster and faster. His lungs were clogged. He tried to breathe through his mouth. It was filled with blood.

Eternity, he thought, with whom? He reached for Leslie, brown flesh against a white sheet. She sang: *Everything a good man needs*. A good eternity. He was falling. Leslie dimmed. His mother's split head appeared. A halo hovered over it.

After Catzker had left Stolz he walked to the bay side of Sea Gate and watched the pleasure boats in the marina bob up and down, smirking their wellbeing at him. He then wandered aimlessly.

The day had heated up. Families headed for the beach loaded down like pack mules with canvas folding chairs, enormous beach umbrellas, picnic baskets overflowing with food and buckets of ice filled with beer and soda pop bottles. God's in his heaven, all's right with the world, for *allrightniks,* he recited aloud.

A boy about Harry's age, wearing bathing trunks and carrying a towel in a paper bag, bumped a bike down outside steps. Seeing Catzker, he looked puzzled. Catzker knew why. His was an unfamiliar face. The boy knew everyone on the block, or even in the next two or three blocks. He was under orders from his parents to report unfamiliar faces to the cruising patrol cars. He pedaled past Catzker, head down, escaping.

Suddenly, nausea bent Catzker over. He retched. A woman at a second-floor window screamed:

"Drunk slob. Manny, call the cops!"

He ran until his heart rebelled against dying. A police cruiser crawled up beside him. The cop called him over.

"You don't live here, do you, buddy?

"No."

"Visiting?"

"Yes."

"Who?"

"Mr. . . ."

"Mr. who?"

"I forgot."

"Your breath stinks."

"I was sick."

"On the street?"

"Yes."

"Get in."

The cop in the passenger seat got out, held open the back door for Catzker and followed him in. He looked down at his billy club, directing Catzker's eyes to his masturbatory movements over the gleaming brown wood.

"This can do a lotta damage," he said.

Catzker nodded.

"You just a bum, or you do something else when you're not puking on good people's streets?"

"Writer."

"Bullshit!"

He's right, Catzker thought.

"OK, get the fuck out. If I catch you in Sea Gate again, you better give your soul to God because your ass belongs to me."

He reached across, opened the door, grabbed Catzker's shirt and shoved him out. He was opposite the Sea Gate fence on 36th Street. Almost immediately, Vince forced him into a car. He kicked a soiled handkerchief, dirty enough to be one of his own. They drove to the Half-Moon Hotel.

Menter snapped his fingers, dealing with something inconsequential:

"Your friend Stolz has gone on a long vacation. Chances are he'll never come back."

Catzker's cried for Aba, and because he could not kill Menter.

"Did you have to kill him?" he sobbed.

"It was business, reputation. How would I look to Shay if he saw Stolz again? It makes me small-time."

"And now me."

"I wouldn't mind, but no. You do the job the two of you were supposed to."

"And my son?"

"Fuck you, your son and your whole whoring family." Menter pounded his fist into his palm.

"Hear me, you kike piece of shit! This is personal. You do the fire alone or there will be no more Catzkers!"

31

CATZKER, FACE AWASH, ZIGZAGGED LIKE A DRUNK, WAILING, "*OY, OY, OY.*" He was relieved to find no one home. He needed time to think, to explain. Explain what? That Aba Stolz, a man with a soul of sugar, had been murdered by a monster who could not be named. It sounded like one of his implausible *romanen*.

To think more clearly, he chose his son's room. After all, his son was the cause of Aba's death. What a thing to think! Yet it was true. But true had nothing to do with truth. Abraham Lincoln was responsible for the death of the actor who shot him. That was true, but not the truth. *Split more hairs*, he told himself in disgust, *then you can scuttle away to land of theory where consequence hurts only the ego.*

A framed picture of the Negro boxing champion hung over Harry's bed. His brown fists were wrapped in white tape as if burned in an accident. Heshele had explained that the tape cushioned the fist's impact when it struck a chin or another bone. Unprotected, a precious finger or knuckle might break, causing the loss of a match or even ending a career of mayhem. At the bottom of the photograph a child's labored penmanship read: *To Heshele, Best Wishes, Joe Louis. Heshele* was written differently from the rest. The letters were separated, unconnected to each other. Catzker saw Aba dictating the letters to an annoyed Louis whose fist was being asked to do other than that for which it had been constructed. How excited Heshele had been, devouring all Aba had said about Louis, staring at the hand that had actually felt Louis's biceps.

Catzker fell on the unmade bed, squashing his face into the spearmint gum smell of his son's pillow. He began to choke and turned over. The ceiling resembled the bottom of a flatboat. He remembered his passage to America as a frightened teenager. He never before had been on a ship. During the rough crossing, he had befriended an equally frightened boy. Together, they had detected dangerous noises that heralded the vessel breaking apart. The boy had reassured him: *I was born in a cowl, Moishe. I have a charmed life. Stay with me and all will be well.*

Freud also was born in a cowl. He was dying of cancer. There was no one alive left to talk to.

He lectured himself: *A man is dead who cannot be pronounced dead because there is no body and questions should not be asked. Yet, a man with many friends will disappear. How long before questions are asked? How can I not mourn Aba and not allow his friends to do so?*

If life imitates art, he thought, *can life imitate trash? Why not? Most lives are trashy. In his* romanen *when a character's situation was untenable, even by the accepting standards of his readership, he either died or disappeared. Disappearance was never questioned. It struck a wish-fulfillment button in the problem-plagued readers. It also had the advantage of possible future reappearance as a changed, rich, philanthropic, happy, observant Jew. He had made it a staple.*

Could Aba disappear? How? He could say that Aba told him that he needed a few years of solitude to write. But if Aba's murdered body were found, he would be implicated. No. In the romanen, *a villain paid. Here the villain was immune.*

He realized he had stopped crying and immediately began to sob again for his callousness. Already Aba was a fictional character, an abstraction, a scrawl of disappearing ink. Shouldn't he go to the police and tell the whole story? Menter was the police. The cripple's words throbbed in his ears: *No more Catzkers!* He was as helpless as the little boy who watched his father drown.

Poland! He had his villain. Aba had told his friends that an official investigation of his immigrant status had resulted in permission for him to apply for permanent residence in the U.S. Only Catzker and Menter knew the truth. The explanation of Aba's disappearance would be custom-tailored to the audience:

The anti-Semitic Poles had reopened the case, claiming Aba was an escaped murderer—in fact, had murdered his own mother. The United States Government, shown trumped-up documentation agreed to deport Aba. The plot was carried out by anti-Semites on both sides. Last night a U.S. Immigration agent and an FBI man had arrested Aba and whisked him away to a Polish ship that sailed two hours later. They had allowed Aba one phone call, like a common criminal.

Now, if the body were discovered, he could swear to Aba's last words. It was Polish rough justice. A ruse to kill a Jew.

Concentrated on rehearsing the story, he did not hear Harry enter the room.

"Someone is sleeping in my bed," Harry chirped in child's voice.

"Heshele," he said, rising "come take a walk with me."

"Where?"

"Just a walk. We will see."

As they walked up Neptune Avenue, Catzker held his son's hand and occasionally squeezed it. Harry saw wet and pain on his father's face. He knew not to talk. His father was elsewhere.

They stopped in front of the Beth Emunah synagogue.

"Heshele," Catzker said, "it is the anniversary of my father's death. I wish to say Kaddish. Come in with me."

A bearded man wearing a black wool suit despite the heat ran up to them. He spoke in Yiddish:

"Blessed are the arrivals. Now we have ten for a minyan."

"I wish to say the Kaddish," Catzker said.

"Exactly, the rest are Kaddish sayers. Now we have the requisite ten."

It was a false minyan. Harry had never been Bar Mitzvah, the prerequisite for being counted in a minyan. His father had made it clear that he was being sent to Hebrew school to learn the tradition and culture of his people. God need not be worshipped. When Harry approached thirteen, he was given a choice as to whether to have a Bar Mitvah. He had refused, thankful to escape the terror of reciting before an audience.

Eight men stood in a semicircle, rocking toward each other. The man in the black suit handed Catzker and Harry yarmulkes and draped them in prayer shawls. All began to recite the Kaddish.

"Yiskadall ve yis kaddash schmay rabbah . . ."

Catzker's words broke through sobs. He rocked and pounded a closed fist into the left side of his chest. It seemed to Harry that he was trying to hurt himself.

"Heshele," his father croaked, "say the Kaddish."

"But you are alive."

"Say it for your grandfather. My father. He loved you."

"But he died before I was born."

"He loved you. Say it!"

Harry began. His father's arms encircled his neck, pulling Harry's cheek against his. His father let out a fearful wail. His head fell on Harry's shoulder. They rocked, praising God.

32

HARRY SAT AT THE KITCHEN TABLE SWIGGING MILK FROM THE BOTTLE, enjoying the smooth, thick glass rim on his lips heralding the rush of cold milk. Closer to the cow.

It was Saturday. His father and mother had not yet awakened. It was a time when Aba, having spent another sleepless hot August night wrestling with a poem, would have charged out of his room and announced a call to the cherry tree.

What would he have asked Harry today? That was easy. *What do think, American boy, about the treaty between Russia and Germany not to fight each other?*

Harry climbed into the cherry tree to talk to Aba. Harry missed him so much that yesterday he had seen a mirage: Aba on the front steps turning his pockets inside out in search of his key.

A few days ago his father had said that Harry must learn to live with the probability that Aba might never return. Even if the Polish authorities released him, which was unlikely, he would be trapped in the European war that was not far off. What chance did a Jew have in a war in which all participants were anti-Semites? Those were the first mean words Harry had ever heard from his father. Hope meant something. The other person could feel it. Harry would continue sitting with Aba in the cherry tree.

Aba grabbed a handful of cherries, stuffed them into his mouth and spit out the pits.

"*Nu*, American boy, who will the Russians and Nazis fight now that they cannot fight each other?"

"The Poles?"

"It should only be that wonderful. But first they will kill the Jews, who are always good for a snack before the main dish."

"Why is it, Aba, that people who have no feelings always get their way? Sometimes I think I have no feelings. Does that make me a Nazi? Or is it better not to have feelings? Does it make me stronger not to cry? I think I must stop crying right now."

It was not working. Aba had no answers. Besides, he now thought of Bama, trapped, prey for Hitler. He needed to dive into the ocean. Bucking the waves, going under, simulating drowning, flailing his arms while the salt stung his eyes and cuts, cleared his mind of everything but the tip of danger.

He walked onto the beach and was about to begin the run into the waves when his name was called. On the boardwalk, Soldier waved his arms frantically, as if performing semaphore.

"What's up, Soldier?," he said, looking up at Soldier's legs and noting but one sock.

"Damn, I got a message for you, from Fifi, Harry. She wants to see you."

"What about?"

"Damn, I don't know."

"OK, Soldier, I'll swim awhile and then go see her."

"Damn, go now."

"What's the rush?"

"Damn, I don't know. But I got a feeling. It's not like when Woody says: *Make it snappy*. She needs to see you. I just know."

"OK, Soldier."

He wriggled into his white polo shirt and carried his pants and sneakers. Soldier met him at the ramp.

"You coming with me, Soldier?"

"Damn, no, but I'll walk a ways with you, if you don't mind."

"You know I don't mind."

It was nine o'clock. The boardwalk below the amusement area was a winter anachronism of old men and women tilting faces and silver sun reflectors toward the guarantor of life. Beyond them, a few early arrivals for a day at Coney chewed on hot dogs and gulped soda pop. A cooling sea breeze reminded Harry of the dwindling days of summer. Soon he would be dismissed by Morey and incarcerated behind a school desk. Aba spoke to him: *Heshele, always begin, even if it is an ending*.

Soldier, whose head usually swiveled like a frightened bird as he spluttered to drown out the noises in his brain, was silent. He walked stiff-legged, knees locked, his eyes vacant, unblinking. Harry thought he must be back in the war. Not a good idea.

"Soldier," he said, tapping him on the shoulder, "soon we'll have Coney all to ourselves. I'll bet you'll like that."

Soldier mumbled: "Damn, fire."

Harry laughed. Soldier knew the routine: end of season, then fires.

"Yeah, Soldier. That's the way it always is."

"Damn, people will be killed."

"Nah, Soldier. Nobody ever dies."

"Damn, this time . . ."

His voice tailed off. He stopped abruptly.

"Damn, got to go now, Harry. Don't forget Fifi."

Before Harry could say good-bye, Soldier had turned and stumbled away. He was getting worse. He would ask Fifi about a doctor for him.

"Sank you for coming," Fifi said, as he kissed her cheeks.

"I always like to see you."

"You are nice *gosse*, 'Arry."

"You are a nice Fifi, Fifi. Did you want to give *un leçon* in French?"

"Une *leçon!* No, not today."

She smiled, then sighed.

"'Arry, I lose much pounds."

Her fat affliction was passing. He wanted to congratulate her, but her expression did not invite happiness. Perhaps she was worried about losing her job.

"I go doctor 'Arry. He say I lose twenty pound of weight. Next time more pounds. Like *contraire* when I *petite*. Inside, I hurt. Zen he tell me I have ze cancer. Zat inside me ze cancer eat everyzing. Soon it eat what I need to live. Zen I *morte*."

Harry had been thinking: How could anyone tell she had lost weight? There was a special freight scale with a square platform at the sideshow on which Fifi sat, registering her five hundred and thirty pounds for all to see, but surely no doctor had such a device.

"Oh, Fifi," he said, looking down at her bare feet and red-coated toenails.

"Be not sad, *gosse*, I like my life. I see much. Know much. And who say doctor have right. Doctors make much *faux, non?*"

"Yes! Fifi, yes!"

"*Certainment*. But 'Arry, I have what you call a longing. Is correct? Somezing I want much to do."

"What is it, Fifi?

"'Arry, is to see ze *magnifique* French ship, ze *Normandie*."

Harry knew the *Normandie*. Its gallant Captain Thoreux was an exemplary loser. Harry had been tempted to allow him to win one race in gratitude for his besting the German record time for crossing the Atlantic. But in the end, he knew that Thoreux, who had won the *Blue Ribband* on the ship's maiden voyage, would understand Harry's maintaining a perfect record of victories.

"Sure, Fifi," he said, "I'll watch the ocean and when I see it coming in or going out, I'll run to get you and we'll watch it from the boardwalk."

"*Non, mon cher,* I want to be close to it. I want to smell it . . . smell *La France*."

"But how?"

"I have read it yesterday arrive in New York. It carry many Americans running from scare of *guerre*. Is now in ze dock. Will you go wiz me to see it? I must be wiz someone when I go from Coney Island."

"Sure, Fifi. I would enjoy that too."

"*Bon*."

She did not move. She scratched her head and hunched her shoulders.

"What's wrong, Fifi? Did you change your mind?"

She pointed to a pair of black patent leather pumps on the floor beside the couch.

"I cannot put on ze shoes myself. Zere is no one in ze house. I cannot ask of you to do such."

He grabbed the shoes and knelt.

"For Queen Fifi, anything."

She rose by executing a series of forward and fall-back thrusts, building momentum which finally pitched her upright. She took his hand.

Gasping and resting frequently, she climbed the flights of stairs at the Stillwell Avenue terminus. She could not fit through the turnstile. The man in the change booth knew her. He told Harry to hold open the exit gate. He did not ask for money.

Their side of the platform was empty. Across the tracks incoming crowds shoved their way to the exits, clearing paths by swinging bags and folding chairs. Some spotted Fifi, pointed, laughed and slapped their cheeks in exaggerated amazement. Harry wished them painful sunburns.

They were alone in the subway car. Fifi sat on a long seat meant for three. The jostling put her flesh in motion. Her dress jumped and jerked as if receiving electric shocks.

At the 55th Street stop in Borough Park, a few Hasidic Jews boarded and sat at the opposite end of the car. They spoke loudly in Yiddish, confident Fifi did not understand their derision. *May my father give you sleepless nights,* Harry thought in Yiddish.

The subway plunged underground into the land of perpetual night. The naked bulbs created dusk. Overhead fans circulated hot, stifling air. Fifi, silent, was a hillock at twilight.

Round wet spots began to spread on her dress. She dipped a handkerchief into a bottle in her handbag and dabbed her cheeks. The strong perfume made Harry sneeze.

"God bless you, 'Arry. You catch ze cold?"

"No. Just a sneeze."

"Alors, *joost* a sneeze. *Joost* zis and *joost* zat."

"What do you mean, Fifi?"

"It is good to be *joost*. Nozing is so serious. In America zere is much *joost*, I like zat. In France much is *grave*. But maybe in America zere is too little *grave*."

The *Normandie* was docked at the foot of West 46th Street. They left the subway at Times Square and walked west on 42nd Street. The movie houses lining both sides of the street were doing a lethargic business, not being air-climatized. The action or horror double features were unlikely companions for the marquee names from another era: *Eltinge, Wallack, Sam H. Harris* and finally *New Amsterdam,* which, like a drowning person experiencing flashes of his past, displayed in the lobby photographs of the *Ziegfeld Follies.*

They crossed under the West Side Highway. At river's edge, the empty dock slips resembled a jigsaw puzzle of varying oblong shapes. He sniffed the water. It was different from Coney: no salt and seaweed. A sharper, irritating odor, like the back of a garbage truck.

Four blocks to his right, he glimpsed out of the corner of his eye the *Normandie*. It was a dead end, blocking everything beyond.

He knew the *Normandie*'s dimensions, as he did of all his adversaries: 1,029 feet long, 80,000 tons, eleven decks, three soaring funnels that receded in height like graceful fingers. However, even the enormity of those statistics had not prepared him for that which loomed. He beheld a place, a part of the world to be inscribed on a map: the black hull, dotted like Swiss cheese by gold-rimmed portholes; shinning white decks; black funnels that gave way to a red crest; the red, white and blue French flags fore and aft, falling and stiffening in a capricious breeze; and, at the water line, the top of the red keel. He was stunned, as if suddenly coming upon the lost continent of Atlantis.

Fifi tugged at his hand and quickened her pace to a speed of which Harry had not thought her capable. Her breath exploded like gas released by shaking a warm soda pop bottle. They reached the ship's bow. Sailors clad in white uniforms and white berets pinned with blue ribbon and crowned with red pom-poms waved from the decks to Fifi, who saluted while shouting an avalanche of French.

"You see, 'Arry, how *magnifique*! I come see her in nineteen and thirty-five, her first time arrived. Zere are zousands people here. Little boats make fountains in air. One little boat pull a big balloon of Mickey Mouse. *Oo la la*, is *drôle*. From *Le Normandie* zey play *Le Marsellaise*. I sing. Many more too."

She began to sing *Le Marsellaise*. Her voice was delicate, wavering. Like that of the little girl in the photo, Harry thought. The sailors joined in. Strollers stopped, cheered and applauded. Fifi bowed, tipping only slightly forward.

The trip back to Coney was catastrophic. The subway, filled with food- and beach-chair–laden families, was a rush hour with marauding children. Fifi had to stand. Her whitened knuckles gripped a stanchion. Her odor, wafted by the fans, circulated through the car. Those crushed against her pointedly held their noses. At stops and starts she lurched, sending a wave of bodies grabbing for equilibrium. When the train pulled into Stillwell, the passengers stampeded. Those nearest her stepped on her shoes, kicked her shins and dug fists into her flesh.

On the platform she walked behind him, resting her hands on his shoulders to steady her collapsing legs. It was like his often-dreamt nightmare of needing to run from danger but managing only tiny steps.

Luckily, when they arrived at her house Otto was leaving. He half-carried her up the steps, sat her on the couch, gave her a glass of wine and then informed them that he must rush to a secret mission for the German American Bund.

"Otto is crazy but no mean," Fifi said, "but sometime crazy make mean."

Her breathing was back to normal but her dress was soaked. Harry refilled her glass. She gulped down the wine.

"'Arry, will you make for me ze promise?"

"What, Fifi?"

"No, 'Arry, I want you say *oui* before I ask."

"*Oui.*"

She formed a delicate kiss.

"'Arry, you come my funeral."

"Oh, Fifi . . ."

"'Arry, I must know zat you come. Zat it will not be only ze freaks and ze people to look how big is my coffin. I wish a friend, a *copain.*"

"Fifi, you said yourself, doctors make mistakes."

"Not zis time. I feel it, like ze worm zat does not stop eating."

"Nah, Fifi."

"*Mais oui.* I must know zere is plain person zere, who, who, I love, and who, who . . ."

"I love you, Fifi."

She cried. Her body shook. She raised her right hand, motioning for Harry to leave. He remained seated. Between sobs, she managed a strangled word:

"Please."

Walking aimlessly, he suddenly thought of his shock and sadness when, as an infant, he had realized that his mother would not always be with him. But now, for the first time, he also remembered the rage at abandonment. Aba, and now Fifi, were abandoning him. For a moment that ancient hate attached to them. He shook his head, wondering at his inhumanity.

He yearned to plunge into the mind-cleansing Atlantic, but he was late for work. Surprisingly, Morey did not reprimand him.

"Gee, kid, I'm glad you made it. I thought you was sick or something, like me."

"What's wrong?"

"Got the aches and the trots. I don't know if I can last."

"So, we'll close?"

"Never close in season," Morey said gravely. "Once you close in season they think of you different. Like you lied to them."

"Oh."

"If I can't make it, you can handle it alone, kid. You're good. Best I ever had."

Hoo hah, Aba said, but it did not lift his sadness.

CHAPTER
33

AT SEVEN THE NEXT MORNING, VELIA CATZKER LAY ALONE IN HER BED daring the nausea to turn her stomach. Throwing up would be an admission of pregnancy. She was not. She was ill. Her swelling belly was a trick of her mother's evil eye. She saw her mother's cynical expression, her head nodding in knowing disgust:

"Again, like a whore. And this time a *momzer.*"

She lifted a pillow above her head and plunged it against her face. That's how mothers kill infants, she thought. It's not painful. You must know about death to be afraid of it. To a baby, it's just going to sleep.

She threw the pillow to the floor and held close to her face a long-stemmed, silver-leaf oval mirror in which she saw the lie of pregnancy: worn gray skin, dead eyes She pulled at her hair. A few strands came out. She held them up to the mirror. Her face was captured in a spider's web.

The misery that is my life, she told the mirror, *is too calculated to be haphazard. This face was meant to be worshipped by wealthy, gallant men. But instead . . .*

The nausea passed. The lie exposed, she could think about what she would think if she were pregnant. An abortion, of course. Fat chance. Moishe would want the child, even if he realized it wasn't his. The father was unapproachable. Protected by a gangster. Aba, the only one who could help, had disappeared into Poland.

From her son's room screeching trumpets and God knows

what other noise pierced her door. Another calculated misery: She, who loved Mozart and Bach, delivered of an admirer of noise.

A minuet played in her head. She wore a sequined white gown. Her tightly pulled bodice boldly lifted her breasts. She glided beneath gaslit chandeliers, held lightly by a smitten prince of . . . of . . . of . . . Countries competed—Austria, Poland, Czechoslovakia, France. She must be careful in her choice. Visions affected life.

She wished to be appreciated as a statue. To be admired and judged as a creation unto itself, unmodified by partnerships or appendages. She snorted, remembering the horror Mane Rosen had sculpted. He called her voluptuous. A fancy word for fat. She had tried unsuccessfully to smash it. Any day now, the sculpture of her as an obese creature would appear in some gallery. She would say that when she sat for it, she had been pregnant with Harry

The front door opened violently. Catzker came barreling through. His face was the color of dough. Ignoring Freud, he raced into the bedroom, where his wife feigned sleep. He shook her. She swatted away his hand, and turned her back to him.

"Velia, please wake up, I must talk to you," he said, smoothing her hair.

"Later," she mumbled into the pillow.

"Velia, the car. I must speak . . ."

"Well," she said, turning toward him, "did you finally kill someone?"

"No. Thank God, no. But what an experience! I don't know if I will ever drive again."

"Good."

He sat beside her.

"Please listen," he said.

She nodded, closing her eyes to indicate anticipated boredom.

"It rained hard this morning. There were many deep puddles. Of course I drove through them. What can a puddle do to something as powerful as a car? Well, after I went through a particularly deep one, I pressed the brake to stop at a corner. The pedal went down and down. It hit the floor. The car did not slow. Luckily, there were no cars or people at the intersection. Finally, when the street began to slant upward, the car stopped. I got out and found a gas station and asked for repairs. The mechanic said I didn't need any. He explained that when a car goes through a deep puddle sometimes the brakes get wet and do not work. He told me to go back and keep pumping the brake peddle to dry out the brakes. Eventually I would feel the peddle rise and I would have working brakes again. He was right. But I cannot forget how I pressed harder and harder and the car just glided along as if it had free will! I was behind the wheel of an uncontrollable car, made so by an inconsequential puddle. Velia, it was like one of those slow-motion nightmares that do not end until you wake with a scream and a pounding heart. I could *hear* my heart!"

"Maybe if you hit someone, you would stop this foolishness."

"Velia, don't you see how shaken I am?"

"Yes, yes. So terrible. One moment of an uncontrollable car. My whole life is an uncontrollable car."

"Velia, this is not human. What is becoming of us?"

She flared her nostrils.

"Not becoming. We have become."

"What?"

"Little people. Tiny people, who are stepped on as a matter of habit. Sentenced to a life of misery."

"Why do you exaggerate? We have to eat. We have a fine son. We have each—"

"Other," she cut him off. "What does that mean? I'm sure I don't know."

"It means love."

"Love! Then love is a slum. Love is more than two hours a day on a stinking, crowded subway. Love is to try and blind myself to tomorrow, to the rest of my life."

"Don't you feel my love for you? Heshele's?"

"You sound like one of your miserable *romanen*. I'll tell you what love is. The love of a king who would give up his throne for me. That is the kind of love due me."

He swallowed hard. During the past five months he had increasingly feared for her mental state. She always had courted fantasy, but ever since her transfer out of Barbetta's office—the affair with Barbetta had obviously soured—the border between dreams and reality had been crumbling.

She boasted of many identities even to people who knew her background. People who had known her parents! She had been born in St. Petersburg to the Romanovs, into the Prague branch of the Hapsburgs, in Warsaw to the Chopins, Each lineage spawned its own story, but with common threads: heiress to glory and splendor; adulation of her beauty which led to many brokenhearted suicides; then a cruel twist of fate (usually a peasant uprising) that forced her to run for her life and be thrown up on the shores of poverty and vulgarity in Coney Island.

Catzker could not imagine that she expected to be believed. Eventually he came to a more frightening conclusion: at any given time she believed the persona presented.

She was a fanatic moviegoer and excellent mimic. Even alone with him, she began to present a parade of royalty: Marlene Dietrich as *The Scarlet Empress*, Norma Shearer as *Marie Antoinette*, Claudette Colbert as *Cleopatra,* Greta Garbo as *Queen Christina.*

Three weeks ago, he had come home to find her blind drunk, admiring herself in a mirror. Although it was a mild summer night, she wore her Winter Palace costume: a black seal coat and matching fur hat. Tips of blond hair peeked out from beneath the hat, forming a semihalo on her forehead.

"Hello your majesty," she had said, rotating her head to show him her profile, which many had told her was indistinguishable from that of Renée Falconetti in *The Passion of Joan of Arc.*

He had said nothing.

"Why so quiet, little tsar?" she said, removing her hat and shaking her hair like a wet dog. "Let us have some of that, how you say, champagne, with the tiny bubbles in it."

He recognized Garbo in *Ninotchka*. Velia also claimed the Romanov crown jewels.

She dropped her coat at her feet, like a stripper beginning her act, revealing a contour-hugging black ankle-length dress. A string of white pearls encircled her breasts like a geographic marker. She gyrated toward him. Jean Harlow.

She had stopped just short of him, squinting, puzzling his identity, then twisted her face in haughty disgust.

"You are not my tsar. You are a peasant. I will have you shot," she had slurred, before passing out at his feet.

Catzker reached across the bed to take her hand. She pulled it away.

"Velia, it is good to dream, but . . ."

She cut him off.

"Sure, I talk nonsense. I'm just a stupid woman. You and your genius cronies, you know everything. *We must do this . . . and we must do that*. Everything but we must work, make money and live like human beings."

"Velia, you are in one of your moods. It will pass."

Nausea rose from her stomach and stank in her mouth.

"Not just a mood. Permanent. You want to know what will become of us? Soon there will be no more *us*. There will be you, who will remain as you are for the rest of your life. And there will be me, finally me, the me that was meant to be. Someone will save me."

"Velia, don't talk like a crazy woman."

"And why shouldn't I talk like a crazy woman? Would a sane woman live like this! When I ran from you thirteen years ago, I was sane. No, still crazy because I took him"—she pointed to Harry's room—"with me. What has happened during those years? Exactly nothing. We walk arm in arm. People say: *What a beautiful couple*. Beyond that there is nothing. The beautiful couple disgusts each other. At least one half does. I should have left the two of you to stink up rooms with your feet together."

He sighed.

"Velia, we must get away. Refresh ourselves."

"Sure. *We must* again. We have enough money to ride the subway. It doesn't go to Tahiti."

"Listen, in Pennsylvania is a Baron de Hirsch farm, where boys are trained to become farmers in Palestine. The paper wants me to write an article on it. The three of us could go. It would cost nothing. We could spend a weekend walking in the country, refreshing ourselves, getting back to what we were. Heshele said he would like to try farming."

"Another wonderful idea: Jewish farmers to plow up a Jewish homeland. This is what Baron de Hirsch wastes his money on? The only thing Jews can grow are beards. Do you want to make that"— again she pointed toward Harry's room—"a Jewish farmer? Why not a blind aviator?"

"I just thought some good country air . . ."

The nausea overtook her. She ran to the bathroom and threw up. He followed her, asking if she were ill. The idiot, she thought. I have no privacy even in sickness. Perhaps he would like to watch me shit.

"Get out of here," she screamed. "Become a farmer!"

34

THAT AFTERNOON, MENTER AND WOODY WERE PLAYING *RUMMY YUMMY*, the card game Menter had invented especially for the two of them. The cards lay on the back of a nude whore from Rosie's, crouched on her hands and knees between them. Her mouth was buried in Menter's crotch. Woody held her thighs and pumped lightly inside her.

Menter took a card from the top of the deck, set it among the seven cards fanned out in his hand and discarded one, face up. He cautioned the dwarf:

"You're rockin' the boat, Woody, gettin' too excited. Maybe we ought to switch."

Woody stopped moving and shut his eyes.

"Never fails. All I gotta do is think of Fifi nude and I calm down."

"Let's switch anyway," Menter said. "I'd like some target practice."

He tapped the woman.

"Gert, about-face!"

The whore, a woman of forty with stretch marks of mother-hood on her flat stomach, rotated slowly so as not to upset the cards. She butted Woody's hard penis upward and, on its descent, caught it in her mouth like a dog trained to flip a bone resting on its snout.

"Bravo, Gert!" Menter shouted.

Encircling his penis in a loose fist, he moved his chair left and right, as if it were the hinged air gun of an arcade target game.

"Gotta watch the aim. Don't want the wrong hole—or maybe I do."

He rolled himself forward slowly.

"Perfect bull's-eye. Give the man a Kewpie doll."

Woody drew a card and discarded. The familiar pain of a stymied orgasm knotted his stomach. However, he was not allowed to come before Menter.

Woody was sure that Menter faked a screaming climax because he had no feeling down there. But if Menter saw him reaching the edge of orgasm before the howl, he would crash the whore to the floor, and order her back to Rosie's, leaving him with aching balls,

The phone rang.

"Get it Woody," Menter said.

The dwarf took tiny steps so as not to agitate his pain.

"Hello . . . Vic, it's a guy named Frank Bruno."

"Now, Gert," Menter said, "just stay like that. Maybe put a few fingers up and rub a little to stay warm. That's a good girl."

He took the phone from Woody, who began to walk toward Gert.

"Stop right there. Gert don't like it without me. Ain't that right, Gert?"

The whore lifted her chin and nodded.

"Hello Frank," Menter said.

Menter closed his eyes and listened, interjecting only a few yeses or grunts, while his finger traced the holes in the speaker like a man reading Braille. Woody tiptoed back to Gert. He pumped furiously.

"Bingo!" Menter shouted, throwing his arms over his head and clasping his palms together like a victorious prize fighter. He looked at Woody and shook his head:

"Scram, Gert!"

Woody clutched her buttocks. The whore jumped to her feet. The cards floated down. One fell on Woody's penis and stuck. She grabbed her clothes and dressed while stumbling toward the door. Menter owned Rosie's. He punished with a weighted cane and lighted cigarettes.

Woody helped Menter dress. He felt as though he had been

kneed in the testicles. He walked toward the bathroom.

"Gonna play five against one," Menter said. "Kid stuff. But, what the hell, on a day like this, go ahead. But don't take all day."

"You dwarfs are plenty horny." Menter said, as Woody walked back into the living room. "I guess it's because your bodies are too small to hold it in. Normal people like me, we've got staying power. That's what it takes to be a man."

Woody nodded. Menter reminded him of Molly, *the singin' whore,* who always put on a show for her customers by screaming that no one did it to her that good before and she loved it so much that if it wasn't for Rosie she wouldn't take any money. If you shoved a cannon up Molly, she wouldn't feel it. He had caught Menter staring jealousy at his ample cock.

Menter lit a cigarette, giving Woody his Roosevelt profile.

"You know why FDR's a great man?"

"'Cause he's president."

Menter slapped his forehead.

"No. But he got to be president because he knows how to get the most out of everything he does."

"Oh."

"And now it's my turn."

Is he going to tell me that he's going to be president, Woody thought? Sure he'll be president, right after he gets a hard on.

"To do what?" Woody said.

"To mix business with pleasure."

Menter wheeled himself around the room, shouting: "Oh, boy, oh, boy!" He stopped at the telephone, lifted the receiver and said:

"Right in there. A gift from heaven. Thank you, Frankie."

Woody wished Menter would get over whatever it was that was making him crazy. Jerking off had only increased his need for the real thing. He needed a woman. He needed Rosie's.

"Woody," Menter said, "I'm goin' to make a lot of dough from this fire. That was always true. But now I also get to rid the world of disgusting freaks and a kike."

"What? I don't understand."

"The fire-setters. The freaks, Soldier, that kike writer. They all die. My friend Adolf would be proud of me."

Menter took a long drag on his cigarette and, without inhaling, let the smoke escape his mouth. A translucent cloud covered his face, then curled its way through his hair. The top of his head seemed to be smoldering.

He's crazy, Woody thought. I'm tied to a crazy man. So what's new? Crazy men always called the tune, especially for dwarfs. What was sane? His dumb brother in Hollywood making that all-midget Western, *The Terror of Tiny Town*?

"How you gonna kill all those people?"

"I ain't gonna kill 'em. They're gonna' kill themselves."

"Huh?"

"Oh, yeah. We're goin' to make them a suicide cocktail: kerosene, gasoline, naphtha, acetone, and shake well. *In the hands of an experienced torch*, Frankie told me, *it's surefire*." He laughed at his cleverness. "A good torch knows the mixture gives off vapors that explode like a bomb. So he soaks a long rope or leaves a paper trail that slowly crawls to the doused spots. And when it goes boom he's walkin' the street. But amateurs, they just sprinkle it around and then throw a match, thinking they got time to get out before everything goes up. They think that because *you, Woody,* tell 'em that's the way it is. But the real way it is"— he clapped his hands together loudly—"is when it goes boom, they go boom and the world is rid of a shitload of freaks and worse."

He means it, Woody thought. He wants to kill six, seven people just like that. I got no feelin' for nobody, but I ain't no murderer.

Menter raised his left palm in front of his face and spat on it.

"I'm readin' my fortune," he said. "It says there are happy days in store for me. But one thing is wrong: there's a gutless dwarf who could fuck me up because he's scared shitless."

He spit again.

"My fortune says to get rid of him. To put him in the ground and it will be smooth sailing. Whaddya think about my fortune, Woody?"

Maybe I could skip town, Woody thought. Sure, I'm tough to find. Blend in with everybody. Christ, if I could only get to Rosie's and clear my head.

"It must be some other dwarf your fortune is talkin' about. This one is with you one hundred percent."

"That's good, Woody. Make sure you don't go talkin' to that other dwarf. He's bad news."

"Sure."

"Now, here's what you do. You buy as many one-gallon gas containers as we need. Bring 'em here. Frankie will fill 'em just right. Then you get the word out that the fire setters should come to your bike shop to pick them up. We already told 'em to just sprinkle it all around and throw a match. You tell 'em that we got the best stuff. That it'll take five minutes before the fire really gets going, because that's how the stuff in the containers is mixed. They got plenty of time to get out before it starts. Got it?"

"Yeah, I got it."

"And just to make sure you say it right, Vince is going to hang out with you for a while, listen to your instructions."

Woody nodded.

"Good boy, Woody. You're a lucky dwarf. I'm king of Coney, and you're right there with me. We'll shovel shit down everybody's mouth."

"Great!" Woody said.

Menter crooked his index finger.

"Now come here and give me some luck."

Woody lowered his head over Menter's lap. Manicured nails burrowed under his hair. His scalp felt filthy.

"I hope you don't have any cooties," Menter said.

Woody let his head fall a bit more, enjoying the odor that lingered on Menter's crotch: the smell of where he would soon be, and where Menter was useless.

CHAPTER
35

HARRY AND HIS MOTHER WALKED TO THE NORTON'S POINT TROLLEY stop. He was still unconvinced that they would board the trolley as the first leg of a two-hour journey to Yankee Stadium to see the Yankees play the Detroit Tigers.

Five years ago she had promised to take him to a baseball game. However, all subsequent requests were ignored. Eventually, he had stopped asking. Then, yesterday, she had stunned him by asking:

"Can we go to a baseball game tomorrow?"

"But it's a Wednesday, you work," he had reminded her.

"I'll take the day off. I'll call in sick. It's a long time since I played hooky."

The surprising answer was further evidence of a change that recently had come over her, altering previous dogma. She no longer chastised him for leaving his clothes scattered on the floor. In fact, did not even notice a stray garment. She had stopped screwing up a sour face to express disgust with him when he cracked his knuckles or drank milk directly from the bottle.

On several occasions he had looked up from reading to find her staring at him as if he were a stranger, a curiosity. It had been weeks since she had yelled at him for playing his records too loud and once she had come into his room, listened and asked:

"What is that? And what do you find wonderful about it?"

"It's Benny Goodman and his band playing *Sing, Sing, Sing,*" he had answered, "and it makes me feel like I can do anything I want to, that anything is possible."

"That's a good feeling," she had said, "I'm happy for you."

Now, missing work. Unheard of a month ago!

He would have preferred Ebbets Field and the Dodgers, but they were playing on the road, and he was not about to risk a postponement. But the loss of his beloved Bums would be compensated for by the chance to see Detroit's Hank Greenberg, the first great Jewish baseball player.

"You will explain the game to me during our trip there," she had said. "Tickets must cost a lot and I want to get my money's worth."

Seated next to his mother on the trolley, he opened a notebook, drew the diamond and identified the positions.

"You see," he said, "this is the defending team and where they stand. If the batter hits the ball in the air and they catch it before it hits the ground, he is out. If he hits the ball on the ground and they throw the ball to the first baseman before the batter reaches first, he is out . . ."

He accompanied his words by sending his index finger in a parabola that culminated at the outfielder catching the fly ball, and jabbing it progressively forward to indicate the ground ball, the batter running, the shortstop throwing the ball to first base.

Her eyes were not on the diagram. They were on him. Her expression was more melancholy than usual. He wondered if she was regretting her impulsive act, especially since the temperature was around ninety degrees.

"Now if the defending team puts out three batters, they become the offense and the opponents the defense. Understand?"

She did not answer. She had not heard. Something in his face seemed to fascinate her, absorb all her attention. Perhaps she was struck by his resemblance to her. He sometimes looked at her and wondered if nature's magic carried with it an obligation of closeness. He closed the notebook.

"Why did you stop, Harry?" she said, still staring at him.

"I didn't think you were listening."

"Oh, but I was. Maybe not to the words, but the voice. You explain like your father. You get caught up, excited."

"Is that good?"

"Only if someone is listening." She laughed and stroked his cheek.

They boarded the express subway to the Bronx. It was twelve-thirty. They were the only passengers in the car.

"This is better than the rush hour I travel in every morning," she said. "Some people don't wash too often. How do you get to school?"

"I ride my bike."

"Of course. What do you do, Harry?"

"What do you mean?"

"All the time I don't see you. What's your life like?"

"Oh, I do homework. Ride my bike on the boardwalk. Eat hot dogs at Nathan's with the money you leave and tell me not to."

She laughed.

"Jokes, like your father."

"Don't you like jokes?"

She didn't answer. She tilted her head back and closed her eyes, as if inviting sleep, then opened them and asked:

"Will you miss me?"

"When? Are you going on a trip?"

"No. I just meant that when I die before you, which is the normal way of things, will you miss me?"

"But I'll be a man by then, probably an old man. I don't know how an old man would feel about that."

"He would probably feel the same as a young boy."

"Well, if he would feel the same as a baby, then the answer is that I would miss you."

He recounted his memory of the realization that she would not always be with him and the infant's wail it had provoked. She nodded her head.

"Do you remember that?" he asked, eagerly. "Do you remember what you did?"

"I can't say that I remember that specific time. But if you cried, I picked you up. That was my way."

"I'm glad."

"You're a funny kid."

"Why?"

"Well, I just saw you turn a painful memory into a happy one. A perfect about-face. I wish I could do that."

The game was scheduled to begin at three-fifteen. They arrived at the stadium at two-fifteen. The crowd was thin. He led her to the bleacher entrance.

"Are these good seats?" she asked.

"They're the cheapest."

"For my first and probably last baseball game, I want better. I want the best!"

They bought tickets for the lower boxes behind first base, which allowed an unobstructed view into the Yankee dugout. An usher led them to the seats and brushed them off with a cloth.

The Tigers were taking batting practice. Hank Greenberg stood behind the batting cage, waiting his turn. He pointed him out to his mother, who looked at him and said:

"He is more Jew than baseball player."

"How do you mean?"

"Oh, he is big and strong, maybe the strongest one there, but those eyes, those sad eyes . . . and that large nose for sniffing danger . . . that's what he is mostly about."

Greenberg stepped into the batter's box and sent tremendous drives into the left-field stands. The crowd *oohed* and *ahed*.

"Is he allowed to do that ? . . . hit the ball where no one can get it," she asked

"He sure can. That's the best you can do. It's a home run."

"He takes no chances, your Mr. Greenberg. He hits the ball beyond any plot that has been hatched against the Jew."

She showed little interest in the rest of the Tigers and the Yankees until one Yankee came running in from the outfield to take batting practice.

"Who is that?" she asked, pointing, her voice suddenly animated by excitement.

"Joe DiMaggio."

"He is a god."

"A god?"

"Yes, Harry. See how he carries himself as if the air dare not resist him. He glides so lightly. I can imagine him standing on water and not sinking."

DiMaggio sprayed a few line drives and a home run.

"He shows so little effort, yet the ball travels as far as when hit by the others who grunt and twist their faces. Oh, he is certainly a god."

DiMaggio left the batting cage and walked to the Yankee dugout. He took off his pin-striped cap and smoothed his hair.

'He is a funny-looking god," his mother said. "His head has not yet caught up with the rest of him. But it will. It will."

"Have you seen many gods?" Harry asked.

"A few."

"Is Pop a god? Is Aba?"

"No, Harry, They chase God. They try to catch him and open him up so they can see what makes him tick and copy him. It doesn't work."

In the top of the first inning, Greenberg hit a tremendous home run into the left-field pavilion. Two men scored ahead of him. But his mother had eyes only for DiMaggio.

"Your Jew," she said, "played it safe, but the god was not fooled. He never moved. He knew the ball would be out of reach. He'll get even."

She was prophetic. During the game DiMaggio roamed the outfield like a restless spirit, denying fly balls to the left and right fielders as though the entire outfield was his domain. He had ten putouts—one short of the major league record—and at least four remarkable catches that brought the crowd to its feet. After each ovation his mother said:

"See Harry, they recognize a god."

At the seventh-inning stretch, his mother craned her neck to peer into the Yankee dugout. She laughed.

"What's funny." Harry asked.

"The god is hiding and smoking a cigarette. Is it against the law for baseball players to smoke?"

"I don't think so."

"Then he hides his nervousness. He is wrestling with being a god."

On the subway ride home, his mother asked:

"Are you happy, Harry?"

"Not so much these days with Aba and Bama gone and probably in danger."

"Sadness is what I know about. I'm an expert. Did I make you sad?"

"Sometimes."

"Did I ever make you happy?"

"I guess."

"Do you forgive me, Harry?"

"Oh, Mom, for what?"

"For *I guess.*"

When they descended from the Norton's Point trolley and began their walk home, Harry said:

"Thanks for taking me to the game."

She did not answer immediately, but took his hand in hers, squeezed it and then said:

"It was the least I could do."

In the Cherry Tree: August 6, 1939

Aba: *Heshele, what do you think of Albert Einstein?*

Harry: *He looks like my grandfather.*

Aba: *Anything else?*

Harry: *He knows things no one else knows.*

Aba: *What things?*

Harry: *Since he is the only one who knows these things, we cannot know what he knows that we do not know.*

Aba: *Who told you this?*

Harry: *A teacher. Not exactly in those words, but that is what I understood.*

Aba: *Einstein has written a letter to President Roosevelt.*

Harry: *Explaining what he knows?*

Aba: *In a way. He told President Roosevelt that it is possible to construct a bomb out of atoms.*

Harry: *What are atoms?*

Aba: *They are little things that are all around us. They make up the world.*

Harry: *And we can scoop them up and make a bomb?*

Aba: *Perhaps.*

Harry: *President Roosevelt should not believe Einstein.*

Aba: *Why?*

Harry: *If it were so easy, we would explode atoms on the Fourth of July instead of cherry bombs.*

Aba: *President Roosevelt will believe Einstein.*

Harry: *Why?*

Aba: *Because he offers him magic.*
Harry: *I once saw a magician make a woman disappear.*
Aba: *Einstein says he can make the world disappear.*
Harry: *Can he?*
Aba: *Only he knows.*

CHAPTER

36

4:15 AM: WOODY OPENED HIS EYES TO YELLOWING PLASTER DANGLING from the ceiling. He felt limp, as though he had not slept at all, yet wisps of dreams played hide-and-seek around the edges of his mind. Dreams tired him. He was exhausted.

He dressed. In the bike shop, the warm air thickened the smell of grease. He ran his palm along a few bikes. A hammer and perhaps a crowbar had been the tools of repair. Soldier believed in the resurrection of all bikes. He would smile and say: *Got to get them doing like they was meant to.* Then he would pound them into brotherhood with W.C. Fields's bent cue stick.

If the bike did not perform, Soldier was not discouraged. *Fixed things ain't the same as new,* was his anthem. Soldier might have been talking about himself, although Woody doubted that anyone ever had tried to fix *him,* despite the gold medals and red and blue ribbons in his drawer.

Soldier, fully dressed, slept, eyes wide open. Woody puckered his lips under Soldier's nose to confirm a warm tickle of life.

Soldier dribbled nonsense. He heard *nurse* just before Soldier jumped up and ran into a wall.

Woody stood on the bed and pulled the unraveling string attached to the light bulb. Twenty-five watts outlined, as if in an underexposed, grainy photograph, Soldier flattened against a wall.

"Soldier," he said.

Soldier did not turn.

"Damn, is that you, Woody?"

"Yeah."

"Damn, are you a dream?"

"No, Soldier. I'm here."

"Damn, did you touch me?"

"Yeah, I wanted to get you up."

"Damn, no one ever touches me when I sleep. I was sure it was a dream."

Soldier walked to the bed and sat down.

"Damn, is it time to go, Woody?" he asked. His eyes were unfocused.

Can I kill Soldier? Woody had been trying to escape the question in sleep, only to have it unhinge sleep. His first response had been rote: *Why should I give a fuck about anyone? Did any one ever give a fuck about me?* But there had been a nagging coda: *Soldier does.* It exasperated him. He had spoken aloud to himself as if to an idiot: *it's only because he's as crazy as a bedbug, which makes him better off dead.*

It hadn't worked. It was in Soldier's eyes only that he did not see himself reflected as a deformed person. Soldier truly treated him as just another human being, another guy.

But if Soldier did not die in the fire, Menter would have Soldier and him killed to silence them.

"About time to go, Soldier."

"Damn, ever been caught in a big fire, Woody?"

How had he found out? He's smarter than he lets on. Even he's a phony, Woody thought, glad for the excuse to pass a death sentence.

"No, Soldier. Why you askin'?"

"Damn, I was. In France. The hospital I was in burned down. Lucky I could walk. Damn, a lot of guys who couldn't, they died. I carried some out. It was like carryin' a baby. Damn, they was so scared and holdin' on."

"Fuck it!" Woody shouted.

"Damn, I'm sorry you didn't like the story."

Woody drummed his fingers on Soldier's forehead, hearing

the hoofbeats of his staple fantasy of becoming a jockey. Soldier's
flesh was cold and slightly moist, like a dog's nose.

"No, no, Soldier, your story is OK. Now listen to me: you ain't
gonna start no fires. There's been a change in plans."

"Damn, some other day?"

"No, never."

"Damn, we gotta tell everyone else."

"No."

"Damn, how come, Woody?"

"Don't ask questions. I give you an order. That's it."

"Damn, they gonna get hurt?"

"Nobody gets hurt."

"Damn, I smelled what's in the can. It's dangerous."

"You think ya start a fire with soda pop?"

"Damn, OK, Woody, I believe you."

"Now you stay right here," he said, pounding the bed. "You
don't move. Even if you hear fire engines, you don't move. Right
here. Understand?"

"Damn, I understand, Woody."

Soldier stretched out. Back in his own room, Woody opened the
bottom drawer of the dresser and felt under the entwined tangle of
shirts, socks and underwear. He lifted out a .32 caliber pistol, held it
upright by its mother-of-pearl handle, eyeing it suspiciously. The seller,
a house robber who specialized in deserialized guns, had guaranteed its
lethal accuracy to six feet. He had his doubts. However, it did not matter. The gun would be pressed against flesh. He pressured lightly the
gun barrel against his chest and squeezed the trigger. A small click
sounded. There were no bullets in the chambers. Now he had the feel.

4:25 AM: Soldier, prone on the floor, arms fully extended to grasp
an imaginary rifle, wiggled toward the door as he had snaked along
the earth and barbed wire of Château-Thierry. Outside, he crashed
into a public phone booth, dropped a nickel in the slot and dialed.

4:27 AM: Moshe Catzker, walking past the phone to the bathroom, decided to let Heshele sleep.

"Hello," Catzker said.

"Damn, don't—" a voice shouted.

"What?"

The caller had hung up.

My readers are deranged, Catzker thought. My profession is becoming dangerous.

4:27 AM: Woody snatched the phone from Soldier and slammed it into its cradle.

"Who'd you call?" he demanded.

"Damn, I called but didn't talk to nobody."

He held up the nickel with which he had intended to call the freaks' house.

"See."

Woody slapped at the coin and said:

"You're a nut case. Now let's go. And no fuckin' tricks."

"Damn, where we goin'?"

"Back to the store."

"Damn, why?"

"To lock you in your room."

"Damn, ah, Woody."

"For your own good, you nut case."

4:35 AM: Fifi rocked herself backward, pressing against the pillows of the couch, and spoke to the group standing in a semicircle before her.

"'Allo Otto, my *Hercule*, Jo-Jo, *le beau chien*, Olga, *ma petite*, Jamie, such pretty mouzess, *sacre bleu*, Albert-Alberta, *mon frère, ma soeur.*"

Otto looked down at the gallon containers scattered about like chaotic road markers. The strongman punched his chest.

"*Ach*," he said, "is noding ve do. Jews make fire in Coney all de time."

Fifi extended her arms toward Otto, who pulled her upright.

"I walk out wiz you. Today, we all togezer. Zen . . ." She closed her eyes tightly.

She led them into the street and stood, like a one-person

receiving line, kissing each one and waving them on their way. Walking together, brown shopping bags tucked into their sides, they seemed a bizarre group of successful bargain hunters. At the corner they looked back and waved to her. She climbed the steps. The weakness had worsened. She was not sure she could make it.

5:01 AM: Moshe Catzker looked at his watch, rolled off his side of the double bed, rested his flat feet on the floor and slowly stood up. If he rose too rapidly, he would become dizzy and his varicose veins would ache, which they did anyway. He was startled by his wife's bloodless, white face. Layers of cold cream, he remembered. Her labored, noisy breathing had bloomed into steady radio static. Nothing more unfeminine than snoring, he thought. As unfeminine as a long, uninhibited fart. If she knew her nose's indiscretion, she would cut it off.

He gathered up his clothes, which lay in a chronological bottom-to-top undressing pile—shoes, socks, shirt, pants, underwear—and carried them to the kitchen. He removed canary yellow pajamas—a gift from a color-blind reader—and dressed, while eyeing the gas range and wondering if it could ignite the flammable liquid he had hidden behind the books in the living room. It seemed improbable, but impossible was another story. He decided against a glass of tea.

He removed the books, one of which was *Moll Flanders*. He had not read it in years and hardly remembered it. Was that Defoe's fault or his? He would reread it and let Defoe know.

He put the can in a shopping bag and walked into the dawn. He shivered. Soon it will be hot enough, he told himself, as his eyes floated overhead to observe Catzker schlepping. To fight fear, he composed:

On a warm summer's morning in the town of——, an ardent youth, Moishe——, hurried toward a crime. He carried a can of gasoline with which he intended to burn down the pawnshop of Katya——, who had stolen all the poor youth's family heirlooms.

Being a serious, bright student, he had prepared himself with answers in the event of being stopped by the police. His would explain that his car had run out of gas and he was on his way to remedy the situation. On the tip of his tongue were words that would set policemen's minds at ease: clutch, brakes, tires, the esoteric gear shift. How he would account for the presence of an automobile in mid-nineteenth century Russia was a more difficult task. But the Lord would provide for the righteous. Hadn't Father Zossima taught him that?

The reader may well ask how a young man named Moishe became associated with Father Zossima. Yes, he may ask. But the writer feels himself under no obligation to answer.

Why always jokes? His wife's constant lament brought his eyes back to earth.

Because, he answered, *if things are a joke, then I am not.* But things were not a joke. Aba was dead and Heshele was in danger.

So kill me, he thought. *I am not Proust. Am I even Sholem Asch? Probably not. Does that make me worthless? In my own eyes, yes. The world does not agree. That is because it likes jokes. What is the bromide? Deep, deep, down, he's shallow.*

He cut across the Norton's Point trolley barn, thinking. By this afternoon Heshele will be out of danger. Nothing else really matters. So much for morality, ambition and literature. Aba, resurrected, smiling maliciously, jabbed a Yiddish thumb and said: *Moishe, we are failures manqués.*

5:11 AM: The pack had been migratory for almost seven months. After Bear had been killed there had been a series of battles to determine the new leader. Victors fought victors while losers healed their wounds. Only the Weasel King, nursing his bullet-torn leg, did not participate. Three days into the fighting, WK, limping slightly, rushed at two snapping gladiators, gripped each in turn by the neck and threw him aside. The new leader had emerged.

WK had led the pack away from the summer dangers of Coney on a trek along lonely areas abutting the Belt Parkway. They ate garbage, rats, mice, cats and an occasional squirrel. Humans stood respectfully rigid as the dogs loped past them.

Now, heading back to Coney, the pack was racing across a dirt-caked, litter-covered field. Lindy, his three legs often leaving the ground to keep pace, skidded to a stop to dig at earth of a deeper color and clean of debris, like a disinfected wound. He unearthed a fleshless skull. Disappointed, he butted it away with his snout. It rolled, coming to rest on the jawbone. The sunrise turned it into a jack-o'-lantern.

5:20 AM: Joe Baker dreamed a bridge, attached on only one side to land, the other endless, disappearing. In that void was sleep. He blinked his eyes, crossing into wakefulness.

He had no home. He slept in disabled trolleys in the Norton's Point repair barn. A trolley just taken out of service usually had coins wedged into the seats, in dust-filled corners, or even under the coin machine. With these finds and the money people gave him for gargling numbers, he maintained his diet of Devil Dog cakes, Baby Ruth candy bars and chocolate milk. His only other need, a whore at Rosie's, was supplied by Menter for doing whatever Menter ordered in front of a lot of people.

He had been making friends with numbers ever since he could remember. Words stuck in his throat, fought with each other and broke into sharp pieces that cut off his breath. When the ladies at the orphanage had asked him to say words, he could not.

Numbers were like sweet, squashed Devil Dogs. But when he would tell the ladies *numbers* they would just stare at him. Once, a lady whose face looked as if it had been pinched by a giant clothes-pin, had said: *I understand, it is a revelation,* and then read to him from a book she said was *Numbers*. He had spit on the lying book.

He sat in the conductor's seat and steered the trolley. Suddenly a man carrying a brown bag appeared and walked through the barn. His lips were moving. One, Joe thought. He was the *one* person of the day, bringer of another *one* day.

5:25 AM: Lohu and Mohu sat on the shoulders of two tall Manchurian sailors, swinging their legs freely, playfully kicking the sailors' chests. They looked down at the Pacific Ocean. Behind, no longer visible, sat San Francisco. Lohu pointed to the horizon.

"There," he said, "is Japan."

Mohu thrust his thumb over his right shoulder, saying:

"And there is Coney Island."

The twins were the only passengers on the freighter *Namura*, bound for Yokohama with a cargo of scrap metal. Determined to escape setting the fire, the twins had told Haya Takamura, their friend at the Japanese consulate, that they must leave America. At first Haya had been angry, reminding them of unfinished work. However, when they had explained the possibility of arrest, he had relented.

Lohu inhaled deeply.

"It is a very great pleasure to remove the stink of the white man from one's nostrils."

"We should be given a medal for spending so long among them," Mohu said.

"I am sure we will get a medal. We have done as we were told. That is rewarded."

Haya had praised their photographs, taken on their many carnival tours, of potential targets which would be of great help if, as the rulers of Japan suspected, the United States attacked Japan.

The twins laughed and struck their palms against the sailors' shoulders like jockeys rating a horse. In apparent response the sailors moved forward until their stomachs pressed against the guardrail. The twins giggled. They seemed to be flying over the ocean.

The sailors bent over the rail, put a large hand on each of the twins' buttocks and flipped them forward. They fell shrieking into the ship's heavy swell, disappearing quickly, as if under a magician's cloak.

5:30 AM: Commissioner of Parks Robert Moses opened his eyes to the color splash of the russet drapes in his Gracie Terrace apartment, cursing the restlessness that had denied peaceful sleep. He sat up and looked at his wife, Mary, asleep in her bed. How old she has gotten. How coarse. She could be one of those hatchet-faced reformers or social workers who complained that his parks were not sited in Negro neighborhoods or where poor whites lived. Neglect, they said. Neglect, hell! What would filthy Negroes or dumb Swedes do with parks? Piss in them or fuck on the benches like monkeys or rabbits. If the reformers wanted green for their wards, let them use paint.

He parted the curtains. A tug pulled a freighter up the East River toward the towers of *his* Triborough Bridge, where even at this early hour there was light traffic. He imagined the excitement of families getting a first-light start on *his* highways to *his* inland and seashore recreational facilities. He inhaled deeply the sweetness of his thoughts, moving phlegm to his windpipe. He coughed till red-faced.

The bridge's magnificence was a galling reminder of his lack of major projects. A park here, a park there, but nothing monumental whose grandeur and purpose would erase from memory what previously had existed. Perhaps, he thought, Coney Island.

5:36 AM (**Warsaw time**): In the kitchen of her apartment on Nalevski Street, Rebecca Fishman Rabinowitz stuffed cleaned carp into an iron grinder and turned the wooden handle. She thought of Heshele standing beside her and crushing down on the fish. She missed him. How so sweet a nature had emerged from the bitter, tramp belly of her daughter was a mystery. It was as if he were the son of her younger daughter who had died during the plague in Warsaw. The wrong daughter had died.

As she brushed the last of the clinging flesh into a bowl, she heard distant thunder. She hoped it would not rain, as she wished to shop among the pushcarts on Mila Street. In America, Heshele often had gone shopping with her, proudly carrying two heavy bags.

The thunder came closer. It was a strange kind. It did not rumble but was sharp, like the crack of a million whips. Heshele's mother was petrified of thunder. As a child she had cowered in a basement or under a bed. In America she had run to the movies.

She fears God's wrath, Mr. Fishman would say. Why should an innocent child fear God's wrath? she had wanted to ask, but knew her place. Yes, she admitted to her daughter, even you were innocent and I loved you.

She went to the window to look for lightning. Suddenly the room was filled with harsh whistling that hurt her ears. She saw the building across the courtyard crumble as if put through a grinder. The floor shook. She looked down. The ceiling buried her.

5:46 AM (**Warsaw time**): Horst Petzel, former radio operator on the ocean liner *Bremen*, scanned the Polish countryside from the cockpit of a Stuka bomber. The sky was a curved, blue canopy, unbroken by clouds or other aircraft. He was lost. Somewhere, his fellow pilots flew in tight formation. Perhaps they wondered if he had been shot down. More likely, they were shaking their heads and laughing: Petzel has blundered again.

Petzel had volunteered for the Luftwaffe rather than the more logical choice, the navy, because he imagined the sky a vaster sea. Petzel's soul was warmed by endlessness. On the *Bremen*, he would stare at the sea, imagining a perpetual journey in a portless world and whisper: "World without end, Amen."

The sky had not disappointed. He sped from infinity to infinity, daydreaming under the spell of nothingness. His mind traveling, however, brought his wings dangerously close to the next plane in the group or, as now, lost the formation. He had been marked as a likely washout as a pilot, but the order to invade Poland had saved him.

As he had bombed Warsaw, the sight of a park had reminded him of a soft green field where he and his father had flown paper planes they had folded into being. During the reverie, Warsaw and his group had disappeared. His instrument panel flashed one remaining bomb.

He saw a village, flew over it, closed his eyes to make a game of it, and released the bomb. It spiraled down. Wood and flames defied gravity.

In the village, people hid, anticipating more planes and bombs. None came. The plane disappeared. It was an act of God, the people said, that only the house where the Antichrist had murdered dear Pavel Sienkewicz had been erased from the face of the earth.

5:51 AM: Luigi Barbetta stood before an eight-foot-high tailor's mirror, practicing a speech to be delivered in three days, on Labor Day. He would be addressing his own union, but the speech would be carried on radio to most of the Eastern states. It would be the most important speech of his life.

He stopped to scrawl some revisions in the text. He missed Velia Catzker. She was a fast, dedicated typist who could decipher his handwriting. Why had she ruined their relationship? Women are not part-timers, he thought, regretfully. They want dinner and breakfast. He continued:

"In our union, we have Ukrainians, who sing in their native tongue *The Dnieper Weeps and Mourns*; German Meistersingers; Neapolitans, who parade the effigy of their patron saint, San Gennaro; Poles, who dance the polka and mazurka; Jews, who celebrate their escape from bondage in ancient Egypt; Swedes, who set a table of smorgasbord; Czechs, who place their hats in the kitchen sink to be filled with Easter eggs; Romanians, who celebrate on their native country's Independence Day, May tenth; Irish, who parade in praise of Saint Patrick; Greeks, who maintain the Old Country authority of the *koumbaros,* the godfather; thousands who celebrate, on *Columbus Day,* the *Día de la Raza*, the Day of the Spanish Race; and the Negroes, who have made Harlem a world-famous cultural attraction."

He checked his list of ethnics to ensure against offense by omission, pleased with himself for hiring a college kid to research all that crap. Wait, the idiot had left out the Russians. God, there were thousands in the union. Back to the library with him. No, there was the celebration of the Russian New Year. Fuck the kid and his books. He knew life. He read on:

"We welcome, indeed, prize this wonderful mix of cultures. It

is from this diversity that we draw our strength. We are a living testament to our nation's motto: *e pluribus unum*—one from many."

"Luigi," his wife's mannish voice shouted from the bedroom,
"who the hell are you talking to?"

He did not answer.

"Oh, you're at the mirror again. I'm surprised you can still
look at yourself, you son of a bitch. I think I'll tell all your brothers
and sisters what a miserable, whore-hopping shit you are. Think
about that, great man! One day I will."

5:52 AM: Velia Catzker had heard her husband leave the house.
The idiot is driving again, she thought. She lay in bed staring at the
dirty ceiling that had not been painted in five years and then slowly
begun to nod her head, as if it were regulated by a precise inner
mechanism. She rose, put on a pink silk robe and pulled from the
darkness of her closet an alligator-skin case, whose dimensions she
knew precisely: nineteen inches long, twelve inches wide, four inches deep, weight, twenty-three pounds.

It was a twice-stolen object.

In 1913 her mother had snatched it from under a dozing
Polish aristocrat who, before nodding off, had informed Mrs. Fishman, the only other person in the compartment of a train traveling
from Cracow to Warsaw, that she, a contessa, shared compartments
with no one. However, stupid railway officials had failed to provide
her with her usual sleeping compartment, her due for even short,
daylight trips. To prove her point, she had opened the case which,
she said, always was carried by a stupid maid who had got herself
lost in the railway terminal, and displayed the wine-red silk sheets
and pillowcases. Mrs. Fishman had grabbed the booty and left the
train at a stop outside Warsaw, confident that the woman could not
describe her because she never had looked at her.

It had crossed the Atlantic and rested in the bottom of Mrs.
Fishman's closet as an anti-gentile trophy. Velia had removed it
during her mother's brief hospitalization for heart palpitations in
1936. It had never been missed.

She snapped open the two gold latches at either end of the case, uncovering three tiers of silver bottles, jars and flasks fitted snugly into a velvet lining. Dead center was her favorite, a modified Florentine flask, capped by an eggcup-size spirits holder screwed tightly into threading cut into the glass.

She lifted gently two silver-backed hairbrushes—one oblong, one round—and running them along her temples, felt soothed as if stroked by the delicate fingers of her favorite nun, Sister Lorna. She slowly rotated, each in its turn, three tall flasks and three deep silver jars, finger-tracing the words on their raised nameplates: *eau de cologne, lotion lys, crème pour les mains, poudre 1, 11, 111*. One nameplate was blank. There she had planned to etch: *cold cream*, the ointment that made her feel like a girl.

She slid out two square, alligator-skin–covered boxes. The deeper was reserved, awaiting diamond earrings, gold bracelets and hypnotic jeweled pins. The shallower box contained mascara and a brush that still clung to a few strands of the contessa's gray hair.

From a small box, she lifted an enamel, gold-lined thimble, on which was painted in polished reds, blues, browns and whites a pastoral pastiche of barns, mansions, graveyards, windmills and cloaked men on horses and donkeys. The scene, she was certain, depicted the countryside around her convent, confirming fate's role in placing the case in her hands. She lifted a silver pillbox, inset with an opal, and extracted a cough drop, which she had put there because of its appropriate golden color.

She held a pewter-encased magnifying mirror over a silver jar, revealing a delicately etched *Hermès*, and beneath, illegible to the naked eye, the artisan's signature: *St. Dupont, bis Rue de Dieu, Paris*.

She bunched together under the mirror all the flasks and jars. Each silver lid reflected the initial *V*, etched like a bird's wings soaring upward. *It had been fate.*

She threw the mirror against the wall, wanting to smash its faithless promise. But it struck sideways, settling on the floor under a rain of grimy plaster.

From her bureau drawer she removed a small object and put it into the pocket of her robe. She ran a very hot bath, took off the robe, stood sideways in front of the bathroom mirror and spit on her motherhood.

She eased herself into the hot water which rose to the tub's rim. Under the water she held her father's straight-edged razor—which, for reasons unknown to her, she had kept.

Lifting it, she pulled the blade from its imitation pearl sheath and ran her thumb along the cutting edge, feeling honed ferocity. Closing her eyes and crying softly as she had for many doomed, titled movie heroines, she drew the razor's edge across the mass of veins on her left wrist. There was an initial jolt of pain, which passed quickly. She rested her head against the porcelain rim and felt her life flowing out like ocean waves defying the retracting tide. She begged the nuns to take her into the sky, even though she had done this. They understood and beckoned.

5:52 AM: As Leslie and Willie drove across the state line from Pennsylvania to New Jersey, Leslie lit a reefer and inhaled a long suck ending with a loud kiss. She carefully removed the flimsy paper from her lips and pushed it into Willie's mouth until he secured it. The virtuoso breath control that made him the envy of every jazz reedman pulled the orange sparks within a singe of his lips. Leslie removed the minuscule butt as Willie gulped, whale-like, the soporific smoke.

They were returning to New York from a gig in Philadelphia, where they had planned an overnight stay at a hotel until word had reached them that cops, hungry for headlines, would arrest them for dope possession. At two-thirty, after the last show, they had sneaked out of a back entrance of the nightclub and into their car, not daring to pick up the luggage at the hotel. Leslie wore her white gown; Willie, a one-button-roll electric blue band uniform. Dumping the marijuana was useless. The cops had plenty of their own to plant.

Now in New Jersey, Willie rammed the gas pedal heavily.

The car backfired, lurched and exploded forward. They felt no speed, the reefer having worked its soothing magic, bending reality into a slow-motion dream.

The car radio was tuned to *The Milkman's Matinee*, which sometimes played their records. As they approached the George Washington Bridge, the disc jockey cut in to read a bulletin reporting the imminent invasion of Poland.

Willie squealed with delight.

"Hee-hee, the white folks is after killin' one t'other."

"What you got against white folks?" Leslie said, mocking him with minstrel-show delivery.

"Nothin', if they dead. Alive, they dangerous. Like a rattlesnake with no rattle."

"I think I goin' to turn you in. You a Red or somethin'."

"I just a somethin'."

He slid his hand under her gown and probed from place to place.

They rushed up the stairs to her apartment, heated heroin and injected themselves. Omnipotent and immortal, they threw off their clothes and lay side by side, floating in the tide of a warm internal bath. Willie scratched his head and stared quizzically at his fingernails, searching memory.

"Didn't that DJ say Boss Charlie is killin' in Poland, and ain't that where your Jewboy stud come from?"

Leslie patted her pubic hair.

"You got it, lover."

"How can you let a white cat fuck you?"

"How come you always beatin' on white chicks?"

"That's different."

"Why?"

"Because it is."

"You got a solid answer for everything."

Willie cupped a hand on her breast.

"I ain't seen him around. You get dragged with his little white dick?"

"Other way round. He done disappeared."

Willie popped her nipple between his fingers. He squeezed and massaged.

"What did the cat do?"

"He's a poet."

"Like moon and June."

"No, he want to rhyme moon and gun."

"Can't do that."

"Maybe not, but that don't stop him from tryin'. And he was makin' music too. I heard it."

"Like what?"

"Like I don't know. When it got in your ear it was music. Willie, you know damn well what I'm sayin'."

Willie turned on his side and flattened his palm on her pubic hair. He massaged the hair clockwise and the breast counterclockwise.

"They say only drummers can do that. You got youself a drummer and the best pair of chops in the universe. Yeah, I dig what you say about music. Tell me some words."

"It was a cryin', laughin', listen-to-me language. It was blues."

"Down Mississippi they say: *A Jew ain't nothin' but a nigger turned inside out.*"

Willie mounted and began to penetrate. Aba loved me, Leslie thought. I wonder if he's dead. Bye-bye.

Inside her, the heat and fullness set off furious motion.

"Buck me, Mama!" Willie shouted.

"I'll buck you through the ceiling, sweet Papa!"

5:57 AM: Catzker had memorized Woody's instructions: *Douse the middle well. Leave enough for a thin line of drops, like a fuse to the middle. Toss the can in the middle, light a match and throw it on the fuse drops.* The dwarf had assured that the mixture provided much time to escape.

He bent over the trail of liquid and struck a match from a book that advertised the Cafe Royal. It lost the phosphorous head on contact. The second lit, but was immediately extinguished by a draught from the open entrance door.

He cupped his hands over the match. When it flared he threw it into the trail. He turned to run. An explosion slammed him to the floor. How hot I am, he thought, before realizing that his clothes and hair were on fire.

He screamed *Gevalt!* and punched at his hissing hair. Flames shaped like daggers surrounded him. Among them Aba appeared: cool, untouched. He pointed an angry finger:

"Liar! You promised to see that Heshele grew up straight and tall."

"He will. He will!" Catzker shouted as flames singed his tongue.

SIREN'S FIRST WAIL: Woody put the loaded pistol in his pocket and walked to the Half-Moon. In the lobby, the deskman, a retired cop, said:

"Hi Woody, sounds like a big one."

"Sure does."

"You goin' up to see Menter?"

"Yeah."

"He told me you was comin'."

Menter, wearing a red silk bathrobe and a fireman's hat, let him in. From the terrace they saw thick smoke rising from the Midway. The air tasted bitter. Menter coughed.

Which is the best way? Woody thought. *Behind him, right through the back of his head. How would that look to a jury? Not a crime of confrontation, self-defense, but a calculated execution. No, it had to be in front, face to face.*

"Well Woody," Menter said, running his tongue over his lips, "can you taste it?"

"Yeah."

"Hey, what's with ya. You ain't grievin' for that nut case, Soldier?"

"Why the hell should I?"

"That's the spirit."

Menter's right hand appeared from under his robe. He pointed a long-barreled pistol at Woody.

"Now dwarf," he said, moving the gun from side to side, "reach into your pocket and pull out the piece. And pull it out by the barrel. Little shits can't hide things like a gun, you should know that. Now, slow and by the barrel."

Woody nodded. He brought the pistol to daylight.

"Now what do I do with it?" he asked.

"We'll bury you with it," Menter said. He squeezed the trigger of his pistol six times—three at Woody standing and three against the fallen dwarf's forehead. He wheeled himself to the house phone, cursing while it took twelve rings before pick up.

"Yes sir, Mr. Menter."

"Yes, sir, my ass, you lazy mick. Call the cops and tell 'em that kike dwarf tried to kill me, but I got 'im first."

SIREN'S FIRST WAIL: Soldier heard Woody leave the bike shop. He tugged at the door of his locked room. It didn't budge. He used his head as a battering ram against the thin wood. The wood began to crack. Splinters pierced his forehead. He punched a hole and climbed through. Woody had not locked the front door. He ran toward the beach.

SIREN'S FIRST WAIL: The clanging and shrieking vibrated in Schnozz's hangover-ridden head. He pressed a pillow against his ears. *Whaddya makin' so much noise about,* he thought, *it ain't no fire. When Dreamland burned down, that was a fire. Christ, we used to have two shows of a simulated fire in tenements every day at Dreamland. Guess I'll go see what this Girl Scout's campfire is all about. They make it sound like the end of the world.*

SIREN'S FIRST WAIL: Harry was mired in a nightmare. A fire drill was scheduled at school. The alarms went off. Harry discovered it was a real fire. He tried to warn everyone. They thought it was a joke and scolded him. He ran into the street, waving his arms, calling for fire engines. Finally they came into view, but did not slow down, whizzing past him blasting their sirens. He awoke to the same sound.

End-of-season fires were expected in Coney. But never before cashing in on the Labor Day weekend. This one, Harry thought, must be special.

He put on bathing trunks to cool off in the ocean if the heat of the flames became too intense. He needed to piss, but the bathroom door was shut. His mother was soaking in a bath. Not to be disturbed. He would piss on the beach.

"I'm going to see the fire, Mom!" he screamed at the door, not waiting for a reply.

A cover of black and gray smoke lay over the sun. As he ran along the beach the fumes attacked his throat. By the time he was parallel with the fringe of the amusement area, he was certain that the fire was on the Midway. From a spectator's point of view, this was unfortunate since the Midway was set back from the beach. But a fire of this intensity would jump all over the place.

Harry stopped parallel to the Midway. Behind the boardwalk row of concessions, smoke so dense it seemed solid rose like a reverse tornado. Explosions were followed by flames leaping, stretching, as if to burn the sky. The Cyclone, suddenly an intricate design of kindling wood, was as yet untouched, but in danger. The onshore wind intensified, blowing most of the smoke off the beach toward Luna Park, whose spires disappeared.

In the distance he saw a familiar stiff-legged gait. As Soldier drew closer, Harry made out splinters of wood ridged with dried blood imbedded in his forehead.

"Father, father!" Soldier shouted.

Harry smiled.

"Yes, father," he said.

"Tried to tell him! Tried to tell him!" Soldier was screaming. Spittle flew onto Harry's face.

Harry put his hand on Soldier's shoulder. The splinters explained his words. His agitation had even eliminated his prefatory *damn*.

"You must have had a nightmare, Soldier."

315

A look of utter helplessness, like Charlie Chaplin done in by an assembly line, clouded Soldier's eyes. He fell at Harry's feet, pounding his head on the hard sand, driving in the splinters deeper and surrounding them with seashell fragments and sand.

The flames were gigantic. Harry wished his father were here. But he had declined before, saying that to enjoy witnessing human catastrophe was unwholesome, and he hoped that Harry would grow out of it. Then, as usual, he had thrown in a quote, not from Freud but from another Vienna wise man. It had stuck in Harry's mind: *Man could only have fire when he could control his urge to urinate on it.* Harry did feel like pissing again. But he could hold it. Chalk one up for Vienna.

"Fire, fire, this ain't no fire."

Schnozz was coming toward him shouting and waving derisively at the Midway.

"Dreamland, that was a fire. Dreamland, something great was lost. What's this? A few shacks, skee ball, darts, hit the milk bottles. Baby games. You know, Harry, I told you."

Schnozz wore one black and one gray sneaker.

"Did I ever tell you about the Somalis I brought over to Dreamland?"

Harry showed no interest, but once Schnozz was wound up there was no stopping him.

"Let's see. Yes. I came upon them in a tiny village in British East Africa. I was trapping animals for the sideshow. Fact is I was checking out some native tales about a two-headed lion. Said it had two fully developed heads growing like a Y out of its neck. Wouldn't have believed them—didn't really anyhow—except they said it had two different-colored manes, one red, one yellow. That got to me. Didn't think natives could think like carny folk.

"Anyway, we come on these thatched huts and there are these Negroes, who are black and blue. But I mean as blue as the sky over Tahiti. I look more closely and I see the blue is kind of something attached to their bodies, like growing maybe an extra skin.

They speak a little English and are nice and friendly, so I ask them how come they're blue? They laugh and let me feel their bodies. The blue parts are ridges brought about by rubbing blue clay in wounds to kill the pain. All the time all I can see is a sign saying: '*Wild, Blue Men of Africa.*'

"I made them a proposition. I bring them over to Coney and put them in a sideshow. About a hundred agreed to come. But they had conditions you wouldn't believe. Get this: no breaking up of families. If Mama and Papa come, so do the kiddies and their schoolteachers. Hell, I didn't care if they transported their whole village, huts and all. All I could see was Blue Men, a hundred Blue Men.

"They was as great a hit as I knew they would be. And they got bluer and bluer because I hit on the idea of paying each one by the number of ridges they could raise.

"Now comes the best part. All the time they're saving their money, and it was a considerable sum. One day they come up to me, thank me for helping them out and tell me they're going home. I offer them more money, but they say they got enough. Couldn't do anything to stop them. Later I heard they all bought plantations. Became rich, some even millionaires. All because they knew how to turn blue."

Harry saw them: old, blue men, moving gently on rocking chairs, enjoying a late-evening pipe on the terrace of magnificent mansions.

"Schnozz," Harry said pointing to Soldier, "he's having a fit. Keep an eye on him. I want to get a little closer to see what's burning."

"Ah, Harry that ain't no fire."

"I know, Schnozz, but I just want to see."

"OK Harry, I'll watch him."

Harry moved to the soft sand. The flames were menacing the Cyclone, thrusting and retreating like a dueling swordsman. Soon it would go up. The most spectacular show he had ever seen.

He turned to check on Soldier. He still beat his head into the sand. Schnozz knelt beside him, saying:

"Fire, fire, this ain't no fire."

Harry turned back to the hissing orange curtain. A limerick Fred Krause's older brother had recited captured his mind, insisting on sound. He repeated it aloud, raising the volume, until he was shouting:

There was a young man of St. James
Who played the most horrible games;
He lit up the front
Of his grandmother's cunt
And laughed as she pissed through the flames!

"*Nu*, WONDERFUL AMERICAN BOY, HOW DOES IT FEEL TO NO LONGER BE a boy but a man?" Infantry platoon sergeant Harry Catzker smiled as he recalled Aba's words, spoken in the cherry tree on Harry's thirteenth birthday.

Tomorrow, he would lead the platoon into Buchenwald, the first concentration camp in the path of Allied forces. He had convinced himself that Aba would be in that camp. After all, he never had been reported dead. Fate had chosen that they be reunited in this place they had shared on the symbolic day of Harry's manhood, when Aba had offered a parable on German insanity:

"Centuries ago, Goethe and his friend Eckermann would lean against an oak tree in a forest four miles above Weimar, gaze down on the soft, green fields below and discuss life and literature. When that forest was cleared to construct Buchenwald, the tree, now the famous Goethe oak, was spared. A protective fence enclosed it."

Upon entering Weimar on April tenth, Harry had asked for directions to the oak, only to be told that it had been destroyed by an Allied bombing raid.

The platoon, assigned to root out diehard German resistance between Weimar and Buchenwald, rose early on April eleventh. Harry's men appreciated his knack for killing the enemy while minimizing risk. However, some were uneasy with his quick trigger finger which blasted Germans obviously on the verge of surrender or perhaps even a split second after their hands were raised. Captured prisoners never were allowed to unclasp their hands from behind their necks or sit or smoke. Conversation with them was forbidden.

The camp's tall iron gate loomed. Harry made out the legend stretched across its top: *Jedem das Seine*. His Yiddish translated it: To each his own. A good omen. Aba and he surely would be reunited. To each his own.

Before Harry passed through the gate, a stink clogged his nostrils, overflowed to his tongue and palate and nauseated him. When he came upon the decomposing, naked corpses piled like cordwood and the milling crowds of pus-soaked, fleshless human beings who barely filled the rags hanging from their bodies, he vomited.

Retching, he bolted for relief to a courtyard and almost knocked down an inmate, who recoiled, then stood rooted. Harry escaped the horror he beheld by creating a fiction: here was the elemental man—eyes, ears, nose, limbs—God's first stab at it before surrounding the essential parts with softening esthetic.

He could be Aba, Harry thought; individual identification is impossible, "Aba?" he whispered.

The man's eyes expressed bewilderment.

Aba, Harry realized, was the Hebrew word for father.

"I can speak Yiddish," Harry said. *"Ich ken redden Eidish."*

The man's eyes widened. "Are there many Jews like you?" he asked.

"Yes, many."

The man smiled, yet tears filled his eyes.

"I thought there were only Jews like me left."

He shuffled forward. He buried his forehead in Harry's shoulder. Harry felt no weight, as if a light breeze had brushed him. Harry delicately encircled the man's waist. They rocked, sobbing.